Reviving the World Court

The Procedural Aspects of International Law Series
RICHARD B. LILLICH, editor (1964–1977)
ROBERT KOGOD GOLDMAN, editor (1977–)

Reviving the World Court

Richard Falk

University Press of Virginia
Charlottesville

THE UNIVERSITY PRESS OF VIRGINIA

Copyright © 1986 by the Procedural Aspects of
International Law Institute, Inc.
200 Park Avenue, New York, New York 10017

First published 1986

Printed in the United States of America

Library of Congress Cataloging-in-Publication Data

Falk, Richard A.
Reviving the World Court.

(Procedural aspects of international law series ;
v. 18
Includes index.
1. International Court of Justice.   I. Title.
II. Series.
JX1971.6.F28   1986   341.5'52   85-31451
ISBN 0-8139-1084-6

Contents

Editor's Foreword

This volume, the eighteenth book in the Procedural Aspects of International Law Series sponsored by the Procedural Aspects of International Law Institute, is the second contribution to this series by Richard A. Falk, Albert G. Milbank Professor of International Law and Practice at Princeton University's Center of International Studies.

What distinguishes this book from other scholarly works on the World Court is Professor Falk's novel approach to assessing judicial effectiveness by reference to the character of contemporary international society and the consequent importance of jurisprudential adjustments in matters of judicial style and orientation. His principal argument is that the Court will not become an effective institution in the international order until it abandons its traditional adherence to orthodox Western legal doctrine and begins to help fashion and apply a non-Western jurisprudence which reflects the diverse cultural and ideological realities of the global political system.

It is from this perspective, shaped, in part, by his experiences as a counsel for Ethiopia and Liberia in the *South-West Africa* case, that Falk critically appraises the Court's work and examines the controversy and strains inherent in attempting to resolve conflicts through international adjudication. In this regard, he particularly focuses on the Court's handling of the *South-West Africa, Certain Expenses,* and *Iran Hostages* cases as examples of the "big case," which he characterizes as "a controversy of major significance among the actors in the political arena" (p. xiii). Perhaps the most dramatic instance yet of the "big case" is Nicaragua's ongoing action against the United States. The Reagan administration's decision to withdraw from further proceedings once the Court denied its jurisdictional objections reveals not only the administration's aversion to international law and institutions, but also the depth of the controversy that can be generated by the Court's hearing the "big case."

Reviving the World Court is an imaginative and insightful work by one of this country's preeminent international legal scholars. Professor Falk's vision of the Court's potential role in international life surely will be shared by students of the Court and by those persons committed to the peaceful settlement of disputes through international adjudication.

I want to acknowledge with thanks the considerable time that Richard Gittleman, my previous Dean's Fellow, devoted to the editing of this book. I am particularly indebted to Richard B. Lillich, Howard W. Smith Professor at the University of Virginia Law School, for arranging for the publication of this volume.

ROBERT KOGOD GOLDMAN

Washington, D.C.

Preface

At first glance, yet another evaluation of the role of the International Court of Justice (which will be referred to mainly in this study as the World Court, or simply as the Court) is not an attractive project. The subject has already drawn more than its share of printers' ink.

Yet the World Court has persisted as an international judicial institution for more than half a century in a divided world never more than minutes away from nuclear catastrophe. Its existence is a tantalizing embodiment of a different and preferable world, if only. . . .

Less grandiosely, even if its overall role has been marginal to the main issues of the day, the Court has played a significant role between the 1950s and 1970s in the conflict process that has unfolded between South Africa and the organized international community during the United Nations period. Appropriately, this conflict is understood to make manifest the utter inadequacy of judicial methods for coping with important international questions and to illustrate the genuine potential controversy going on in international society, centering on the degree to which apartheid as an official policy for state and society is or is not a matter of sovereign right. Sovereignty, self-determination, human rights, the conditions of peace, and the role and capabilities of the United Nations are among the issues raised regarding the former mandate of South West Africa, now known as Namibia at the international level.

These issues also have been discussed quite extensively in the scholarly literature. My excuse for adding to this corpus arises from a particular blend of concerns that have not yet been adequately addressed. These concerns arise out of prior scholarly inquiry and professional experience. To put in perspective, the study that follows, it might help to indicate briefly the three main features of this background.

First, I have had an abiding interest in the way judicial insti-

tutions in general relate to the international legal order. This
interest reflects my judgment that much of the current approach to international legal studies is misleading because it
relies upon an image of law derived from some selected aspects of legal experience in well-ordered and structured domestic societies. My argument has been that international law,
in contrast, works on the basis of a logic or dynamic that
reflects the statist character of international society, that it
depends on reciprocity and largely voluntary patterns of compliance. This outlook of mine was fashioned, in part, by an
effort to interpret the way in which domestic courts in the
United States tangled with international law issues in the
course of the protracted litigation arising from Cuba's expro-
priation legislation of the early 1960s. It resulted in my book
The Role of Domestic Courts in the International Legal Order, which
was written in the heat of controversy, published under the
auspices of the Procedural Aspects of International Law Institute, and introduced by Richard Lillich, who encouraged the
whole process, despite his sharp divergence from certain of
my ideas. In an important sense, this present effort is a sequel
to the earlier book, applying the same view of law, hopefully,
"seasoned" by the intervening twenty years, to circumstances
of international adjudication and similarly encouraged, to put
it mildly, by both PAIL and Richard Lillich.

The second explanation that shapes my concerns is a more
personal one. During 1965 I served as one of several counsels
on the legal team that represented Ethiopia and Liberia at
The Hague in the legal battle being waged against South Africa over the status of its mandate to administer South West
Africa. This experience was enlivened and deepened by working under the general direction of Ernest A. Gross, a gifted,
well-connected lawyer/diplomat. Such tutelage made me especially aware of the way politics mix with law in a controversy
of this sort. It also made me aware of the reality of the International Court of Justice as an institution: its absurd formality
and archaic quality; the deep sense of pride and commitment
shared by its judges, who agree on little else; and most of all,
the remoteness of this judicial atmosphere from the changing
currents of international life. If only the Court were located in
Cairo or Bombay, its entire modus operandi would be definitely different by now. I was struck also by the odd spectacle
of white American lawyers representing this preeminently

black, Third World cause—not only by the racial disjunction, but also by entrusting the direction of such litigation to a prominent American diplomat / lawyer, who, while personally abhorring apartheid, was still closely identified with one of the two governments in the world (the United States and the United Kingdom) *with the most to lose* by the collapse of the status quo in southern Africa. Such an anomaly was quite standard in World Court practice, but it tells us some important things about both the Court and the Third World. I hope that the lapse of years, since the unexpectedly adverse judgment in 1966, have diluted my partisanship without altogether extinguishing the special weight of such prolonged direct exposure to the Court in action.

The third background element has been my preoccupation during the last two decades with the contours of global reform. It so happened that while living in the Netherlands in 1965, I was working with Saul Mendlovitz on a series of edited books published under the title *The Strategy of World Order*. We felt keenly the provincial quality of trying to grasp the dynamics of global reform from an exclusively American position in time and place. Ever since, we have been trying to globalize our inquiry into world-order politics. One main outcome of this commitment has been the World Order Models Project, which has gone through a series of stages since its founding meeting in New Delhi back in February 1968, yet has always sought to build toward a social movement for global reform. My own participation in this work produced a series of writings, including: *This Endangered Planet: Prospects and Proposals for Human Survival* (1971) and *A Study of Future Worlds* (1975). In this work on global reform, I have been struck by the low place accorded "law," either as a dimension of some future better world, or as an instrument for getting there. Despite my own legal training, I confess that law slipped to the periphery of my efforts to develop an appropriate world-order perspective, and it was even more neglected by my colleagues from other parts of the world in the World Order Models Project. Here, in this study of the World Court, I return to a concern with law and legal institutions, undoubtedly influenced by intervening studies of the politics, economics, and sociology of the world political system.

My hope is that this background yields fruitful results. At least, perhaps, these prefatory remarks can serve as an explanation for writing a book on this subject. But to explain an undertaking is not to justify it. My real purpose is to bring law and judicial methods back into the mainstream of planetary activity committed to the urgent possibility of bringing about a just and peaceful world, if not by the year 2000, then at least by the middle of the twenty-first century. Such an objective may seem remote from the world of the 1980s, especially as it is being shaped during the Reagan years. Never before has the United States been governed by leaders who are as ideologically opposed to reliance in foreign policy on international law and cooperative methods. Such an ideological stance has caused this leadership to repudiate bargains generally favorable to the United States, such as the law of the seas treaty. For practical as well as normative reasons, it seems especially important at this time to advance the case for an increased role for international adjudication. If we are to proceed with a positive type of political development in international life we will have to find an array of peaceful means to deal with disputes among states. It is in this vein that the World Court can be studied to discern its largely untested potential.

The plan of the book is to outline a conception of the actual and potential place of judicial settlement in international life. Chapter 1 seeks to lighten the burden of exaggerated expectations that have afflicted the identity of the World Court throughout its more than sixty years of existence, a burden imposed largely by high-minded international jurists of distinction. Because too much was hoped for, disappointment and disenchantment have been inevitable, not just within professional ranks but, more damagingly, among the general public. To be helpful, a student of the World Court first of all must examine the institution more cautiously, balancing what has happened against what should have been expected.

Chapter 1 also seeks to develop an approach to the appraisal of the work of the World Court. The emphasis is on the importance of optimal judicial approach to a mandate and organizational character derived from the United Nations Charter and a stature that depends on a suitable relationship with the political organs of the United Nations, the Security Council, and the General Assembly. The need for such a balance is accentuated because the Court today is precariously poised in a diverse and dynamic global setting. To be explicit about these elements of the World Court's overall situation helps us to better understand and evaluate the tensions embodied in the adjudicative process itself.

Such an approach is then applied to the circumstances of "the big case"—a controversy of major significance among the actors in the political arena. Chapter 2, accordingly, looks upon the controversy over the status of the mandated territory of South West Africa (later Namibia) as a dramatic instance of "the big case." The analysis tries to explain the implications for judicial style, especially in relation to the institution's quest for respect given the absence of direct enforcement mechanisms, of recourse to the World Court in this particular instance. In effect, the chapter seeks to demonstrate concretely why entrusting a big case to the Court is itself controversial and complex.

Chapter 3 is an extended inquiry into how the World Court responded in fact to the controversy about the disposition of the mandate at its various stages. From the outset, it was evident that contending images of judicial function were presented by the judges at The Hague. One element that emerged, however, in the various opinions of 1962, 1966, and 1971 was an intense disagreement about what it meant to conceive of the International Court of Justice as a judicial arm of the United Nations. My objective in examining this ongoing dispute is to illuminate wider concerns by a detailed assessment of this single controversy.

In chapter 4, another big case, *Certain Expenses* of 1962, which arose from the financing of controversial United Nations peacekeeping operations, extends the analysis to a new context. In the case of the South Africa dispute there was a strong normative consensus operating in the political arena. As a consequence, a judicial departure from that consensus, as occurred in the 1966 *South-West Africa Cases* decision, generated reactions of dismay. If the consensus is fragile, as in *Certain Expenses*—in which the Soviet Union and France were among those refusing to honor earlier peacekeeping assessments—then a Court determination, no matter how pleasing it may be to one side, is unlikely to be effective, especially, perhaps, if the outcome takes the form of an Advisory Opinion.

Part of the intention of chapters 3 and 4 is to explore the relationship between judicial and political approaches to conflict resolution. It is arguable that a judicial outcome adverse to a strong consensus may have a positive impact by accelerat-

ing the political process, whereas a judicial outcome supportive of a slim majority is likely to stifle the political process
altogether. Such an ironic conclusion applies only to that special category of disputes where public attention exists, which I
have labeled the big case.

Chapter 5, written in collaboration with Jack Sanderson,
considers the American invocation of the Court in the Iranian
hostage crisis. This was clearly a big case, where the world
community was actively concerned about a highly visible dispute and where a threat of war existed. Iran refused to participate, alleging bias and one-sidedness. The Court proceeded in a conventional way to confirm the American claim,
which in this instance had already been unanimously endorsed
by the Security Council.

The majority made no effort to consider Iranian grievances
against the United States, even as these related to an earlier
severe abuse of embassy premises with regard to the sovereign
rights of Iran during the 1953 pro-Shah coup. The majority
also did not suspend inquiry in response to American unilateral actions, including the use of military force undertaken
pending the judicial proceeding. The Court's decision was in
many respects staged by the United States as a public relations
event. Even the United States, the clear winner in the litigation, held off on enforcement efforts in the Security Council,
evidently acknowledging that such efforts would inflame
rather than contribute to the resolution of the conflict. Should
the Court properly have acted differently than it did? Would a
wider inquiry have produced a more useful outcome? Such
questions, of course, can never become more than conjectures
about what might have been. However, in a broader sense, the
Court could have taken the opportunity to examine the encounter in its entirety, thereby linking for public understanding the issues of diplomatic immunity with those of Great
Power interventionary diplomacy. Without such a linkage the
law seems lame and one-sided, and can contribute little to the
search for a reasonable resolution of the crisis.

Chapter 6 draws upon the analysis of the earlier chapters to
examine why the World Court has fared badly as an international institution. Part of the conclusion here goes back to the
first chapter's reminders about the limited compatibility of
third-party approaches to international disputes within a system of sovereign states. On the basis of a closer look at sub-

stance, chapter 6 adds a cultural assessment to this structural
one. It argues that the entire international legal process, as
embodied in The Hague, is alien to the non-Western world,
that the jurisprudence of the World Court is inevitably Western, and that even those few Third World judges who differ
from the majority in specific instances do so by reliance on
standard Western sources. Furthermore, even Soviet and
Marxist judges have seemed ideologically intimidated or indifferent and have failed to evolve any kind of socialist judicial
orientation. In this central sense, the Court's legitimacy is a
product of Western heritage; what makes it legitimate in
Western countries also makes it alien, if not illegitimate, in
non-Western countries or in polities where Marxism is the
governing ideology or an influential ingredient of intellectual
life.

The argument of chapter 6 is that the way to think of
strengthening the World Court is through representativeness
at this deep level of perspective on law itself that derives from
culture and ideology. We in the West are so imbued with our
provincial notions that we believe, generally in good faith, that
a predominantly Western legal tradition is objective and uni-
versally acceptable. My study draws such convictions into question, at least in the context of asking how the World Court
might be strengthened as an institution.

Note, finally, that such an assessment is as much an indictment of the non-Western world as of the Western world. Colonialism has collapsed. Formal non-Western judicial representation exists. Whether the locus of the Court in Western
Europe and its reliance on English and French as working
languages must be changed is one policy question left unresolved in the text. Another, far more serious, question is resolved—the World Court cannot be revived without the awakening of non-Western governments to its potential importance
and the commitment of their representatives on the Court to
the development of a non-Western jurisprudence, including
authoritative sources. At this point, the West needs to understand and the rest of the world needs to awaken to this fundamental level of reconstructing reality.

Recourse by the Sandinista government in Nicaragua to the
World Court as a means of challenging and exposing the character of United States interventionary activities represents a
fascinating recent development. The Nicaraguan leadership,

whatever their motives, perceived the Court correctly as a
forum within which to press their allegations against a superpower in a war/peace setting. As such, it is the first time that a
Marxist-oriented government has invoked the Court, presumably on the double assumption that international law was on
its side and that this world judicial body would apply the law
in an impartial fashion. There is every reason to regard Nicaragua's initiative as based on a pragmatic assessment of bene-
fits and losses, given their situation, including their inability to
respond militarily to U.S. policies.

Nicaragua's pragmatic intentions are confirmed by their reliance on mainstream legal counsel drawn from the United
States. The main task of developing and presenting the Nicaraguan case has been left to two U.S. lawyers who would
undoubtedly describe themselves as non-Marxist, if not anti-
Marxist—Abram Chayes, former Legal Advisor to the Secretary of State during the Kennedy years, and Paul Reichler, a
Washington-based attorney with a Harvard law degree. From
the perspective of this book, Nicaragua's recourse to the Court
is at the very least a brilliant move in the struggle to convince
world public opinion that they are victims of illegal U.S. activities and that their approach is to seek a peaceful settlement to
the conflict. In some respects, the Reagan Administration has
cooperated with this strategy by its boycott of the proceedings
after losing out in its effort to convince the Court to deny
jurisdiction. Arguably, however, Nicaragua would have gained
even more in the court of public opinion if it had prevailed in
a legal battle that had the added drama of U.S. participation.
In any event, however the Court may eventually decide, the
Nicaragua initiative has opened up a whole new conception of
the relationship between international law, judicial remedies,
and the pursuit of national interests by non-Western, radical
governments. Such a development should not be overinter-
preted. Nicaragua's move was pragmatic. It involved no attempt to influence the Court to adopt a Marxist or Third
World approach. On the contrary, the posture of the case as
argued represses any special ideological identity or perspective
on law and the proper functioning of the international judiciary. I think it reasonable to assume that had Nicaragua
rested its argument on more ideological grounds its prospects
for success would have diminished greatly.

In the end, then, this book stands for the view that international law, to evolve at this stage of history outside of settings based on technical interaction, must become as pluralistic and diverse as the world in which it exists. The unity of international law under Western aegis had some intelligibility in an imperial world order; however, this had been largely lost as a result of the active participation of so many non-Western states. But participation, to be effective, must be more than the narrow assertion of national interests. Participation should understand national interests in light of the distinctive quality of cultural and ideological identity. The assertion of such cultural autonomy, to complement the autonomy of political independence, would undoubtedly provoke some hostility in the West. In fact, gropings in this direction on the Court have been steadfastly ignored by the dominant (Western) literature of interpretation. Judge Alvarez, who repeatedly argued to this effect, has been, in the main, viewed as a Latin American curiosity rather than as a jurisprudential pioneer.

Nowhere has this postcolonial awakening been so little acknowledged as in the international legal system. And nowhere in this system have the authentic cries of non-Western voices been so little heard as in the International Court of Justice. Despite its record of cultural and judicial myopia, the International Court of Justice could play a positive and significant role in international life, provided only that it becomes in practice as globalist as its treaty of incorporation purports.

Reviving the World Court

CHAPTER I

The World Court Assessed
as Dream and Fact

I shall repeat a hundred times; we really ought to free ourselves from the seduction of words!

FRIEDRICH NIETZSCHE, *Beyond Good and Evil*

After thirty-five years of growing disappointment over the record of the World Court, the brilliant forecast made by those
who worked out the conception of the United Nations at the
close of World War II reminds us how different, and more
hopeful, prevailing sentiments were at the time: "In establishing the International Court of Justice, the United Nations hold
before a war-striken world the beacons of Justice and Law and
offer the possibility of substituting orderly and judicial processes for the vicissitudes of war and the reign of brute force."[1]
Of course, this passage can also be read to stress its cautionary
elements. The prospective World Court was only described as
being able to provide "beacons" that "offer the possibility" of
displacing the war system by judicial methods of conflict
resolution.[2]

Nevertheless, that cast of mind that substitutes the force of
words and projects of law for the realities of behavioral
change is a pronounced tendency in international legal discourse, especially in relation to the subject matter of adjudication. Even distinguished international lawyers have encouraged, however unwittingly, this fundamental confusion right
up to the present time. Louis Sohn, for instance, writes that

> [t]he alternative of war or of other military or naval action, which
> not long ago was resorted to at the slightest provocation, is no

[1] Doc. 913, IV/1/74(1), 13 U.N.C.I.O. Docs. 393 (1945).
[2] In fact, there had been more than twenty years of experience with the almost
identical predecessor institution, the Permanent Court of International Justice. Drop-
ping the word *Permanent* was, in part, a belated ironic comment on an earlier generation of false hopes.

longer available. The Charter of the United Nations proscribes
the use of armed force, except as a collective measure in the
common interest. . . . The only remaining method for adjusting
conflict by therefore, settlement of disputes by peaceful means,
several kinds of which are at the disposal of the parties in
conflict.[3]

Naturally, if you believe this, then the World Court is inevitably bound to seem to be a major actor on the world scene; but
if you do not believe this kind of reasoning, it is difficult to be
optimistic about the Court's prospects. What is amazing about
Professor Sohn's assertion is the extent to which words of legal
intent, however lacking in prospects for their realization, are
accepted at face value as actually producing consequences.
Surely some 115 wars later, we now know that the Charter
provisions and the institutions created pursuant to them have
not transformed the war system, nor have they even produced
a surge of international judicial activity that seeks at least to
take the Charter norms seriously. Quite the contrary. We now
know, perhaps too well, that judicial procedures play only the
most marginal role in damping the fires of war in international conflicts.

Even Kotaro Tanaka, who added so much to the stature of
the jurisprudence of the World Court during his period as
judge, has written that the failure of governments to commit
themselves to the compulsory jurisdiction of the World Court
is "an unthinkable anachronism." Why? Because "the Charter
of the United Nations stipulates the principle that, in accor-
dance with its purpose to maintain international peace and
security, all members shall settle their international disputes
by peaceful means and that the International Court of Justice
is the principal judicial organ of the United Nations."[4] The
unthinkable anachronism is the failure of the members of the
United Nations to carry out their Charter pledge, *rather than
the pledge itself*. Perhaps former Judge Tanaka intended his
words to be mostly hortatory, a plea uttered in desperation
that governments should, at long last, take the Charter seriously. If governments persist in this neglect, Tanaka seems to
be arguing, then we must expect the worst kind of chaos in

[3]Sohn, *The Role of International Institutions as Conflicting-Adjusting Agencies*, 28 U.
CHI. L. REV. 205, 206 (1961).
[4]Tanaka, *The Character of World Law in the International Court of Justice*, 15 JAP. ANN.
INT'L L. 6 (1971).

international life. Yet his phrasing illustrates the major false premise of this cult of legal optimism, namely, mistaking words for actions.

Even the great Hersch Lauterpacht gives aid and comfort to those who would deduce political effects merely from the linguistic domain of legal pronouncement. Lauterpacht writes that

> [t]he function of law is to regulate the conduct of men by reference to rules whose formal—as distinguished from their historical—source of validity lies, in the last resort, in a precept imposed from outside. Within the community of nations this essential feature of the rule of law is constantly put in jeopardy by the conception of the sovereignty of States which deduces the binding force of international law from the will of each individual member of the international community.[5]

Here the problem is explained by arguing that the function of law is jeopardized by sovereignty as *cause,* rather than *effect.* In fact, the conception of sovereignty is itself a generalization of—or if one prefers, a rationalization of—international experience. It is also true, though with less force, that enshrining this experience of sovereignty in doctrinal form helps to shape and sustain expectations for newcomers to the international scene as well as for the traditional actors.

Leaders of ex–colonial states, for example, believe that the claim of sovereignty is an essential aspect of their assertion of political independence. The insistence on sovereign rights is also a practical instrument to promote autonomy, given their heritage of colonial subordination. If, however, we imagine a doctrinal vacuum, then perhaps some leaders of such states, especially leaders of comparatively weak states, might be more disposed to promote their independence through the partial embrace of doctrines and structures of cooperation. Indeed, the power of the nonaligned movement can be perceived as a creative reconciliation of the demands of sovereignty with a form of internationalism appropriate for Third World countries in the hierarchical structure of the world political system.[6] My objection to Lauterpacht's characterization of sover-

---

[5]H. LAUTERPACHT, THE FUNCTION OF LAW IN THE INTERNATIONAL COMMUNITY 3 (1933).

[6]That is, the Third World countries, despite their diversity of endowment and outlook, share a historical experience of dependency and a contemporary reality of technological inferiority, as well as a natural desire to stay out of the entanglements of

eignty is that it encourages legalistic approaches to reform by
implying that weakening the doctrine of sovereignty is tantamount to restricting the operative discretion of states.

Only slightly less distorting is "the naive realist" view that
awesome developments in the area of military technology and
international morality make recourse to force virtually unthinkable and, therefore, create openings for peaceful alternatives, including international adjudication. For instance, C.
Wilfred Jenks ties such an argument directly to a rationale for
accepting the compulsory jurisdiction of the International
Court of Justice: "for strong and weak alike there is now no
effective redress for the victim of injustice except due process
of law; only if we are convinced that we will be more sinners
than sinned against have we a continuing interest in rejecting
compulsory jurisdiction."[7] Such an assessment of the supposed
diminished utility of force exaggerates the impact both of nuclear weapons and of modern normative prohibitions on patterns of international diplomacy, and mistakenly associates
what impact there has been with an increasing disposition to
entrust national concerns to third-party procedures. Such assessments embody an unfortunate mixture of wishful thinking
and a poor sense of geopolitics that confuses our expectations
about the role of international adjudication in the present
world.

These comments serve as a basis for considering the Charter
of the United Nations and its relation to our subject, the role
and prospects of the International Court of Justice. In part,
the Charter is an instrument that reflects the immediacy of the
context of its drafting, both the widespread suffering of
World War II and the victors' conviction of the need to recon-

---

"the old world." In this latter instance, recall the sentiments expressed by George
Washington (actually derived from Thomas Jefferson) in his farewell address on the
importance of this fledgling United States avoiding entangling alliances with the established powers of Europe. Hence, to band together loosely for limited shared purposes has been one way for Third World countries to combine the virtues of cooperation with those of independence.

[7]C. W. JENKS, LAW IN THE WORLD COMMUNITY 155 (1967). Earlier in the same
passage Jenks writes that:

A powerful state can no longer secure justice for itself by the strength of its own
right arm without so transgressing the modern law of nations and so offending the
ethos of contemporary international society that it is almost bound to lose far more
in general prestige and influence than it can hope to gain in the particular case;
Id. at 155. For standard realist views on these issues, see K. KNORR, ON THE USES OF
MILITARY POWER IN THE NUCLEAR AGE (1960); R. OSGOOD & R. TUCKER, FORCE
ORDER AND JUSTICE (1967).

struct the international order so as, in those oft-quoted words of the Charter's preamble, "to save succeeding generations from the scourge of war." This noble sentiment undoubtedly was sincerely held by many leaders and by the public, yet the commitment to its realization was not understood, nor were its implications capable of being implemented politically at any stage. An effective peace system, along the lines envisioned by the Charter, calls for certain minimal steps, including some sort of veto-free police force in the United Nations and a dispute-settlement process that includes compulsory jurisdiction as a last resort and a genuine expectation of enforceable judgments. The refusal to make compulsory jurisdiction for the Court an automatic incident of membership in the United Nations or, perhaps more importantly, the unwillingness of even the great champion of international adjudication, the United States, to accept compulsory jurisdiction in unconditional form, is indicative of the real limits on a movement for global reform in the post–World War II period.[8]

In the background of these limitations stands the hostile attitude of the Soviet Union to this entire conception of a centrally guided world-order system built out of Western domestic experiences with law and order. For Soviet leaders and for the Eastern bloc of countries, binding international arrangements were perceived as thinly disguised traps, legal in form, political in content. In their view, international institutions proclaimed a pseudoobjectivity and a pseudoneutrality, while, in reality, they operated as political arenas in which the socialist countries often found themselves a small, beleaguered minority. Thus, the price of Soviet participation in the postwar arrangements was the credible assurance that the substance of their sovereign rights would be secure. Given the stature of the Soviet Union as the world's second leading power, it was implausible to suppose that the Charter vision could be realized, even had it been the case—which it was not—that this vision was seriously avowed by the other principal international actors. In truth, perhaps only the United

---

[8]For a helpful review of the San Francisco mood, including the private reluctance of *any* of the major governments to get swept away by their public rhetoric into making far-reaching commitments to accept third-party procedures, see the careful report in 1972 by Helmut Steinberger for the Max Planck Institute for Comparative Public Law and International Law in Heidelberg. Steinberger, *The International Court of Justice*, in JUDICIAL SETTLEMENT OF INTERNATIONAL DISPUTES 194–201 (H. Mosler & R. Bernhardt eds. 1974).

States government had genuinely high hopes for the United Nations, and those hopes were based partly on the somewhat controversial and atypical idealism of Franklin Roosevelt and partly on an unrealistic belief held by a portion of the American leadership that the wartime alliance could be extended past 1945. These views were challenged at home by a near majority (or at least a blocking minority) who had distrusted internationalism ever since Woodrow Wilson made the League of Nations his pet project.[9]

Despite its treaty form, a series of legal procedures were established by United Nations machinery, the effective use of which depended on the convergence of a multitude of sovereign initiatives. The whole Charter vision, which included outlawing force (art. 2[4]), requiring peaceful modes of dispute settlement (art. 2[3]), making the Court a principal organ of the United Nations (arts. 7, 92) with the role of resolving disputes dangerous to world peace and of advising the other organs of the United Nations as to legal questions (arts. 93, 94, 96), fell stillborn at the drafting stage. Some important states were hostile per se to the idea of international adjudication, and *all others* were, at best, hesitant and ambivalent. On such a political foundation only limited results could be expected, certainly far less impressive than the grandiose norms of the Charter calling for the substitution of peaceful settlement for discretionary violence.

Even in 1946 the United States stood firm on traditional grounds of sovereign rights; without United States initiative, where would the reforming energy come from in the world system? The real importance of the Connally Reservation—allowing the United States to determine for itself when disputes fell within its domestic jurisdiction and hence could be withdrawn from the World Court—then, was symbolic; it was to strip away illusions about what could be expected from the United Nations system.[10] It was not the American insistence on

[9]*See* Steinberger report, *supra* note 8, at 199, for judgment that the United States, Great Britain, and France "also were agreed [that is, along with the Soviet Union] in their rejection of compulsory jurisdiction" at the San Francisco stage. For the general background, see D. YERGIN, THE SHATTERED PEACE: THE ORIGINS OF THE COLD WAR AND THE NATIONAL SECURITY STATE (1978).

[10]As Leo Gross puts it, "surely the claim of the United States to be the champion of the free world and a staunch supporter of the rule of law in international relations will have a hollow ring unless and until the United States removes those crippling reservations" on its acceptance of the International Court of Justice's compulsory jurisdiction.

a self-determined domestic jurisdiction as an exception to the
Court's compulsory jurisdiction that gives the Connally Reservation its significance, but rather the extent to which this formal act (unrepudiated to this day) registered and dramatized
the persistent unwillingness of states—large and small, Western
and non-Western, socialist and nonsocialist—to loosen their
grip on sovereign discretion over all matters of national interest
and policy. The *whole system* of states remained unready to fulfill, even in minimal form, the promise of the Charter. In doctrinal terms, the Westphalian logic remained paramount.[11]

Despite the dangers of conflict in the nuclear age since the
Charter founding, the role of peaceful settlement has diminished, especially involving recourse to the judicial sphere. As
Jenks has put it: "Since the Second World War remarkable
advances have been made in virtually every sector of international organization except the judicial sector . . . ."[12] Jenks insists that the progress of law in international affairs correlates
closely with the progress of extending the compulsory jurisdiction of international tribunals: "submission to law through the
acceptance of recourse to international courts and tribunals is
an essential complement to the renunciation of force in international relations."[13] One important feature of Jenks's view is
the argument that from the Alabama Claims award of 1872
until 1930, "there appeared to be a long-term trend toward
the acceptance of a larger measure of compulsory jurisdiction"
and that "[s]ince 1930 virtually no further progress has been
made."[14] It is the apparent growth in law-oriented behavior
during the sixty years from 1880 to 1930 that seems to have
created the mood of legal optimism.

Whether, as Gross also notes, the Connally Reservation "struck a most damaging blow
at the Court" becuase "it expressed a virtually total lack of confidence in the Court" is
open to question. No serious demonstration of a causal relationship between the
Connally Reservation and the actual business of the Court has been attempted as far
as I know. Hence, the mere assertion seems largely polemical, rather than analytical.
See Gross, *The International Court of Justice: Consideration of Requirements for Enhancing
Its Role in the International Legal Order*, in THE FUTURE OF THE INTERNATIONAL COURT
OF JUSTICE 38, 39 (L. Gross ed. 1976).

[11]R. FALK, A STUDY OF FUTURE WORLDS (1975); for its defense, see J. VINCENT,
NON-INTERVENTION AND INTERNATIONAL ORDER (1974) and H. BULL, THE ANARCHIC
SOCIETY (1977).

[12]C. W. JENKS, THE PROSPECTS OF INTERNATIONAL ADJUDICATION 1 (1964).

[13]*Id.* at 114.

[14]*Id.* at 13, 14. *See also* N. POLITIS, LA JUSTICE INTERNATIONALE (1928) for depiction
of this favorable trend. For a more recent review of this historical trend, see R. P.
ANAND, INTERNATIONAL COURTS AND CONTEMPORARY CONFLICT 11–66 (1974).

This optimism was well-expressed by a German international jurist, Hans Wehberg, who, in the middle of World War I, wrote an essay urging the establishment of a permanent court of international justice. Wehberg was impressed at that early time by trends toward international economic interdependence that he believed would necessitate a continuous expansion of the international function of law. In general, Wehberg's outlook was conditioned by a positive view of international history:

> When we recall that before the year 1800 no international congress worthy of the name had met with the object of regulating the legal relations of groups of states, and that, on the contrary, since 1815 about two hundred congresses of states with an ever-increasing number of participants have taken place, we recognize clearly the line of development, that an ever-stronger union of states upon a legal basis is coming about, and that the day is no longer far off when the most important fields of international interest will be ruled by law.[15]

Given this optimistic vision of the future, the establishment of a permanent international court was expected to be an important step. As Wehberg notes, "[i]ts creation will necessarily be regarded as a striking victory of the modern peace movement, which has advocated it incessantly for decades,"[16] and further, such a court

> will strengthen the belief of thousands that the nations must hasten to an ever higher stage of their development and that their policies must assume gradually a nobler character. In this way it will once more be shown that all great ideas prevail in the course of the centuries, and mankind must only have perseverance in order to reach its highest growth.[17]

This expectation, quite normal at the time, is now relevant mainly as an exhibition of naive optimism. Then, however, given the upward trend of peaceful dispute settlement, the wide public support for moving ahead with a permanent court, the relatively small number of international actors, the urgent, widely shared sense during World War I that alternatives to war must be found, and the absence of the sort of ideological split in international society brought about by the

[15]H. Wehberg, The Problem of an International Court of Justice 2 (1918).
[16]Id. at 245.
[17]Id.

Russian Revolution, it was quite natural for the more liberal segments of the Euro-American elite to expect that the next fifty or sixty years would produce a much more law-oriented world-order system. And, of course, the establishment of the Permanent Court of International Justice in 1920 appeared to confirm this positive line of interpretation. The political climate for serious global reform seemed present to a degree that has not been duplicated since.[18]

One might still have believed that the 1930–45 period demonstrated only that Wehberg's projection of legal growth was too mechanical and linear, and regarded that regressive interval as an aberration, a consequence of the fanatical quality of totalitarian leadership, especially in Hitler's Germany. In this spirit, it was still possible to expect the underlying secular trend toward internationalism to be reinforced. After all, the totalitarian challenge was defeated, the ravages of the Second World War had been even greater than those of World War I, and the United States was apparently convinced this time that it must participate formally and prominently in the United Nations, the sequel to the League of Nations. The advent of nuclear weapons shocked people, even governments, into the realization that a third world war could mean a permanent catastrophe even imperiling human survival. In such circumstances, it was natural to regard the role of international adjudication as critical to the future of world peace. "The failure of the international community to develop a system of third-party law-making comparable to that of the national community may well prove to be the fatal error of our civilization."[19] Underlying this view was the important recognition that conflict inevitably would persist and disputes would continue to arise, and that nonviolent modes of conflict resolution would be needed if violent ones were to be avoided. This view claimed many adherents for the adjudicative mode. This mode has the potential for impartiality, fairness, and flexibility, and even decisiveness, in the sense of reaching results.

Why then, we must ask, has the apparent decline in reliance upon adjudicative processes that began in 1930 continued until the present time? What has happened in international rela-

[18]For a typical expression of this outlook that snatches legal optimism from the jaws of geopolitical pessimism, see C. W. JENKS, *supra* note 7, esp. chapters 1, 2, 5, 8, and 12.

[19]T. FRANCK, THE STRUCTURE OF IMPARTIALITY 46 (1968).

tions since the publication of Wehberg's book in 1918 that
would make his outlook, if written today, seem silly and naive?
A half century has elapsed since 1930. We can discern clearly
a countertrend culminating at some future time in disintegra-
tion and collapse. Indeed, pessimistic outlooks today hold
sway in much of the West, supplanting earlier optimism based
on the expectation of inevitable progress.[20] The positive, serious prospect for adjudication is now only relevant to elements
of functional interdependence and international cooperation
in such spheres as oceans regulation, investment disputes, and
space exploration. The legal outlook, and with it confidence in
the adjudicative method, today seems almost irrelevant to the
big picture of war-avoidance in international relations.

Charles De Visscher seems on target (as he so often is) when
he writes in a well-known passage that "all things considered,
the present slowing down of judicial activities must be attrib-
uted much less to a deterioration in their spirit or to the im-
perfections of their methods than to external factors of a
strictly political nature which paralyze the role of all international law in international relations."[21] In part, De Visscher
argues that the earlier optimism as well as the later pessimism
both arose from the same optical illusion, namely, the mis-
taken belief that international adjudication *could ever have had*
the prospect of eroding the political prerogatives of sovereign
states. It evidently seemed that way to interpreters earlier in
the twentieth century, possibly because their sense of trend
was based on the recent origins of international mechanisms
for the settlement of disputes among states. A period of apparent expansion relative to the more convenient settlement
of nonvital disputes took place without really raising questions
of sovereign prerogative. Perhaps De Visscher's dichotomiza-
tion is excessive, arising from an overly sharp distinction between "political" and "legal." The essence of his view is that
the structure and logic of the state system imposes an outer
limit on the applicability of the adjudicative mode to international affairs. If our sights are lowered, then adjudication can

---

[20]R. HEILBRONER, AN INQUIRY INTO THE HUMAN PROSPECT (1974); THE PREDIC-
AMENT OF MAN (E. Goldsmith & E. Gee eds. 1974); D. MEADOWS, THE LIMITS TO
GROWTH (1974); R. FALK, THIS ENDANGERED PLANET: PROSPECTS AND PROPOSALS FOR
HUMAN SURVIVAL (1972); THE GLOBAL PREDICAMENT (D. Orr & M. Soroos eds. 1979).
[21]De Visscher, *Reflection on the Present Prospects of International Adjudication*, 50 AM.
J. INTL. L. 474 (1956).

fulfill its modest role as an incident to routine diplomacy. De Visscher argues against an all-or-nothing view of international adjudication. The International Court of Justice is a resource that can be used for certain limited purposes, but its existence and potentiality should not be confused with the quest for a just and peaceful world.[22]

These "external factors of a strictly political nature" to which De Visscher refers relate to the changing character of international society. The world-order system of the late nineteenth and earlier twentieth centuries was a simpler affair, yielding simpler solutions. A relatively small number of actors dominated the world, actors who shared generally a religious, cultural, and political tradition that they believed superior to others, and who were confident that a science-based industrial economy would continue forever to make the material conditions of life easier. The application of reason to human affairs was believed to have displaced the authority of religion and led reformers to suppose they could devise solutions to solve all societal problems. Juristic rationalism was merely one symptom of a larger societal disorder, that of presupposing the capacity of reason to fashion sensible institutional solutions for all human problems.[23]

The Russian Revolution climaxed a continuing process of undermining confidence in rational reform. Marxism-Leninism, as a philosophy and then as an ideology, challenged the legitimacy of the entire jural temperament and its underlying theoretical presuppositions, even as applied to domestic life. It grounded its hopes for change on armed struggle and saw capitalist society as deeply driven by class conflict. Law and the state were the political instruments of the ruling classes that were engaged in the exploitation of dependent classes and peoples. Such a structure could not be reformed precisely because the reformers were among the exploiters. It could only be smashed. This is not the place to discuss shifting Marxist and different Soviet views on the role of international law, but all these views place their trust for change upon revolutionary

[22]See ON THE CREATION OF A JUST WORLD ORDER (S. Mendlovitz ed. 1975) for a series of culturally distinct perspectives on global reform. Note the failure to mention international adjudication in any sustained serious way at any stage of the World Order Models Project.

[23]See W. THOMPSON, AT THE EDGE OF HISTORY (1971); W. THOMPSON, EVIL AND WORLD ORDER (1976).

social forces. The only proper socialist relationship to the institutions of the existing legal order, including the United Nations
and the Court, is to *neutralize* their capacity to serve as instruments for international class domination. Operating from a
minority position, the Soviet group has participated in the world
legal system to facilitate its own ends and to neutralize the
system's claims to intervene in the historical process. In this
sense, the Soviet government has never repeated its error of
1950, when its absence from the Security Council enabled that
organ to create a mandate for the defense of South Korea. This
ideological and geopolitical split in the West since the Russian
Revolution has nullified the consensus on the means and ends
of global reform, especially on the place of law and international institutions in this process.

With the collapse of the colonial system, the process of dis-
sension has spread further. Non-Western outlooks have become important in international affairs. The heritage of international law has been regarded with skepticism because it formerly provided a legitimating rationale for colonialism and
was associated with the functioning of what the non-Western
world agreed to be an inequitable international economic
order.[24] At best, this legal heritage was regarded as an unfa-
miliar product of an alien civilization. The new states of Asia
and Africa and the more emancipated states of Latin America,
despite their array of differences, have established a Third
World identity that has been able to muster considerable solidarity on many international issues. Underlying this solidarity
is often a kind of Marxist-Leninist interpretation of international history, which prevails even in countries where the governing elite is rabidly anti-Marxist and pro-Western. The essence of this Third World outlook in relation to law, in some
ways typified by the predominantly conservative alliance of oil
producers, the Organization of Petroleum Exporting Countries (OPEC), is that struggle and political power are the main

[24]It is misleading or polemical to regard sovereignty-oriented participation in the
world system as "reactionary." A normative assessment depends on the clash of values
between those who dominate the world system and those who seek, above all else, to
preserve their autonomy. In general, both postures are reactionary in some respects
and progressive in others, depending on the normative statement correlating "reactionary" with "sovereignty" contained in the following statement by R. Y. Jennings:
"New States are naturally concerned about sovereignty and independence and, to that
extent, reactionary. . . ." Jennings, *Report,* in JUDICIAL SETTLEMENT OF INTERNATIONAL
DISPUTES, *supra* note 8, at 36.

engines of meaningful change in the current world system and that law and judicial remedies represent snares and delusions. The Third World brings a new agenda of economic priorities into the international arena that fractures further the illusion that reason translated into international institutions is the path to peace and justice.

The growth of the socialist sector and the number of states comprising the Third World has given these outlooks a *majority* position in most United Nations organizations, most prominently in the General Assembly. Hence, it is not surprising that in recent years it is the United States and, more generally, the advanced industrial nonsocialist states of the northern hemisphere that view the General Assembly as a hostile arena, one that operates to achieve political ends regardless of legal rights and duties.[25] The 1974–75 General Assembly debates on the new international economic order highlighted the split and antagonism between North and South. With political control of the General Assembly in hostile hands, the strategy of the United States began to resemble earlier Soviet strategy, namely, acting to neutralize opponents, rather than to strengthen one's own position.

In such an international environment, it is not surprising that there has been a decline in the legal disposition of the United Nations in comparison with the League of Nations, including a decline in the status and function of international adjudication if comparison is drawn between the Permanent Court of International Justice and the International Court of Justice.[26] To be successful, a legal order de-

[25]Compare with this the positive attitude toward the General Assembly taken by the United States when it drafted, proposed, and celebrated the adoption of the Uniting for Peace Resolution in 1950. G.A. Res. 377(V), 5 U.N. GAOR Supp. (No. 20) at 10–12, U.N. Doc. A/1775 (1950). Can we honestly claim that in terms of Charter norms the Assembly was more "responsible" then than now. By what principles? It seems to depend on an inversion of political control, resulting in a new set of priorities associated with the will of the new majority. But is it less genuine, less valid, even less constitutional than the earlier outlook? For some consideration of these issues, including the shift of United States attitude, see THE UNITED NATIONS 249–300 (R. Falk & S. Mendlovitz eds. 1966); on interpreting the changing interplay between the Charter and the United Nations as an active, evolving entity, see Falk, *The United Nations: Various Systems of Operations*, in THE UNITED NATIONS IN INTERNATIONAL POLITICS 184–230 (L. Gordenker ed. 1971)

[26]For discussion and documentation of this decline, see Steinberger, *supra* note 8, at 211–24. *See also* Stone, *The International Court and World Crisis*, 536 INT'L CONCILIATION 31 (1962): "Despite the existence for two generations of ample institutionalized facilities and inducements for submission of disputes more or less tractable to settlement by

pends on an underlying agreement among its members as to
the acceptability of the existing political framework. There
may be grievances, even wars, in a successful legal order, but
the framework of values that guides the behavior of actors is
not drawn into question.[27] When such a consensus no longer
exists, the legal process loses its capacity to generate respect
from the community as a whole. Its role becomes marginalized, and tears of regret and frustration are shed by its former
champions.

Perhaps it is understandable that anyone who has endured
nine quiet years in the damp gray confines of The Hague
would emerge from that experience with a grim determination to promote the Court despite current adverse conditions.
Even so venerable a figure as Philip Jessup declared after his
distinguished service as judge that the Court "unfortunately
does do 'very little business'—not because of its 15 men of as
many minds and of many tongues, but because the sovereign
States of the world are not much inclined to submit their
controversies to final judicial settlement. They are unsure of
the validity of their claims."[28] Of course, it is true that sovereign states are disinclined to use the World Court, but to rest
the explanation for that on their being "unsure of the validity
of their claims" seems wide of the mark. It would be more
illuminating, I believe, to connect this disinclination to an uncertainty as to outcome. For many Third World governments,
their general doubts about the international legal order pre-
cede and shape their attitude toward the use of the World
Court in a particular instance. There is in effect a prior concern with the one-sidedness of international law that needs to
be resolved before it can be said that governments withhold
their disputes from international adjudication because they
have doubts about the validity of their claims. The refusal of
the post-Shah Iranian revolutionary government to appear be-

law, the record of state willingness to accept third-party judgment has shown a distinct
retrogression." Jessup, *The Untried Potentials of the International Court of Justice*, in THE
SEARCH FOR WORLD ORDER 215–27 (A. LEPAWSKY ed. 1971), argues for greater reliance on the Permanent Court of International Justice by the League Council than on
the International Court of Justice by the Security Council or the General Assembly.
For a relatively early perceptive assessment of this trend, see Bloomfield, *Law, Politics,
and International Disputes*, 516 INT'L CONCILIATION 257–59 (1958). For another consideration of this decline, see Gross, *supra* note 10, at 27–36.

[27]H. KISSINGER, AMERICAN FOREIGN POLICY (1977); S. Hoffman, *International Systems and International Law*, 14 WORLD POL. 205–38 (1961).

[28]P. JESSUP, THE PRICE OF INTERNATIONAL JUSTICE 71 (1971).

fore the Court in relation to its seizure of American hostages represents an extreme instance of legal alienation, a posture that went far deeper than the anticipation of judicial defeat, given the manifest violation of sovereign rights surrounding the practice of diplomatic representation (see chapter 5). Some disputes between states relate to technical questions of boundaries or historic rights, or arise between parties that share a common orientation toward traditional international law, yet disagree about the facts or the application of a rule or principle to a given set of circumstances. In these instances, Judge Jessup's observation seems accurate, as even states with no real reason to fear the Court's approach to the content of international law often seem hesitant to entrust their disputes to a procedure of judicial settlement.[29]

In a one-sided normative situation such as the one that exists between the international community and South Africa on the issue of apartheid, divergent images of what is valid international law can be overlooked because an overwhelming political/moral consensus reinforces the legal contentions of the antiapartheid position. If the Court rejects this position, as it was perceived to be doing in its 1966 judgment, an attack upon the Court is unleashed, not a movement to reconsider the legal validity of the prohibition of apartheid.[30] The experience of the United States Supreme Court in cases involving fundamental societal outlook also illustrates that such a reaction is equally to be expected in relation to judicial activity at the national level. When an international dispute touches on a subject where no overwhelming political/moral consensus exists, then the effort by the World Court to fill the vacuum is almost certain to fail. This was illustrated by the inability of even a strong majority in the General Assembly to induce United Nations members to follow the guidelines set forth in the Court's Advisory Opinion in the *Certain Expenses* cases.[31]

Every independent judicial body has this problem of community acceptance, but it is accentuated in the case of the World Court. As Julius Stone observes, "[t]he International Court lacks the comfort of an efficient legislature and its tasks

---

[29]*Id.* at 44: "How often in international affairs it is thought better to let a matter drift than press it to a conclusion which might offend one or another party."

[30]*See South-West Africa Cases* (Ethiopia v. S. Afr.; Liberia v. S. Afr.) (Second Phase), 1966 I.C.J. 6 (Judgment of July 18).

[31]These two cases will be discussed in detail in chapters 2 and 3.

are correspondingly heavier. It also lacks the comfort of shar-
ing the ethos of a close-knit homogeneous community in per-
forming its own law-creative role."[32] The absence of a legislature increases the pressure for judicial creativity, while the
heterodox character of international society increases the prospect that adverse judgments will be perceived as invalid.[33]
These two handicaps inhibit governments from submitting to
the Court disputes for judicial settlement. There is no likelihood of the rapid rectification of these conditions. This leads
Julius Stone to advocate "greater modesty and more ambition"
vis-à-vis the International Court of Justice; he advocates accepting the downward trend as an inevitable reflection of divergent attitudes towards national interests and justice, while
endorsing a search for long-term international reconciliation
upon which an effective legal order alone can be founded.[34]
His juridical prescription is to give a new emphasis to regional
modes of adjudication as an interim approach, thereby allowing states that share a common normative outlook to avail
themselves of a congenial judicial forum where problems of
predictability and acceptability are likely to be less severe.[35]

Nevertheless, Stone's main view is an echo of De Visscher's
emphasis on extrinsic factors. Stone complains that so much
writing on the Court "offers machinery as a solution when the
real problem is a politico-economic one." In such circumstances, there is no short-term prospect for giving international adjudication under global auspices a serious role:
"While therefore it is recognized that the Court, along with
international law itself, is in crisis, it cannot be said that this
crisis is pivotal in the general human crisis."[36] This element of
modesty is much needed. Stone seems to be correct in arguing
that any attempt to push the World Court into a real relationship to the present global crisis "would almost certainly destroy the Court itself, leading to still deeper disillusionment
and frustration." Stone concludes that "[t]o preserve an institution is to preserve its potentialities as well, even if these are
still remote from the immediate crisis of our actual world."[37]

[32]Stone, *supra* note 26, at 40.
[33]On this issue, see H. LAUTERPACHT, THE DEVELOPMENT OF INTERNATIONAL LAW
BY THE INTERNATIONAL COURT OF JUSTICE 394–400 (1958); C. W. JENKS, *supra* note 12,
at 312–15.
[34]Stone, *supra* note 26, at 46.
[35]*Id.* at 53.
[36]*Id.* at 60; *see also* C. W. JENKS, *supra* note 12, at 758–60.
[37]Stone, *supra* note 26, at 64.

The political process in international relations might conceivably lead to a political climate in which the Court could begin to play the kind of role envisioned for it by the Charter. The politico-economic structures of the international order may evolve over time in such a way that international adjudication will again appear to be able to be used as a central building block for global reform. In the meantime, it is best for the Court to mark time, to maintain its integrity as an institution, and not to bemoan its current neglect, which is mainly a consequence of forces over which it can exert little or no control. Along these lines, R. Y. Jennings writes that "the situation of the Court would be healthier" if its main activity "could be seen as resting on a foundation of far more humdrum and routine court business. . . ." Hence, "[o]ne remedy may, therefore, be not just more, but also duller, work for the Court."[38] Stone's view, in contrast to De Visscher's, does not appear to be that the *statist structure* of the world order system is itself a decisive obstacle to the growth of international adjudication.

Leo Gross is another scholar who also reacts strongly to the obvious inability of the Court to uphold Charter expectations. He notes the trend away from legal and institutional approaches to the problem of peace over the course of the century and creatively proposes a different way of appreciating the role of the Court than that set forth in the Charter:

> [I]t would seem that the commonplace assumption of arbitration and adjudication as a substitute for war or other methods of coercion should be abandoned. The proper role for the Court lies in promoting unification in the interpretation and application of international law, both customary and conventional, and contributing thereby to the rule of law and greater integration of the international society.[39]

By such an altered role and expectation, the Court "except perhaps in rare cases," would not make "a direct contribution to peacemaking but an indirect one by strengthening the underpinnings of law on which a secure peace can eventually be based."[40] Such a change of perspective makes for both a more

---

[38]Jennings couples this with the idea of using "some system of chambers to deal with lesser cases of first instance, perhaps with a right of appeal to the full Court," so as to make recourse to the International Court of Justice less formidable to the government officials contemplating such a move. Jennings, *supra* note 24, at 38. Such an approach is one form of preserving the larger potentialities of the Court, which involves keeping it as alive and active as possible, even if on a level of modest significance.

[39]*See* Gross, *supra* note 10, at 27.

[40]*Id.*

realistic and a more favorable account of the Court's record to date, fulfilling at least partially Julius Stone's plea for greater modesty, although, as Jennings wryly notes, "I am not sure that a reputation for law-making is always as attractive to the litigants as it is to professors."[41] In any event, Jenks and Lauterpacht have demonstrated in major scholarly works just how impressive and influential the cumulative contribution of the Permanent Court of International Justice / International Court of Justice has been to the development of international law.[42] Nevertheless, we are left with a somewhat sinking feeling that the rules of the game have been so dramatically weakened that it no longer means very much to be pronounced a winner!

Perhaps, in the end, it is better to share the view of Manfred Lachs, Polish jurist and former president of the Court, who sees the Court as "a great international experiment" that will require "time and experience to mature."[43] Judge Lachs is especially eager to reject the views of those who are disillusioned because the Court has failed to live up to earlier expectations of its becoming a pillar of world peace. He wants to substitute an appreciation of what has been done by the Court for a preoccupation with its shortcomings. This perspective invites attention to both sides of Stone's mandate, for modesty in the immediate period and for ambition in the longer haul.

There is some sense, however, that "waiting for the Court" will turn out to be "waiting for Godot." One is hardly encouraged by Jenks's flights of rhetoric, admittedly written for a Teheran audience in the setting of Pahlavi Iran, that "[w]e need a 'white revolution' developing insistently the law as we have inherited it into an accepted and effective common law of mankind."[44] We now know that the shah's White Revolution brought neither justice nor peace to Iran, but was an ideological stance that may have misled the outside world as to what was going on in Iran, although it evidently persuaded very few of the Iranian people. What Jenks presumably had in mind, a remnant from the more formalistic idealism of the League period, is a revolution from above with respect to foreign policy and international relations. It is one variant of the position, so popular on American patriotic holidays, that

[41]Jennings, *supra* note 24, at 37.
[42]*See* C. W. JENKS, *supra* note 12; H. LAUTERPACHT, *supra* note 33.
[43]*Quoted in* Jennings, *supra* note 8, at 56.
[44]C. W. JENKS, *supra* note 7, at 55.

treats governments as if they were destined to be enlightened in the long-term, and, therefore, eventually embody in official conduct those imperatives of interdependence that Hans Wehberg set forth more than sixty years ago.[45] Such expectations of enlightened responsiveness is one version of Anglo-American liberalism. As either prediction or prescription, however, it is myopic and unconvincing when extended to the role of international institutions in a global setting.

Governments are bound by short-term cycles of accountability to their national electorates (or if they are authoritarian governments, to the equally short-term expectations of their elites or party mechanisms). What is enlightened in international life is overwhelmingly defined by what is acceptable to the domestic polity, and is likely to be in fact selfish, shortsighted, and nationalistic in world-order terms. Such a generalization is even more likely to be true in periods of economic stringency and decline of the sort being experienced by the very societies assumed by liberal ideologists to have the greatest stake in constructing a peaceful and just system of world order.[46]

More serious, however, is the naiveté of the view of Western elites and their perceptions of self-interest and national interest in a world of gross economic disparities; ideological heterodoxy; Third World militancy; geopolitical rivalry between the superpowers and their blocs; population pressures; and anxiety about the cost, availability, and safety of energy resources, as well as growing concerns about the debt structure and the general viability of the international financial structure. There is less and less "political space" for "enlightened" foreign policy. Throughout the trilateral world in the late 1970s we have witnessed the triumph of political outlooks that reject liberal approaches in favor of tougher and more selfish leadership orientations. Despite the idealistic outreach of

[45]For the contemporary emphasis along the same lines, but with international economic functionalism largely replacing legalism, see M. CAMPS, THE MANAGEMENT OF INTERDEPENDENCE (1974), much of the work in The 1980s Project, and some of the studies of the Trilateral Commission, a private body organized on the initiative of David Rockefeller.

[46]Jenks, to be sure, recognizes that in the economic sphere it will be easier to be enlightened if the world pie is growing rapidly, so that adjustments on behalf of the poor can be made out of the increment in the additions to the wealth of the rich. See C. W. JENKS, supra note 7, at 156–59. In these pages Jenks argues that enlightened behavior vis-à-vis compulsory jurisdiction of the International Court of Justice must be reinforced by and coupled with enlightened statesmanship by the rich and powerful toward the poor and weak.

Jimmy Carter's human rights diplomacy during the first two years of his presidency, the United States, especially among Western countries, has been generally on the geopolitical defensive with respect to global reform. Contingency plans for forces for military intervention in the Persian Gulf are endorsed by a bipartisan consensus of American leaders. In other words, even on the basic issue of verbally accepting the Charter's prohibition of nondefensive force, we find a new unchallenged insistence even in the United States on sovereign prerogatives to protect vital economic interests, even if such protection means using military forces in a foreign country in a situation where there is no creditable claim of international legality.[47] This interventionary mood is relevant because it suggests that the state most ideologically committed to third-party approaches to order within its own society and in international life has abandoned such leadership in practice and partly also in language.[48] The point here is that even a "white revolution" (perhaps rarely more than widow dressing) from above is not in the offing; on the contrary, the direction of the movement in international relations is from third-party (impartial) to first-party (unilateral) procedures, to rely upon Thomas Franck's helpful classificatory scheme.[49]

There is another aspect of the liberal perspective that bears on how to think about the future of the World Court and, more generally, about the future of law itself. It is the position that incremental change works, albeit gradually, and that its cumulative impact has a significant reforming effect. Roger Fisher, in his major creative work on securing compliance with international law, offers us this generalization: "Past experience indicates that the world is more likely to move toward improving the international law system by bits and pieces rather than by adopting at one time a comprehensive revision of the United Nations Charter."[50] This affirmation is made in

[47]For one interpretation of this development, see Falk, *The Prospects of Intervention: Exporting Counterrevolution*, 28 NATION 22, 659–62 (1979). *See also* articles in the same "Special Issue" by LaFeber, at 656–59; Halperin, at 668–71; Klare, at 671–76; and Grendzier, at 689–95. Carter, *The State of the Union*, WEEKLY COMP. PRES. DOC. 114–80 (Jan. 21, 1980).

[48]For a trenchant account of the earlier and more extreme United States repudiation of the Permanent Court of International Justice, see D. FLEMING, THE UNITED STATES AND THE WORLD COURT (1945).

[49]T. FRANCK, *supra* note 19, ch. 1.

[50]R. FISHER, IMPROVING COMPLIANCE WITH INTERNATIONAL LAW 22 (1981).

the face of the grudging agreement of the experts that despite confident earlier expectations, third-party procedures and international adjudication have declined consistently over the past fifty or so years.[51] No empirical reality to the contrary seems capable of discouraging the truly committed gradualist.[52] We have no reason whatsoever to suppose, at present, that we can confidently work by bits and pieces to build a sufficiently secure future. Of course, some specific bits and pieces are positive contributions to the quality of international order at a given moment, but the cumulative trend is the reverse, and needs to be acknowledged and appraised. Positive incremental contributions have been *more* than offset by wholesale negative developments.

Small steps may, however, in Jenks's phrase, at least "unfreeze the position" of the present circumstances of the Court, allowing a possible new dynamic to take shape.[53] Whatever hope exists for the future of the Court may be found here. The objective situation is, however, currently adverse for such changes. Past trends are discouraging. No consensus on what can be done exists or is likely to be forthcoming. What is worse, policy-making officials in *all* sectors of international society are unconcerned, even indifferent, to the fate of the Court and the legal system it represents. Comprehensive approaches to global reform almost totally neglect the legal and third-party dimension of change.[54]

Nevertheless, the World Court exists and is accepted as a permanent part of international life. The present drift of international relations is dangerous and unsatisfactory for most actors. An unpredictable event might galvanize the entire international system in a positive way. A leader who captures the world's imagination with a serious, although domestically risky, commitment to international third-party approaches might serve as a catalyst. A single case comparable in magnitude to the *South West Africa Cases,* in which an International Court of Justice decision is seen as preventing bloodshed or

---

[51]*Id.*

[52]The same observation applies to the parallel contention made by advocates of arms control in the face of more than three decades experience with a quickening arms race and a rising risk of nuclear war.

[53]C. W. JENKS, *supra* note 12, at 764.

[54]Illustrative neglect is evident in such diverse writings as those of the World Order Models Project, the Club of Rome, Foundation Reshaping the International Order (RIO), The 1980s Project, and the Trilateral Commission.

national humiliation, could reopen, on a political plane, the case for third-party approaches so well prepared on a scholarly plane by such authors as Thomas Franck, Roger Fisher, Philip Jessup, C. Wilfred Jenks, R. P. Anand, and many others.[55] In this spirit, procedural innovations, movements for the repeal of the Connally Resolution and similar constraints on third-party approaches, sensitivity to confidence-building appointments to the bench of the World Court, and encouragement of an expanded reliance on the Advisory Opinion jurisdiction of the Court to review controversial constitutional issues arising within the United Nations system are all *potentially* constructive moves during this waiting and watching period.[56]

Whether such steps *actually* turn out to be constructive depends on our ability to strike a balance between judicial craft and function and the political configurations that animate international society at the present time. This idea of balance, the guiding idea of the chapters that follow, is relevant in at least four separate contexts:

1. *an inner balance* to be struck by the Court between efficiency and respect for sovereign rights on such matters of judicial practice as delay, expense, and deliberative process;[57]
2. *an inner balance* to be struck in the jurisprudence of the Court between jurisprudential coherence and political responsiveness;
3. *an intermediate balance* to be struck between the Court as a judicial organ and the overall United Nations system of which it is a part;
4. *an outer balance* to be struck between the adjudication function and the wider currents of international life, especially those in the political and moral spheres.

[55]See their important works, *supra* notes 19, 50, 28, 7, 12, 14.

[56]On specific proposals for reform, see Gross's work *supra* note 10, JUDICIAL SETTLEMENT OF INTERNATIONAL DISPUTES, *supra* note 8, and C. W. JENKS, *supra* note 12; on the idea of expanding reliance on advisory opinions, see Jennings, *supra* note 24, but consider also the realist concern about reliance on legal methods to resolve political disputes at this stage of United Nations development. *See also* discussion of *Certain Expenses* adjudication, chapter 5.

[57]On the latter, see Lillich & White, *The Deliberative Process of the International Court of Justice: A Preliminary Critique and Some Possible Reforms*, 70 AM. J. INT'L L. 28 (1976).

These ideas of balance represent an attempt to reconcile integrity and creativity within the judicial sphere of international society. The proposition on which such an approach rests is widely shared, namely, that either too little or too much "political" responsiveness is damaging to the role and stature of the World Court. In different respects and for different reasons, the Court was not responsive enough in the *South West Africa Cases* and in its *Certain Expenses* Advisory Opinion and probably was overly responsive in the *Namibia* Advisory Opinion. The boundary line drawn between too much and too little is necessarily controversial, reflecting, among other factors, a judgment about critical arenas. If one's primary concern is with the governmental arena of a particular state (say, South Africa's or the Soviet Union's), the assessment of responsiveness moves in one direction; if one's primary concern is with the Security Council or General Assembly, assessment moves in the opposite direction. Part of an adequate conception of balance means having some coherent way to relate and rank the main political arenas relevant to the international legal order in different substantive circumstances. Many of these concerns have been traditionally discussed in terms of the relations between law and politics in international disputes.[58]

There is a persisting confusion about the nature of law in international society. When Jennings writes: "[w]hat seems to me more damaging than ideological differences has been the flight away from the idea of the rule of law in international society which has been a characteristic of the United Nations period"[59] he is implying that there exists an established, acceptable, objective international legal order. Many leaders and officials of governments, however, regard law as a political and moral instrument that must be assessed strictly by its effects and purposes. In their eyes, its validity depends on its responsiveness to their agenda of demands, claims, and priorities. For those who invested their efforts in setting up the earlier legal order, such a challenge appears to be directed at law itself, instead of being a challenge to particular laws or to a specific legal order. Without an international legislature, however, only war and political actions exist in international soci-

[58]*See, e.g.,* the useful review in Bloomfield, *supra* note 26.
[59]Jennings, *supra* note 24, at 37.

ety to push forward new attitudes towards international law beyond the consent-constrained and agreement-oriented traditional system.

Part of the problem faced by the World Court in these circumstances involves its ability to inspire confidence. If it adheres to Jennings's conception of law as humdrum routine, then the Court seems doomed to be hopelessly anachronistic, an identity that is constantly being suggested by its architectural structure and geographical presence in a conservative citadel of the old order, The Hague. If, contrariwise, it reflects too strongly the revisionist views of the majority in the General Assembly concerning the need to reorient law to serve the revolutionary goals of the Third World, then the still-powerful forces of tradition will be deeply antagonized. The personnel of the Court reflect this split, and because not much middle ground exists, the search for balance involves learning to walk a tightrope.

CHAPTER II

The World Court and the Big Case— With Special Reference to South West Africa / Namibia

> . . . *language*, here as elsewhere, will not get over its awkwardness, and will continue to talk of opposites where there are only degrees and many subtleties of gradation . . . .[1]

Nietzsche contends that the very syntax of our language produces an artificial and misleading tendency in its speakers to polarize reality into categories of "this" or "that." Nothing illustrates this tendency in legal inquiry more than the dichotomy between "legal" and "political." This distinction can only be drawn properly by degrees and subtleties of gradation depending on context, whether the reference is to arenas or to issues.

At the same time, along with the distortion that is habitually produced by overdrawing this distinction, a natural pressure exists to clarify and identify limits, in this instance, limits upon the judicial function. Some issues in dispute between states seem ill-suited to judicial resolution because their essence concerns controversy over what the law *should* be. The character of these legislative claims generally will be disguised by the initiating party to adapt these claims to the normal conception of judicial function, which is confined to the determination of what the law *is*. The strain on judicial function is greatest here if the overall international community is watching and waiting for the court's judgment. In most such cases, nonjudicial arenas are better suited to express the legislative or reformist mood of the international community. As Roger Fisher puts it, "[t]he greatest talent of the law appears to be to deal with questions when they are small and to keep them small."[2] The

[1] F. NIETZSCHE, BEYOND GOOD AND EVIL 35 (Vintage ed. 1966).
[2] R. FISHER, IMPROVING COMPLIANCE WITH INTERNATIONAL LAW 16 (1981).

epitome of "the legal," at least in the reigning West, is to resolve
conflict by way of adjudication. In judicial arenas, parties to a
dispute are supposed to be the beneficiaries of a third-party
settlement; what is involved is a disinterested appreciation and
application of existing legal rules and principles to the controversy. After several decades of legal realism, it now is generally
accepted that adjudication inevitably involves a generous ad-
mixture of judicial discretion—what is sometimes more affir-
matively described as "judicial innovation," "judicial creativity,"
or even "judicial legislation." We now also know that to speak
about disinterested judges is to make reference to their integrity with respect to the dispute, to their willingness to listen with
respect to opposing arguments, and to their willingness to suspend formal judgment until the parties have had their day in
court. Disinterestedness cannot mean neutrality in any fundamental sense toward the issues at stake. In fact, it does not and
cannot mean neutrality with respect to values at stake, given the
normative character and sensibility of human beings. A judge
necessarily has an evolved view of human society that includes
an elaborate series of subviews on issues of social justice, state
power, peaceful change, and judicial function, all of which inform his judicial outlook. Indeed, the greatest judges are those
who bring their worldview into play without sacrificing any of
the elements of judicial craftsmanship, which is a shorthand way
of describing those qualities of demeanor and analysis associated with proper behavior in the judicial arena.[3]

Part of the reality of judicial process is constituted by the
complexity of fact and law. There are many interpretative
paths that reasonable men and women might choose to reach
a judgment. Logic entails almost nothing once fact/law complexity is present. It is the uncertainty of the law that generally explains the impulse to litigate a claim even in a well-
structured domestic society. If the law were "obvious" and
the capacity to identify who is "right" in a dispute quite clear,
then it would rarely be attractive to incur the costs and bur-
dens of litigation. This uncertainty is acknowledged and
made manifest in the allowance made for dissenting opinions
in most judicial bodies that operate independently, that is,
free from political control. Uncertainty is also expressed by
the provision of an appeals procedure. Reasonable judges
selected from homogeneous socioeconomic backgrounds can

[3]On the issues discussed in this paragraph, see B. CARDOZO, THE NATURE OF THE
JUDICIAL PROCESS (1921); R. WASSERSTROM, THE JUDICIAL DECISION (1961).

arrive easily at contradictory assessments of what a court's judgment should be.

In the background of our discussion, then, is that sense conveyed by Roger Fisher that law contributes most to society when it disposes of the routine and when it can operate quietly, relatively free from public pressures, to reach a particular decision about a disputed point. When public pressure exists it is either confirmed by the judgment, whereby the losing party becomes naturally convinced that the judicial process has been corrupted, or it is defied, and then the public repudiates the results of adjudication as a fiasco, meanwhile trying through popular procedures to reshape the judicial process or the foundation upon which it rests to assure greater responsiveness to the general will. Even so conservative a jurist as Sir Gerald Fitzmaurice has written, while serving as a judge on the World Court, that higher judicial tribunals often will be presented with the type of case "that a considerable element of legal policy will and within permissible legal limits, should enter into the process of deciding them, taking account of the climate of opinion of the day, and of prevailing social and economic tendencies."[4]

The form of this interplay between the political environment and judicial behavior depends on the character of the political system. If it is a highly authoritarian system, then the judge who defies political pressures may soon find himself before a firing squad or in a mental institution. If the political system is more democratic, then the judge who flagrantly defies public sentiments (or even well-organized, vindictive special-interest groups) will be vilified, threatened with impeachment proceedings, and generally rejected and isolated by the relevant community, at least until the storm of protest blows over. Such a controversial judge will, also, of course, be revered by those who share his or her disposition.

Our most important concern here is with judicial effectiveness. If a judicial result appears either to be dictated by the popular mood or to contravene directly that mood, then the result will appear to be less legitimate and will in fact be, to that extent, less acceptable. The acceptability of a judgment is

[4]Fitzmaurice, *Judicial Innovation*, in CAMBRIDGE ESSAYS IN INTERNATIONAL LAW: ESSAYS IN HONOR OF LORD McNAIR 25–26 (1965); not unexpectedly, even in the course of the same essay, he endorses the position of the dissent in the original advisory proceeding of the *South-West Africa* litigation, *id.* at 35–39, concluding that the dissenters, Lord McNair and Judge Read, "demolished with telling ease the arguments relied upon by the majority to support its position . . . ." *Id.* at 38.

enhanced to the extent that assured independent procedures
for enforcement exist. If these procedures do not exist or are
weak, then judicial effectiveness is that much more dependent
on the public acceptance of judicial conclusions, including the
public's sense of the fairness of how the results were reached.
In less momentous contexts and decisions, such issues are not
generally raised because there is no audience to be placated or
antagonized. The parties themselves, win or lose, share a common, prevailing interest in having the dispute settled according to judicial procedures.

In some situations, however, big questions are deliberately
entrusted to the judicial arena, at least by one side. Possibly
the legislative function is stalemated, or one side feels that the
judicial arena would be receptive to its claims, thereby shifting
the balance of attitude and breaking the stalemate in the legislative system. Americans, in particular, are preoccupied with
the legislative and quasi-legislative roles of the judiciary and
with the resultant interplay between these arenas. In fact, the
United States Supreme Court, as the final judicial arbiter of
the United States Constitution, does play a notable and distinctive legislative role, quite often in relation to big issues.
This role was not foreordained in American constitutional history. If reflected the deep commitment early in the republic to
a constitutional order based on the separation of powers and
the system of checks and balances, which led naturally to a
deep commitment to the ideal of judicial independence. It also
reflected the bold and formative role played by John Marshall
and other forceful jurists in the early history of the Court in
asserting the role of the Supreme Court in the American
scheme of government. Later on, it reflected a progressive
view of government in which the law is understood as an
instrument to bring about more liberal and enlightened policies, thereby blurring the legal/political boundary line, as well
as the related judicial/legislative boundary line.[5]

Nevertheless, the history even of the United States Supreme
Court has been one of fire and passion whenever big questions were judicially resolved in a way that challenged the
political will of the public—for instance, when the Court
seemed to resist Roosevelt's New Deal legislative reforms, or
more recently, when it was argued and widely believed that

[5]This line, interestingly, has remained sharp in the context of war and peace, courts
rejecting legal claims arising in relation to war by characterizing them as political.

the Court attempted to put the civil liberties of the criminally accused ahead of effective law enforcement during the period of the Warren Court. Whether the political tactics of the day involved the extreme plans "to pack" the Court by expanding its size, or was accomplished more moderately by appointing new justices holding what was considered a more acceptable outlook, there has been a persistent tug-of-war throughout American judicial history between judicial autonomy of adjudicative institutions and political oversight. This tension seems especially appropriate for the United States. Any more purist conception of judicial function would disrupt that precarious balance between independence and accountability that generally has been maintained and is so valuable to the political process in the United States, despite the stresses and strains that have erupted in agitated controversy from time to time, particularly during periods of heightened social conflict.

Other people in other countries in the world, even those with liberal democratic systems of government, place far less faith in judicial institutions, especially as agents of change, than Americans do. Most states are not democratically constituted in any genuine sense and are ruled by a strong executive that dominates the entire governmental process, including the court system. In such circumstances, the legislative process is rarely more than a rubber stamp for executive fiat. All the functions of government are coercively concentrated in one person or in a small group. These leaders can only be overthrown, they cannot be replaced by normal political procedures. Responsiveness to the will of the ruler is the order of the day, and only very occasionally, usually as a deliberate political challenge, will the highest court in the land defy the expectations of the prevailing political structures. Even in many democratic societies the courts by tradition are not expected to handle big unresolved questions of public policy. There exists in these states a sharper allocation of function between the judicial and the legislative elements. The Courts are confined to the routine and tend to avoid developing the larger implications of smaller controversies. More particularly, unlike the American system, European and Japanese courts do not envision their role as including the mission, admittedly exceptional in any legal system, of overcoming a legislative or political stalemate.

When we shift our concern to international society, many of these same issues emerge in an altered and more severe form. The whole idea of international adjudication is established from the beginning against a background dominated by the doctrine and practice of state sovereignty. Charles De Visscher put this circumstance well:

> From its very beginning, the Court has understood that in the application of the law, as in the establishment of its own powers, sovereignty would be the center and the symbol of resistance, the critical element that it must try to contain without provoking dangerous reactions, to respect without subordinating to it the law of which the Court is the guardian.[6]

On a doctrinal level, the significance of sovereignty is its requirement of consent. A state cannot be obliged to have recourse to any third-party procedure unless its government has given its consent. Consent can take the form of either a particular agreement with respect to the dispute in question or a generalized commitment to accept recourse to third-party procedures, or, possibly, a specific commitment to accept the compulsory jurisdiction of the International Court of Justice for a class of disputes or for all international legal disputes not resolved by diplomacy or local remedies. As was suggested in the preceding chapter, the states of the present world are not disposed to accept such generalized commitments to adjudication at this stage in the development of international society. Indeed, for reasons already set forth, there is a declining willingness to make such a generalized commitment.

As Lauterpacht ruefully observes,

> [g]overnments have not availed themselves of these potentialities of international justice. This is the main reason why the Court has not been in the position to make the contribution to peace which would stem from a general conviction of the members of the international community that no State should deny to other States the elementary benefit of a contested legal right being adjudicated by a tribunal administering international law.[7]

Underlying this observation is a moral judgment that governments, if they only would see the light, would submit unconditionally to the compulsory jurisdiction of the World Court. Such third-party "messianism" supposes that the main obstacle to governments doing that arises from an outmoded insistence by governments on first-party (unilateral) or second-party (bi-

---

[6]C. De Visscher, The Theory and Reality of Public International Law 392 (1968).

[7]H. Lauterpacht, *supra* note 33 of chapter 1, at 5.

lateral; for instance, diplomacy, mediation) images of the relationship between sovereignty and conflict resolution.

Charles De Visscher interprets this same reality of judicial marginality quite differently: "[T]he unconditional undertaking to submit to judicial settlement all disputes without exception would hardly be in keeping with the present structure of international relations."[8] Given the decentralized structure of the state system, he argues that the judicial role is necessarily and appropriately restricted. Governments are not hapless victims of myopic versions of sovereignty; they properly favor those procedures of conflict resolution that are appropriate for this kind of world-order system. By putting Lauterpacht's indictment of state sovereignty alongside De Visscher's justification of its exercise, the issue is posed as a question of contradictory claims toward an explanation of the relationship between sovereignty and adjudication.

In fact, both Lauterpacht and De Visscher contribute to our understanding. As Lauterpacht suggests, we *need* third-party procedures of regularity to secure any kind of peace in a world of sovereign states. The absence of peace, given the availability of the procedures, is a consequence of the refusal of governments to submit disputes to these procedures. From a normative point of view, this refusal is *not* inevitable; it is an exercise of *choice* and *will* and can be altered. Yet, as De Visscher suggests, the logic and structure of the state system— the inequality of its members, their traditions of autonomy, and their competition for power, wealth, and prestige—is inconsistent with the acceptance of third-party procedures for conflict settlement on vital matters. The states' refusal to accept compulsory jurisdiction exhibits their sensitivity to the prevalence of this political condition and is likely to persist, however unhappy it makes the champions of legalism in international affairs, or however foolish it may seem in relation to longer-term human, and even national, interests.

As a practical matter, global deference to state sovereignty is more pronounced than ever as a historical international tendency. Is this view regressive at this stage of the development of international society? From whose perspective? The answers to these questions are not self-evident, especially because the stakes of conflict are high, as even legal idealists would agree.

Socialist countries reject altogether the premises of suprana-

[8]C. DE VISSCHER, *supra* note 6, at 377.

tionalism, viewing international institutions as projections of
class rule and therefore, historically, created to serve capitalist
interests, or the interests of states in which capitalism prevails.
Most Third World countries, even those that are governed by
weak and dependent leaders, generally regard the active exercise of sovereignty as their most effective antiimperialist instrument. Most advanced industrial countries, regardless of
ideology, except in the case of minor disputes with one
another, have been generally reluctant to risk an erosion of
their entrenched positions in the world system by an acceptance of a third-party approach.[9]

The international legal order is relatively unelaborated. The
uncertainty of international law is evident, making prediction of
outcome harder. There is no stream of precedents, tradition, or
a readily accessible corpus of rules that relate the law authoritatively to most of the central issues of international life. In these
circumstances, any submission to the World Court is inevitably
an invitation to judicial legislation and is seen as such, even if the
process is described as "judicial innovation." The international
situation is also shaped by the absence of any acknowledged
legislative organ. The capacity of governments to withhold their
consent from the explicit formation of norms acts as a definite
constraint upon relying on lawmaking treaties as a substitute for
legislation. Because of the importance of sovereignty considerations in regard to third-party jurisdiction and compliance, the
Court has sensibly tended to bend over backwards to accommodate sovereign states as participants in its procedures, especially

[9]The evolution of regional institutions in Europe illustrates the first part of this
generalization. It should also be noted, in qualification of the second part of this
proposition, that there is support by richer developed countries for compulsory third-
party procedures for certain subject matters—for instance, investment and ocean
rights disputes. For more on this, see chapter 7.

[10]The Court's solicitude for the defendant state is, perhaps, most dramatically illustrated by its willingness to allow South Africa to submit incredible quantities of redun-
dant evidence in written form and in oral proceedings. *See* chapter 3. In this regard, the
effort to cast a state in the role of de facto defendant, without acquiring its genuine
consent to the proceedings, is hazardous for the Court from the point of view of its
growth as an institution. This issue is most directly posed in the context of several
advisory opinions. The notion of judicial caution implicit in the *Eastern Carelia* proceedings before the Permanent Court of International Justice was an apt acknowledgment of
these limits, perhaps too easily ignored by the International Court of Justice in the more
difficult—that is, more politicized—environment of its operations. *See Status of Eastern
Carelia Case*, 1923 P.C.I.J., ser. B, No. 5; issues resolved differently by *Certain Expenses of
the United Nations*, 1962 I.C.J. 151 (Advisory Opinion of July 20); *Interpretation of Peace
Treaties with Bulgaria, Hungary, and Romania*, 1950 I.C.J. 65 (Advisory Opinion of March
30): these issues form the crux of chapter 6.

those states cast in the role of defendant.[10] Even if they are in principle committed to compulsory jurisdiction, respondent states, nevertheless will often challenge the jurisdiction of the World Court and submit to its adjudicative competence only after preliminary objections fail. Deference to sovereignty also explains why the Court has tended to give the conflicting parties, especially the accused state, every opportunity to be heard, even if the effect has been to drag out the proceeding, arousing a torrent of public scorn for the baroque quality of international adjudication. Because the stature and role of the Court depends on voluntary patterns of submission and compliance, the parties in conflict exert considerable influence on the proceedings, since part of what makes a judgment finally acceptable is the belief by the losing side that it unqualifiedly has had its *full* day in court.

Given the realities of international competition, it is to be expected that governments will not risk their positions on vital matters very often. The uncertainties of diplomacy seem preferable, even if they include the danger that what is left unresolved can explode into political violence and warfare.

This preference for diplomacy holds especially true for that side that materially holds the cause at stake in the dispute, whether it be territory or rights of some kind. By negotiating, even by stalling, this state can hold onto what it has for the indefinite future. By submitting to a third-party process, it risks having to give up what it has. This risk seems inevitable and necessary in a system where recourse to third-party procedures is an established option. In contrast, it seems gratuitous where the availability of the third-party procedure is itself discretionary. Thus, even if formal consent is somehow present in a dispute that raises critical political issues, actual consent will normally be lacking. De Visscher once again has a helpful formulation:

> When a dispute, though it has a particular and legally definable object, is not detachable, politically speaking, from a serious political tension—when, for instance, it arises between States precisely by reason of this tension or comes to represent the tension to the point of being its manifestation or symbol—it becomes clear that resistance to judicial settlement finds its real explanation in the political tension and not in the refusal to submit to the judge the dispute *in re*.[11]

[11]C. DE VISSCHER, *supra* note 6, at 372.

The expectation that losing would nonetheless constitute an acceptable risk and that an adverse judgment would be authoritative, even if unpleasant, are preconditions for judicial effectiveness at the international level. The international situation is such that a judgment by a Court is seen, at most, as strengthening the political position of the winning side rather than undercutting the legitimacy of the loser.[12]

The problems of securing compliance for this type of dispute are formidable. International law depends for its effectiveness on voluntary patterns of compliance reinforced, to some indefinite degree, by the logic of reciprocity.[13] As long as the issues can be kept small, or made to seem and feel small, securing compliance is generally no problem; governmental bureaucracies incline toward rule-oriented behavior and value occasions for regularity and reliability. But, when the issue is large and controversial or is felt to be so, especially when consent to submit to a third-party procedure is itself imposed as an aspect of the controversy, then the problems of compliance are likely to be formidable. Given the structure of the world system and prevailing views on the exercise of sovereign rights, a formal commitment to compulsory jurisdiction remains a tenuous basis for effective third-party intervention. Much more relevant to the prospects of judicial compliance is the genuineness of consent at a given moment in a particular case and the willingness to participate in the particular context of a given dispute. The movement to achieve a generalized advance commitment to compulsory jurisdiction may be premature at the present stage of international relations, placing an excessive burden on third-party approaches that ultimately depend on voluntary patterns of compliance, *i.e.*, on self-enforcement.

The problem goes beyond assessing the prospects for compliance with Court decisions. There is the related question of the acceptability of the Court's judgments. Given present circumstances in relation to third-party procedures, any adverse judgment about a politically sensitive issue will not be viewed as acceptable to the losing side, no matter how careful and extensive the procedures used to arrive at it. Just how and in

[12]*E.g.*, efforts by the United States to invoke the International Court of Justice in its effort to mobilize support for the release of hostages seized at the United States Embassy in Teheran on November 4, 1979. *See* chapter 5.

[13]*See* R. FALK, THE ROLE OF DOMESTIC COURTS IN THE INTERNATIONAL LEGAL ORDER 14–52 (1964).

what way the judgment is adverse will naturally affect the degree and the quality of the judgment's nonacceptability. It is important to realize and keep in mind, however, that the actuality of sovereignty inhibits any *qualitative* expansion of judicial function at this stage in the development of international society.[14] The time, the expense, and the style of the World Court arguably discourage a *quantitative* expansion in the number of cases handled that might, in time, blur and even begin to erode the boundary that prevents the Court from addressing most politically salient disputes.[15] The World Court's record since 1945 has been conditioned by the global situation, which make judicial arenas inappropriate for highly controversial disputes (the *qualitative* dimension). Because the Court is the principal judicial organ of the United Nations, it is an inappropriate arena for low-salience disputes (the *quantitative* dimension). Caught between the unrealizable expectations of the Charter vision and the inhospitable environment of international relations, the Court languishes in limbo, moving slowly from disappointment to despair and finally onto a plateau of public and even professional indifference.

This qualitative/quantitative distinction touches upon the root of the World Court's difficulties as an institution. The Court, by tradition, is constituted by Charter norms and by its own framework of procedures to deal effectively with *qualitatively* significant political disputes. After all, the Charter is primarily addressed to the question of preventing war. The World Court as "the principal judicial organ of the United Nations" (art. 92) is assimilated into this universe of expectation, and this duty is reinforced by the obligations of chapter 6 of the Charter that member states seek "pacific settlement" of

[14]At least, of the variety associated with the International Court of Justice; such a realization should put the debate on the Connally Reservation into proper perspective. With or without the Connally Reservation, adjudication should be available for routine disputes, and generally not available for political disputes. The same goes for proposals to give organs of the United Nations and other international institutions standing to initiate contentious proceedings in the International Court of Justice. No formal expansion in the scope of judicial competence at the global level can overcome, by itself, structural restraints on international adjudication that arise from state sovereignty as an operative code that limits resolution of serious international disputes to first- and second-party methods. As such, the Connally Reservation may amount to an enlightened compromise on the question of compulsory jurisdiction, given the structure of world order and the prevailing attitude of elite and public opinion. For more on this, see T. FRANCK, *supra* note 19 of chapter 1, at 1–45.

[15]*See* discussion of these questions by Jennings, *supra* note 24 of chapter 1, at 38.

any international dispute that might endanger world peace. As the United Nations shifts its own priorities, the perspectives of what is expected of the Court change correspondingly. Most representatives of the member states in the United Nations expect the Court to contribute to the general purposes of the Organization, as these are constituted by whatever political consensus prevails in the General Assembly and the Security Council at a given time, but certainly not to decide a case in such a way as to undermine or challenge that consensus.

This central dilemma of the International Court of Justice has been accentuated in recent times by the globalization of international relations, by disjunctions between military, economic, and political power and functions, and by the intensification of legislative, reformist pressures within the United Nations.[16] On the one side, the Court is constrained by the persistent, intensifying clamor of sovereign states claiming a discretionary veto over any recourse to third-party procedures. It is also constrained by its own statutory tradition as an organ of international law. This tradition has been reinforced continually by appointing jurists of distinction to the Court, many of whom have regarded the discharge of judicial function in the Court as a professional, technical undertaking. On the other side, the United Nations provides an environment wherein a politcal consensus among governments can be shaped. In at least some circumstances, this consensus is formed in the direction of what the organized international community believes to be the interests of peace and justice. Each organ of the Organization, including the judicial organ, is expected in turn to add its weight to the process of collective decision making. This consensus-forming process definitely characterizes the work of the General Assembly, although the reception and the weight of the consensus depend on whether and to what extent it enjoys the support of all major sectors (the three worlds) of international society. There is a great difference in quality between a nominal assent to a General Assembly position by a state and a serious commitment by that state to the decision as a matter of independent foreign policy. And, of course, a state opposed to a General Assembly position will stress the constitutional limitation of Assembly powers to that of mere recommendation.

[16]For discussion of these disjunctions and their complicating impacts on international relations, see S. HOFFMAN, PRIMACY OR WORLD ORDER? (1978).

For some states, a breakthrough for the General Assembly occurred in the 1960s, when a decisive majority endorsed for the first time the goals of decolonialization and national self-determination and thereby effectively isolated those few states that were trying to maintain the old international order. For other states, this breakthrough was understood as nothing less than a constitutional breakdown, because those with voting power were overriding the concerns of those with financial and military power. This division and its causes persist, and touch on many crucial matters in the United Nations: the status of nuclear weapons, the character of Zionism and apartheid, the obligations of rich countries toward poor countries, and the proper distribution of ocean mineral wealth. In general, the lawmaking claims of the General Assembly have been untested in the judicial setting of the World Court, and there has been little interest in administering such a test.[17] The essence of the test would be whether to accord a quasi-legislative character to the formal resolutions of the General Assembly or to abide by a strict reading of the Charter that limits the Assembly to a recommendatory role.[18] Whether the principle of state sovereignty or the ideal of world community, both given some voice in the Charter equation, tips the balance in the judicial determinations of the World Court will influence decisively its identity as an institution. In particular, it will provide a systematic basis for appraising the most controversial activities of the World Court.

Leo Gross argues that "the central issue" complicating the activity of the International Court of Justice is its "dual function" expressed by the Charter, one of which looks toward the existence of a United Nations Court and the other of which looks toward the Statute of the World Court that is premised upon the quite different idea of the Court as an organ of traditional international law. Such a dualism is paralleled by the competence of the Court, on the one hand to grant Advisory Opinions at the behest of the United Nations, and, on the other, to decide contentious cases arising out of disputes be-

---

[17]See, e.g., Judge Lauterpacht's Separate Opinion in *South-West Africa—Voting Procedure*, 1955 I.C.J. 67, 90 (Advisory Opinion of June 7).

[18]There are other intermediate techniques of validation less extreme than attributing legislative status to General Assembly acts: regarding these acts as evidence of or even as proof of customary international law, or of natural law assimilated into the idea of general principles of law.

tween sovereign states. Dual functioning seemed initially justified by the success of the Permanent Court of International
Justice in reconciling both roles. It has not worked out nearly
so well, however, in the altered circumstances of the International Court of Justice. Gross offers two explanations:

> the links between the Court and the United Nations are much
> closer—some writers call them "organic"—than were those be-
> tween the old Court and the League . . . .[T]he separation [of
> functions in the two types of proceedings] has not and perhaps
> could not be maintained, as illustrated in the *South West Africa*
> cases.[19]

In Gross's view, the Court has done far better in its international law role than in its United Nations' role. The main
reason for the deterioration in the Court's performance of the
latter, affecting the more visible side of the Court's role in
world affairs, is the result of an evolution in "the nature of
post–World War II politics" that "the founders could not
forsee." Gross argues that "the eminently contentious climate
which has settled on the political organs of the United Nations . . . has not been hospitable to the stabilizing function of
the Court."[20] In effect, the relative homogeneity of views represented in the League encompassed a greater willingness to
believe that third-party procedures could be trusted to issue
impartial determinations that would not in its results ever
greatly offend member governments. In contrast, the revisionist consensus now existing in the United Nations, one that
draws its strength from non-Western cultural, ideological, and
even geographical experience, is alien to the orientation associated with the World Court. As a result, the interplay between nonjudicial and judicial arenas in United Nations practice is bound to be controversial and troubled.

What makes this situation so problematical is the seesaw shifting in the balance between the Court's two functions. In the
time of the Permanent Court of International Justice, the
Court's identity as an organization of international law clearly
predominated, even spilling over to the discharge of its function in advisory proceedings. During the current era, however,
the Court's identity as an organ of the United Nations predomi-

---

[19]Gross, *The International Court of Justice and the United Nations*, 120 RECUEIL DES
COURS (Hague Academy of International Law) 313, 320 (1967-I).
[20]*Id.* at 334–35.

nates, even spilling over to its handling of contentious proceedings. In both settings, the view of *proper* judicial functioning
that exists in the political arenas of diplomacy is what is crucial.
When observers note "the contentious climate" of legal discussions in the political organs of the United Nations, they are
describing, usually critically, an atmosphere in which the ideas
of law and adjudication are not associated by participants in
debate with the neutrality of "law" or with the impartiality of
"third-party" procedures, but quite the contrary. Often, in the
United Nations, protaganists insist that standards of justice and
injustice must serve as yardsticks of assessment, thereby deny-
ing the basic liberal contention that third-pary procedures and
law-oriented approaches constitute justice, and thus transcend
politics in this wider sense.[21] This majority position can be understood, although it is not common to do so, as an argument
about law and judicial function, rather than as an expression of
their rejection by those with politicized agendas. We confront
here a genuine jurisprudential conflict. Those who seek to sustain the balance of judicial operations do so in order to assure
the protection of vested interests and entrenched rights; they
attack those who insist on rapid change in the interest of a
greater justice and claim that these people are seeking to destroy third-party procedures, constitutional processes, and judicial function. Those who are responsive to change argue that
only by overcoming the concrete and philosophical domination
of the past can third-party procedures be adopted to be integral
and beneficial to the international order. This argument is
clearly connected with the problems encountered as regards
the voluntaristic element of international legal existence—that
is, the realization that third-party jurisdiction and effectiveness
continue to depend in general and in particular on the voluntary acquiescence of the defendant state.

What becomes a central issue here is the ability of sovereign
right to defy a community consensus. Those governments

[21]One recent commentator, without intending humor, considers that
[a]nother negative development [bearing on the decline of the World Court] has
been the exposure of a generation of international law specialists, including visit-
ing scholars from the Third World, to the so-called "policy-oriented" school of
jurisprudence centered in the Yale University Law School. Couched in the impenetrable jargon of the social sciences, this doctrine reduces law to a mere tool for
rationalizing the policy goals and expectations of the community.
As if the impenetrable mystique of an objective legal order could be preserved,
especially from those impressionable scholars from the Third World! Maechling, *The
Hollow Chamber of the International Court,* 33 FOREIGN POL. 114 (1978).

most insistent on upholding noninterventionary norms and
extending their application to the activities of international
institutions are also those that take the view that law is always
and inevitably a political instrument. The insistence on nonin-
tervention protects the autonomy of weaker states, whereas
the demands for social change uphold the central demand of
poor or victimized states or movements for global reform. In
the ideological background of these claims are the influence
and concrete impact of Marxist critiques of liberal theory, especially the attack on those aspects of the theory that assign a
neutral mediational role to governing institutions and an objective neutrality to law and courts.

In effect, the World Court is caught in a political swirl not
much of its making or in its control. This swirl seems impossible to eliminate. Its effect is to inhibit still further recourse to
judicial procedures and the acceptability of judgments on salient disputes. The Court has (and will have in the future)
differences among its own members that reflect these varying
and even contradictory understandings of what is proper in
terms of judicial function. These are limiting realities, but they
do not necessarily foreclose the growth and development
either of third-party procedures or of the World Court.

Because of these kinds of differences, a balance of outlooks
needs to be represented on the bench of the Court that
roughly approximates the ratio of contending forces in the
world, especially as these are present in the United Nations.
Such a balance would upgrade the responsiveness of the
Court as an organ of the United Nations. Such a gain would
be achieved, perhaps, at the expense of its reputation as a
third-party institution in the Franck sense of a structure of
impartiality.[22] The policy question here is absolutely fundamental. For high-salience litigation, responsiveness is essential
to the viability of the World Court. For low-salience litigation,
such responsiveness is at best irrelevant and at worst corrosive
of confidence in the fairness of the Court as an institution for
dispute settlement. This issue of the internal balance of the
Court has to do with defining its basic institutional role. A
compromise between the two conceptions may not be as appropriate as clearly choosing one or the other. Choosing one
or the other conception of the Court as more significant at this

[22]*See* T. FRANCK, *supra* note 19 of chapter 1.

stage in the development of international relations can establish an institutional identity that is attractive to one or the other type of litigant. A compromise risks making the Court seem ill-suited to both types, too political for low-salience litigation and not political enough for high-salience litigation.

It is important to grasp the fragile character of our images and perceptions of judicial process in world affairs. At present, the absence of cases from the Court docket, the limited acceptance of compulsory jurisdiction, and the failure of the Court to reach "acceptable" decisions in either the *South West Africa* or the *Barcelona Traction* proceedings are understood generally, if temporarily, as persuasive indications of the status of international adjudication. Both scholars and statesmen seem guilty of misplaced concreteness with respect to the Court. It only takes a modest twist of the imagination to consider how the Court would be perceived if its most important case, the *South West Africa* litigation, had been decided the other way, and, more problematically, if the South African government, as a result of its own complex calculations of self interest, had acquiesced in a procedure that resulted in political independence for South West Africa/ Namibia.[23] Rewriting the history of the Court from this altered perspective can help to erode the sense of literalness, even fatalism, that is currently attached to its character and prospects. A new momentum is not foreclosed. Indeed, by acknowledging the possibility of alternative paths, we can influence the diagnosis and thereby the prognosis.

To move toward such a change requires paying attention to the politically charged dispute, the big case around which dominant images and perceptions form with respect to judicial function at the global level. To assist us in this task, it seems helpful to set forth some guidelines on judicial performance in regard to the big case as applicable to the International Court of Justice:[24]

[23]The second branch of this conjecture, if at all plausible, depends on the Court coping with apartheid is such a way that its extension to the mandate is rejected without, in effect, requiring South Africa to acknowledge the invalidation of its own domestic political order.

[24]A suggestive, similar effort to categorize postures toward the International Court of Justice, although in the special circumstances of the *South-West Africa Cases,* was made by D'Amato, *Legal and Political Strategies of the South West Africa Litigation,* 4 L. TRANSITION Q. 8–43 (1967). I am indebted to Professor D'Amato for the imaginative approach taken in his article.

1. The most important guideline has to do with whether adjudication can contribute to the peaceful resolution of the dispute; a priority is placed upon peace, not on justice as technically defined—that is, the objective is to get the issue somehow resolved by third-party intervention of a judicial variety and not by violence. As we have suggested, the grand political issues of the day can always be put in the form of a legal dispute, but a peaceful resolution depends on *both* sides wanting them so formulated and being willing to accept and implement a judicial defeat. As we have further suggested, this peace orientation dominates the Charter, but has been virtually irrelevant to the life of the Court.

2. A secondary guideline, difficult to acknowledge explicitly as an element in an adjudicative context, is to view recourse to the Court as a tactic in an ongoing process of building pressure to achieve peaceful change in a particular situation by nonviolent means. Here peace *and* justice are paramount, and neither can be jeopardized for the sake of the other. This understanding has special relevance in relation to an attempt to overcome resistance to the global will by an entrenched governing elite in a given state and its close allies. Whether such pressure is effective depends largely on relative coercive capacities; the results are not a matter of persuasion, but of applying pressure short of outright force to coerce a solution acceptable to *one side,* although the outcome is quite likely to involve elements of bargaining and compromise. Timing may also be important, providing the target state with a stake in the judicial approach. Thus, to lose slowly may amount to an acceptable compromise for a state that finds itself under increasing pressure to acquiesce in a global demand for change.

3. A third guideline, even more difficult to acknowledge than 2, is to view recourse to judicial remedies as part of a campaign to build support (or at least tolerance) for a particular side in an armed struggle. The purpose of adjudication may be to reinforce the moral claims of a liberation movement, or to build a case for the view that nonviolent alternatives have been exhausted, making the adoption of violent strategies less objectionable even

to states sympathetic with the target society's official position.

4. A fourth guideline, not much considered to date, is to view recourse to adjudication as part of a process of achieving global reform. The expectation here is that the Court can serve as a pedagogic forum within which a poststatist system of world order can be prefigured. Alejandro Alvarez of Chile in some of his separate opinions on the Court seemed to adopt such a posture,[25] as did Hersch Lauterpacht, but in the more restricted sense of using every opportunity of a dispute for a maximum elaboration of international laws.[26]

Against this background, our special concern here is with "the big case"—the dispute that touches on issues of global concern. The judicial treatment of such a case will make headlines throughout the world. The preceding argument suggests that as matters now stand such cases will be rare. They have so far been rare in the history of the World Court, although the question of classification of cases is itself a matter of interpretation. Our inquiry in this chapter is to discuss under what conditions it is sensible to submit the big case to the World Court and to consider the various judicial responses to such a submission. Voluntary submission of the big case is unlikely. Even a law-oriented country like the United States would have been reluctant to have the World Court decide whether some aspect of its Indochina policy violated the Charter and other rules of international law. Access to the Court, therefore, will come about as a result of compulsory jurisdiction (with all its dangers from the real objections of the respondent state) or in the context of advisory proceedings. To date, the Court has been split on whether and how to deal with the big case, a split that to some extent corresponds with the functional schism as to whether the Court should tip the jurisdictional and policy balance in the direction of sovereign prerogative or in the direction of the

[25]See, e.g., opinions in The International Status of South West Africa, 1950 I.C.J. 128 (Advisory Opinion of July 11); Reservations to the Convention on the Prevention and Punishment of the Crime of Genocide Case, 1951 I.C.J. 15 (Advisory Opinion of May 28); Fisheries Case (U.K. v. Nor.), 1951 I.C.J. 116 (Judgment of December 20); Competence of the General Assembly for the Admission of a State to the United Nations, 1950 I.C.J. 4 (Advisory Opinion of March 3); and see also A. ALVAREZ, LE DROIT INTERNATIONAL NOUVEAU (1959).

[26]For an exposition of Lauterpacht's overall attitude toward judicial function, see H. LAUTERPACHT, supra note 33 of chapter 1.

General Assembly consensus, or perhaps whether the Court should struggle for equipoise between the two.

It seems appropriate and helpful to ground this inquiry in the concrete circumstances of the ongoing dispute between the United Nations and South Africa over the administration and status of South-West Africa/ Namibia. What makes this dispute a big case is that it is concerned fundamentally with apartheid as a manner of relating state and society in a multi-racial setting. Faye Carroll is correct when she observes that "the South West Africa case is a reflection of two revolutionary movements which have dominated world politics in recent years. These movements seek the eradication of the last vestiges of colonialism and racial discrimination."[27] What is involved here is *official racism* of the sort embodied in the laws and regulations of South Africa and their extension to South West Africa. What makes this racism particularly inflammatory is that it is blatantly and formally relied upon by a *white* minority to exploit and dominate a much larger *black* majority.[28] Other forms of racial discrimination are widespread in the world; they are more or less tolerated, even if, in some instances, they approximate genocidal extremities. In this respect, General Amin's governance of Uganda, which encompassed severe racist policies, never became a matter of intense Third World concern. However, apartheid is a form of racial injustice that has been condemned repeatedly over the years as fundamentally incompatible with the Charter.

It is also the kind of issue that cannot easily be compromised. South Africa grounds the legitimacy of its political system on the reasonableness of apartheid. Its prevailing white minority overwhelmingly endorses the rationale, if not all of the tactics, used by the government in Pretoria to justify apartheid. Furthermore, given the demographic dynamics between the races in South Africa, the radical outlook of black leaders, and the gross economic, political, and social disparities among the racial groups, any structural move in the direction of racial equality would likely place the white

---

[27]F. CARROLL, SOUTH WEST AFRICA AND THE UNITED NATIONS at v (1967).

[28]Hedley Bull observes, in the course of discussing the special meanings of human rights in the Third World, that "[r]acial equality is above all a demand for the liberation of coloured peoples from subjection to white rule in southern Africa and elsewhere . . . ." Bull, *Human Rights and World Politics*, in MORAL CLAIMS IN WORLD AFFAIRS 87 (R. Pettman ed. 1979).

population in great jeopardy. Hence, South African leaders, including those responsible for governing South West Africa/ Namibia, reject altogether the *substantive* challenge to their policies dedicated to promoting the well-being of nonwhite people, that is, to apartheid. These leaders are also convinced that the repeated attacks by the United Nations upon apartheid are arbitrary, ill-informed, and unconstitutional intrusions of an interventionary character upon "the domestic jurisdiction" and sovereign rights of South Africa. The fact that the focus of action is upon mandated territory softens the constitutional objections, but it does not eliminate the wider implications of challenging apartheid as a legally acceptable way of relating state and society.

This is a big case because the two sides are prepared, if it becomes necessary, to fight and die to uphold their position. It is also a big case because other states and the world community as a whole are vitally interested in its eventual resolution. It is not a context in which the target state (the government of South Africa) is likely to accept third-party procedures except as a tactic of delay, and it is not a situation in which either side would accept, solely on the authority of law, the consequences of an adverse judgment. In such circumstances, we must ask the central question: Why go to the Court? We also need to know: How should the Court respond? How should the United Nations deal with the response made by the Court?

The dispute over South West Africa spans the entire history of the United Nations. In various forms, the Court has made six decisions. The controversy has attracted world attention and abundant scholarly comment, yet remains essentially unresolved.[29] The 1966 decision, perceived as supporting South Africa's main contentions, was greeted with shock and dismay everywhere except in South Africa and by some international lawyers.[30] The anger at the decision in the General Assembly, especially intense among African delegates, was particularly effective politically.[31] Some of the anger was vented directly at

[29]The important scholarly sources are collected in the bibliography in THE SOUTH WEST AFRICA/ NAMIBIA DISPUTE: DOCUMENTS AND SCHOLARLY WRITINGS ON THE CONTROVERSY BETWEEN SOUTH AFRICA AND THE UNITED NATIONS 543–62 (J. Dugard, ed., 1973).

[30]*See, e.g.*, the lead editorial, *South West Africa Verdict*, N.Y. Times, July 20, 1966, at 40, col. 1.

[31]*Summarized in* J. DUGARD, ed., *supra* note 29, at 376–408; *cf.* G. COCKRAM, SOUTH WEST AFRICAN MANDATE 344–61 (1976).

the Court, which was denounced in General Assembly debates. An additional budgetary appropriation the year of the decision was rejected by the Fifth Committee (Administrative and Budgetary questions) of the General Assembly, and later the African delegates openly blocked the election of Sir Kenneth Bailey of Australia to fill the unexpired term of Sir Percy Spender, the arch-villain of the 1966 decision.[32] Greater attention was paid thereafter to the ideological credentials of nominees for judgeships on the Court in subsequent elections, especially the triennial elections held in 1966. In 1971, the 1966 decision was undercut by an Advisory Opinion of the Court that seemed fully congruent with the will of the majority in the General Assembly and that evoked a long embittered dissent by Sir Gerald Fitzmaurice, the sole survivor of the 1966 majority. We have evidence here of a deep long-festering controversy about the role and function of the Court. It remains unresolved despite the greater congruence of outlook between the Court and the General Assembly achieved since 1966 through greater political oversight of the procedure for electing judges to the Court. Had the 1966 judgment come out in favor of Ethiopia and Liberia, as could easily have happened, we would today have a vastly different (although not necessarily more favorable) image of the World Court as an international actor. This "thin line" of perception reinforces my central argument that the course of the history of the Court is vulnerable to rather abrupt changes, for instance, to the emergence of some "new momentum" by the rendering of a popular judgment in a big case or by the rise of an important world leader who would bestow a large measure of confidence upon the Court.

In some important respects, the 1966 decision was "an accident" on a number of grounds that contributed to distorted relations between the Court and the main political organs of the United Nations. Had it not been for a certain laxness in electing judges and the removal from the scene of three judges with clear and known views on the controversy (adverse to South Africa's position)—one by death, one by illness, and one by disqualification—the 1966 decision would assuredly have come out the other way and reinforced the General

---

[32]Gross, *supra* note 19, at 324–25; J. Dugard, ed., *supra* note 29, at 378–79.

Assembly majority.[33] In this regard, I disagree with D. H. N. Johnson, Solomon Slonim, and others who regard the adventitious circumstances of the judgment as irrelevant. With abundant formalism of outlook, Johnson writes:

> It is useless to speculate how judges who are dead, or who, for other reasons, did not take part in the case, might have voted. Every judge is entitled, indeed bound, to "exercise his powers impartially and conscientiously" (Article 20 of the Statute). As for the President, if it falls to him to have a casting vote (Article 55(2) of the Statute), he is entitled to his own view as much as any other judge and if he is in any doubt—not that he was in this case—it is not unreasonable that he should give the benefit of that doubt to the respondent State.[34]

On one level, of course this is technically correct. But that is only one level, and the least discerning level at that. To attempt to restrict scholarly commentary to an explication of the exact judgment as handed down would be to virtually eliminate serious criticism, except that of a very technical character limited to an explication of what was decided.

There are predictive and interpretative guides relating to judicial behavior that help us to better understand what happened to alter the expectations created by the 1962 judgment.[35] These guides involve hypotheses about the consistency of a judge's approach to fundamental issues that are borne out empirically by the fact that for those who participated in both phases, every minority judge in the 1962 judgment on preliminary objections was in the majority in 1966 and vice versa. To overlook these unidirectional shifts in judicial personnel between 1962 and 1966 would impart an excessively "formal" and "analytic" quality to the outcome, and in addition would accord the outcome a finality and authoritativeness that is ill-warranted. It leads commentary toward an *overly* narrow jurisprudential and structural exposition of this big case, whereas a closer scrutiny suggests a much more contingent and illuminating interpretation.

It must be acknowledged, however, that the closeness of the

---

[33]See analysis along these lines in R. FALK, THE STATUS OF LAW IN INTERNATIONAL SOCIETY 378, 420, 388 n.28 (1970).

[34]Johnson, *The South-West Africa Cases (Second Phase)*, 3 INT'L REP. 173–74 (1967).

[35] *See* the discerning essay by Higgins, *The International Court and South West Africa*, 42 INT'L AFF. 573–599 (1966).

1962 judgment on preliminary objections was a warning sign. The mistake in expectations was to suppose that the jurisdictional issues had been put aside after 1962 and that the 1966 judgment would proceed immediately to substance. South Africa did not make that mistake, fully rearguing its jurisdictional objections to the competence of the World Court to try the case, although it was believed at the time that this was done partly to delay and confuse the proceedings. The judges of the Court gave the contending parties little hint that they were still contemplating issues of competence and seemed disinterested in the reargument of these issues, seemingly allowed out of deference to South Africa's sovereign rights to advance virtually any claim in its behalf, however remote from the likely grounds of disposition. Hence, the rationale of the 1966 judgment, as much as its content, aroused consternation and surprise among those who expected a decision on the substance of the allegations.

The narrow approach necessarily leads to a failure to understand the process and political features of the big case that are far wider and more powerful than the simple tactical foray that took place in the Court during the 1960s. Again, Professor Johnson's sympathetic interpretation of what the Court did in 1966 provides me with an example of what it is I am arguing against here. Johnson concludes his essay on the litigation with a series of propositions, the last of which is the following: "In any case, whatever may be thought of the 1966 Judgment, it is now part of the law and practice of the Court, to be ignored by counsel in future cases at their peril."[36] I would argue exactly to the contrary. To treat the 1966 judgment *as if* it were authoritative is to minconstrue the character of the big case and the Court and to overlook the degree to which the coordinate organs of the United Nations can impose pressure on the Court to revise an unacceptable judgment. The outcome of the 1971 Advisory Opinion, after some key personnel changes conceived deliberately in the spirit of revising the jurisprudence of 1966, suggests how wrong it is to suppose that the Court automatically will sustain an unacceptable judgment in a big case. What is at issue is a more fundamental dependence by the Court on its political context than is suggested by Leo Gross's helpful distinction between contentious proceedings that favor respon-

[36]Johnson, *supra* note 34, at 76.

dent sovereign states (the *Lotus* outlook) and advisory proceedings that favor the political climate of the United Nations. The posture of the litigation as contentious or advisory is a factor, but the disagreement as to judicial function emerged initially in the dissenting opinions of Judges McNair and Read in the 1950 Advisory Opinion on the status of the mandate in the United Nations. Lord McNair particularly prefigured the later split on the Court when he characterized the majority's view of the United Nations' right to substitute itself for the League in the workings of the Mandates System as "pure inference," "a piece of judicial legislation."[37] Sir Gerald Fitzmaurice, more than twenty years later, struck a similar note in his dissent in the 1971 *Namibia* advisory opinion case.[38]

My main point here is that the split over judicial function in the big case cannot be sufficiently understood merely by distinguishing advisory from contentious proceedings, although certainly the form of the proceeding should be noted and its specific relevance assessed. Historically, the Court's move in the direction of becoming a United Nations court in the advisory setting, by limiting the *Eastern Carelia* precedent to its facts, represented a definite shift in emphasis compared to the Permanent Court of International Justice period. This shift formally allows the advisory route to be used to circumvent the failure of respondent states to accept compulsory jurisdiction or to arrange for the voluntary submission of a particular controversy.

The absence of enforcement mechanisms in the Court and the United Nations, however, means that the enhancement of judicial competence in the big case may be fruitless from the point of view of judicial effectiveness. The main consequence of trying to mobilize judicial pressures against Communist respondent states (*e.g., Peace Treaties, Certain Expenses*) has been to make manifest the impotence of the judicial process at the implementation stage. In sum, the reality of sovereign rights persists despite the emergence of international institutions. These rights enjoy a wide backing, especially in relation to the obligation to submit disputes for peaceful settlement. To cir-

[37] 1950 I.C.J. 162.

[38] As Slonim observes, Fitzmaurice even supports the literal McNair-Read view of 1950 that the United Nations has never succeeded to the League's supervisory authority. S. SLONIM, SOUTH-WEST AFRICA AND THE UNITED NATIONS: AN INTERNATIONAL MANDATE IN DISPUTE 341 (1973).

cumvent sovereign rights via the advisory proceedings route does not seem to be a constructive technique of conflict resolution except in very special circumstances.[39]

The South West Africa/ Namibia dispute, then, had the characteristics of the big case from the beginning, but in the three advisory proceedings up through 1956, this was obscured by the tactics adopted. Questions of status and procedure under the mandate were put to the Court; the issues of racial discrimination and colonialism, always the world's foremost concern, were kept in the background of the litigation. The Court never responded with unanimity, but the split was always expressed in such a way that on each of the three occasions the majority opinion seemed to reinforce the claims of the General Assembly and to refute the position of South Africa, reflecting, in all probability, the substantive sympathy of the judges for the attacks upon apartheid. In such circumstances, the qualms of the minority were simply overlooked.

These "advisory" determinations were rejected and ignored by South Africa, thereby fostering the impression that more drastic measures would have to be adopted if peaceful change was to be brought about.

On the other hand, the governments of Great Britain and the United States had important material and strategic interests in southern Africa, as well as a variety of cultural ties, that made them very reluctant, even unwilling, to push the South African leadership very hard. Yet it was these two particular governments that possessed the connections and the leverage to make South Africa incur costs heavier than verbal abuse as a consequence of defying the United Nations' majority. There has been a campaign in the United Nations since its inception against apartheid, applied tactically to the mandate over South West Africa. By the late 1950s this campaign was in real need of new tactics in order to build pressure against the regime. It was obvious, given the geopolitical realities of that time and especially the Portuguese colonial hold over Mozambique and Angola, that South Africa was prepared to go on defying the General Assembly indefinitely.

South Africa also refused to cooperate with the attempts of the General Assembly and its agencies to put into effect the

[39]These circumstances have to do with the size, nature, and intensity of the political majority in the General Assembly and with the belief that a *legal* endorsement of its main claims would be politically useful in mobilizing pressure.

operational side of the 1950 advisory opinion: to impose the supervisory authority of the General Assembly over South Africa in relation to its obligations as mandatory power. Indeed, those years of "negotiation" in the 1950s were regarded as having exhausted the possibilities for a diplomatic resolution of the conflict. South Africa maintained its position throughout that the General Assembly was a hostile, usurping body; that the 1950, 1955, and 1956 Advisory Opinions reflected bias against it and were in any event "advisory;" and that the collapse of the League had led to the lapse of the mandate, and with it the end of all obligations of accountability to the organized international community.[40]

In 1957 the General Assembly requested the Committee on South West Africa to explore the possibility of legal action against South Africa. This group reported back that the compromissary provision contained in article 7 of the Mandate appeared to give states who were members of the League at its time of dissolution and who are currently members of the United Nations a right of access to the International Court of Justice in a contentious proceeding against the Mandatory to enforce the provisions of the Mandate.[41] In early 1960, the Liberian government asked the prominent American lawyer/diplomat, Ernest A. Gross, to prepare a legal memorandum on possible legal action against South Africa for distribution at the Second Conference of Independent African States. The Conference endorsed the tactic of seeking a decision by the World Court.

As Ernest Gross himself describes the motivation to seek recourse: "The objective was not to resolve doubt concerning the jurisprudence of the Mandate, which had its firm foundation in the Advisory Opinion of 1950, but to transform a dishonored, though authoritative, Opinion into an enforceable judgment."[42] Note here that the Court is perceived as providing an enforcement lever, *not* as resolving uncertain

[40]*See* chapter 3 for further elaboration.

[41]The relevant portion of article 7 provides: "The Mandatory agrees that, if any dispute whatever should arise between the Mandatory and another Member of the League of Nations relating to the interpretation or the application of the provisions of the Mandate such dispute, if it cannot be settled by negotiation, shall be submitted to the Permanent Court of International Justice."

[42]Gross, *The South-West Africa Case: What Happened?* 45 FOREIGN AFF. 40 (1966); this article was also relied upon for background on the decision to adjudicate described in the last paragraph; for more detail, see S. SLONIM, *supra* note 38, at 167–84.

issues of law. In that sense, the expectation was that the Court
would contribute to the wider process of dealing with a state
that was defying the General Assembly in an area of its special
competence and responsibility, namely, upholding the Mandate as a "sacred trust of civilization." The second aspect of
the decision relating to recourse to the Court assumed that the
Court would go beyond the earlier opinions to take on the
fiery center of the dispute, namely, the status of apartheid in
relation to the administration of the mandate. The basis for
such an assumption was that South Africa had failed as a
consequence of its racist policies to fulfill the basic obligation
of article 2, that is, "to promote to the utmost the material and
moral well-being and the social progress of the inhabitants of
the Territory." Bringing apartheid under the jurisdiction of
the Court, as was almost inevitable given the African auspices,
assured that the litigation would be treated as a big case, and
also excited inflated expectations about what was to be expected from the Court's determination. This inflation of expectations was further guaranteed by South Africa's decision
to participate actively, in the adjudicative process before the
World Court, something that was not at all assured in advance. At last there would be an authoritative judicial determination that apartheid was an unacceptable form of official
racial policy in *any* setting—if apartheid was proved to be unacceptable for Africans in South-West Africa, could anyone
doubt that it was equally unacceptable as applied to the African majority in South Africa itself? The earlier litigation had
avoided, at least directly, this explosive center of the controversy. The questions previously litigated had all concerned
issues of status and procedure relating *only* to the Mandate.

In addition, it was argued that here was a contentious proceeding in which the real moving party was the United Nations, or more specifically, its General Assembly. In no realistic
sense was "the dispute" just between Liberia and Ethiopia and
South Africa. Liberia and Ethiopia were taking advantage of
the compromissary clause to act in a *representational* capacity,
and at each stage in the proceedings, consultations and coordination between them and the members of the United Nations
were carried on. For instance, on December 8, 1960, General
Assembly Resolution 1565 (XV) ["*concludes*"] that the dispute
which has arisen between Ethiopia, Liberia and other Member
States on the one hand and the Union of South Africa on the

other, relating to the interpretation and application of the Mandate has not been and cannot be settled by negotiation."[43] Such an assertion, besides offending a certain feeling that sub judice notions should have been foreclosed from Assembly action during the period of litigation, disloses both the understanding that Ethiopia and Liberia were acting on behalf of "other Member States" as well as themselves and the conception that appropriate forms of negotiation had already been sufficiently pursued. On this latter point, the question is whether the negotiations between the General Assembly and South Africa had satisfied the jurisdictional requirement, because of the absence of any attempt by Ethiopia and Liberia to negotiate *their* dispute, regarded as a distinct reality, arising out of the Mandate directly with South Africa. In effect, this procedural awkwardness has led one apologist for the 1966 outcome to argue that "the real target for criticism ought to be Article 34 of the Statute of the Court [and not the Court itself] which prevents the United Nations from conducting contentious litigation against Member States before the Court."[44] Of course, even if the United Nations were treated *as if* it were a state by the Court, this would not have allowed the UN to initiate a contentious proceeding against South Africa. The compromissary clause of the Mandate obliging South Africa to adjudicate disputes can only be invoked by League members.

In effect, we have here a problem complementary to that of *Eastern Carelia*—to endow the United Nations with the capacity to proceed legally in the World Court requires stretching the conception in article 34 that only states can be parties in contentious proceedings. We are back once again to Leo Gross's dualistic view of World Court, with United Nations' initiatives statutorily confined to the advisory context. The procedural prohibition on the United Nations participating as an active party in contentious cases embodies a jurisprudential safeguard of the position of sovereign states vis-à-vis the organized international community. It also provides a judicial facade that allows states to appear to be amenable to "impar-

---

[43]Vote of 86–0, with six abstentions (Luxembourg, Portugal, United Kingdom, Australia, Belgium, and France).

[44]Johnson, *supra* note 34, at 163 n.9. *Cf.* Gross, *supra* note 19, at 47, who urges such an amendment to the Statute of the Court on the basis of what happened in 1966, invoking the *Reparations* case on behalf of the proposition that the Court has already endowed the United Nations with international legal personality sufficient to discharge its functions.

tial" judicial procedures, while in fact they rest assured that
their policies are exempted from scrutiny at the procedural
stage of inquiry. This prohibition in the name of sovereignty
has been lessened or weakened somewhat in special situations,
for instance, in the situation in which the members of the
organization and the United Nations itself are subject to rights
and duties and in situations, like the case of the mandate, in
which a special fiduciary dimension links the United Nations
directly to a dispute. Yet such a lessening, as several judges on
the Court have contended, can have adverse policy consequences generating bad law.

The problems posed in the *South West Africa* litigation by
recourse to the Court in a big case can be summarized:

First, to use the Court to promote enforcement in a big case
is likely to spotlight its inability to implement decisions against
a recalcitrant state and thereby to foster an image of judicial
ineffectiveness. If enforcement is the reason for the recourse
to the Court, then the costs of delay and expense have to be
vindicated by the prospect that something will be done to increase compliance pressure on the target state.

Second, to suppose that a favorable legal judgment would
have made the General Assembly position significantly more
enforceable against South Africa is, to say the least, an untested projection of faith. Slonim asks the rhetorical question:

> For if the economic and other interests of the major powers made
> the price of adopting any meaningful measures against South
> Africa prohibitive up until 1960, could a Court judgment have in
> any way reduced the price to non-prohibitive levels? . . . One need
> hardly be an economic determinist to conclude that in the heirar-
> chy of values of the states concerned the upholding of the rule of
> law would probably not have ranked so high as to cancel out
> countervailing material interest.[45]

Third, to suppose that the legal issues had already been
resolved by prior proceedings largely outside the Court—
mainly in the General Assembly with respect to the status of
apartheid—created a dilemma for the Court—either to defy
the Assembly and invite censure and retaliation by the af-
fronted political majority or to uphold the Assembly and appear to be nothing more than a subordinate political body.[46]

[45]S. SLONIM, *supra* note 38, at 353.
[46]The South African legal team expertly exploited this dilemma by charging repeatedly that Ethiopia and Liberia were trying to destroy the Court by turning it into

Fourth, to continue in the General Assembly the denuncia-
tions of apartheid and South Africa while the litigation was
pending inevitably politicized the atmosphere of the Court,
building up resistance on the part of those judges and jurists
who wanted to demonstrate the judicial independence of the
International Court of Justice.

Because of these difficulties, Slonim, for instance, argues at
length that the contentious proceedings that took place between 1960 and 1966

> eventuated in a much maligned and misunderstood Court judg-
> ment . . . . The nations of the Third World, in particular, had
> been led to harbor totally unrealistic expectations of what the
> Court could, or should, do and were completely unaware of the
> manner in which the case had actually unfolded before the
> Court.[47]

But was it an abuse of the Court to proceed as Ethiopia and
Liberia did in 1960, with General Assembly encouragement?
Or more precisely, did the political preoccupations of the antiapartheid movement cloud some real obstacles standing in
the judicial path? Was it reasonable to anticipate, as of 1960, a
favorable outcome? And would a favorable outcome have vindicated the Court and the recourse to it as an institution of
justice, even if it did not lead immediately to resolution of the
conflict?

In light of the poltical environment in 1960, including the
advisory jurisprudence of the Court, there was no reasonable
way the applicant states could have expected the sequence of
litigation that culminated in the 1966 judgment. As the most,
they might have expected a tough legal fight on the jurisdictional issues argued in the form of preliminary objections.
That was to be expected, given South Africa's insistence that
the mandate had lapsed and as a consequence, so had its obligations to the organized international community lapsed. To
have lost in 1962, this conflict at the stage of ruling on preliminary objections, would have aroused some political backlash, but immeasurably less than the same outcome did four
years later.

---

a rubber stamp for the General Assembly. In December of 1979 the revolutionary
government of Iran repudiated Security Council Resolution 457 calling for the immediate release of the hostages on the ground that the United Nations' behavior showed
its subservience to the United States.

[47]S. SLONIM, *supra* note 38, at 6.

The 1962 decision could reasonably have been understood, however, as having resolved the procedural issues relating to jurisdiction. Based on such an assumption, the minimum outcome the member states could have expected in 1966 was that the Court would uphold its advisory opinion in the 1950 decision affirming South Africa's obligation to accept General Assembly supervision and to report annually to it. The question of whether the Court would also find that apartheid violated the well-being of the inhabitants of South West Africa was more uncertain, incredible as that may sound to any nonlawyer wondering about the minimum content that might be expected to adhere to a fiduciary obligation by the international community to promote the well-being of specially protected dependent peoples. On the apartheid issue, the Court would need to find an authoritative canon of judicial interpretation that would override South Africa's "good faith" insistence that apartheid contributes to the well-being of the inhabitants of South-West Africa better than other possible administrative schemes.

What was not understood after 1962 was the depth of resistance to the litigation and to its majority-wished-for outcome on the part of those seven judges who had voted in support of South Africa's preliminary objections. The closeness of the 1962 judgment, together with the one-sided effects of the adventitious factors related to the subsequent composition of the Court, created a judicial situation that set the scene for the *de facto* reversal that came in 1966.

If the 1966 judgment had come out the other way, we can only imagine that its grounds probably would have been derived from those expressed in several of the dissenting opinions, especially those of Judges Jessup and Tanaka. We can assume that the judgment would have been applauded in political circles and also would have received a generally favorable reaction from international legal scholars. In all likelihood, South Africa would have responded angrily, but, depending on how far the judgment went with respect to timely relief, might have been willing to comply, if only to stall for time.

The results issued from the Court would have been seen as generally positive, thus posing both a challenge and an opportunity to the Security Council, especially for the Western veto powers. It is likely that South Africa would have resisted any far-reaching adjustment, and after years of frustrating and acrimonious debate in the Security Council, neither compliance nor serious enforcement would have been forthcoming. In that event, the Assembly undoubtedly would have moved toward the revocation of the Mandate, through a series of affirmations similar to those now embodied in General Assembly Resolution 2145 (XXI). It would have so moved perhaps with a stronger legal foundation and greater political support and possibly at a later date.[48] Such a resolution might well have been referred to the Court, as 2145 was, for a confirming Advisory Opinion. Much the same process would have ensued, expressing even more forcibly the deep sense of onlookers that in the last analysis the conflict could only be resolved by military force, no matter what other approaches had been preferred by the aggrieved parties.

And yet, we cannot know. A certain liberal atmosphere prevailed in Washington during the Kennedy and Johnson presidencies, especially on issues of race. As involvement in the Vietnam War escalated in the mid-1960s, there seemed to be a strong American desire to take more positive stands with respect to a variety of Third World issues. There was also prevalent in the American public and in its leaders in this period a conviction that international institutions, especially legal ones, deserved support, provided that they did not make the United States' actions an object of criticism. South Africa, too, might have decided that it could have done better by shifting to a more accommodating approach on the question of the Mandate, especially if its actual internal arrangements were shielded from scrutiny. Until the collapse of the Portuguese empire in the 1970s, a faction of the South African leadership apparently entertained the view that an independent South West Africa / Namibia could be easily contained and that ending this dispute might stabilize the internal South African situation. Other South Africans disagreed, either because they believed it was unnecessary to yield, or because they thought it would be dangerous for the future security of South Africa to do so.

We cannot know how this complex set of circumstances might actually have evolved. It is possible to argue that the political leaders who counseled having recourse to the Court,

---

[48]G.A. Res. 2145 (XXI), 21 U.N. GAOR Supp. (No. 16) at 2, U.N. Doc. A/6316 (1966).

from their perspective, made a reasonable choice as of 1960. They had reason to believe that they had at least an excellent chance of winning, that the legal victory would have been dramatic, and that it might have yielded positive political results as measured by out earlier yardsticks of peaceful resolution, peaceful change, liberation struggle, and global reform.[49]

We cannot judge in retrospect (as so many critics of the litigation have done), as if the 1966 outcome had been foreordained. Nor is it reasonable to suppose, as does D. H. N. Johnson, that those who supported recourse to the Court in the pre-1960 period believed that their prospects of success in the litigation were no better than "a fifty-fifty chance."[50] In my view, the expectation of success was up around 100 percent, after the 1962 decision, on the assumption that the split over judicial function had been resolved when the preliminary objections were rejected in 1962, even if that had taken place by a far closer vote than had been expected. Undoubtedly in hindsight it was a mistake not to examine this reality more carefully in the 1962–66 period, but the Court itself gave very little hint that it was still preoccupied with *whether* rather than *how,* it should adjudicate.

If the perceived changes of success were as low as fifty-fifty, then it would have been a dubious decision to take the dispute to the Court. It has been evident all along, but became especially clear after 1962 when jurisdiction had *apparently* been established, that a judicial refusal to condemn South Africa's behavior would be *politically intolerable.*[51] It would lend funda-

[49]S. SLONIM, *supra* note 38, at 6.

[50]Johnson, *supra* note 34, at 159; a view apparently endorsed by Slonim, *supra* note 38, at 309: Both Johnson and Slonim suggest that given this calculus, it was unreasonable to act shocked by the 1966 outcome; in their view, such a result was made plausible by the close vote on the procedural phase, even if a reversal in 1966 was not to be expected. Johnson and Slonim are critical of those who have heaped a torrent of abuse on the Court and its legal rationale in the latter substantive phase.

[51]Part of what makes it politically intolerable is that South Africa is so isolated with respect to its racial policies and that these policies are so deeply offensive to the overwhelming majority of states in the United Nations. It is quite different from other overtly political issues, such as those arising within a Cold War context, where the minority position is encompassed within a wider view of *legitimate diversity.* The notion of legitimate diversity is admittedly vague, designed mainly to draw a contrast with "illegitimate diversity," that is, a position that is perceived as unacceptable by the great majority of members of the United Nations and by world public opinion. In this regard, somewhat arbitrarily perhaps, the failures of apartheid are viewed as incompatible with constructive participation in the United Nations, whereas the failures of communism or capitalism are not.

mental support to the basic contention of South Africa that its relationship to the United Nations is entirely discretionary with respect to the Mandate. Such a decision would appear to rebuff the entire course of action undertaken by the General Assembly. Given the intense feelings about apartheid that exist in the world and the central role of the General Assembly in the antiapartheid campaign, it was apparent that the Assembly would react with great anger to any Court judgment helpful to South Africa. Such a storm, although probably not too important with regard to the technicalities of the dispute, would definitely lower the status and the morale of the Court, and because of that would be very costly. As it turned out to be.

In conclusion, then, there was no advance indication that the World Court would handle the *South West Africa Cases* as it did, or that it will handle such a case similarly in the future. Had the expected outcome occurred, it would have been perceived as helpful and as just, even if, as was likely, South Africa evaded its responsibility to comply with the judgment and with whatever implementing decisions were subsequently taken by the Security Council.

Putting this conclusion in more abstract terms, the *actual* outcome of the *South West Africa* contentious litigation was an unlikely option among many plausible outcomes.[52] Yet the image of the International Court of Justice has been significantly impaired by it and by the misleading interpretations of both scholars and political figures that the actual outcome was a charcteristic, if not actually a necessary, response by the Court to the big case. To some extent, this damaged image has been repaired by the subsequent effort to reconstitute the personnel of the Court in subsequent elections of judges and by the more acceptable Court response to the request in 1970 for an Advisory Opinion. Nevertheless, the earlier image persists. This is undesirable to the degree that it is important to preserve whatever unused and untested potential exists for third-party adjudication on a global scale in the world community.

In my view, we lack the experience, tradition, and consensus

[52]The actual outcome was not, of course, the only undesirable outcome possible. The Court might have gone on to assume jurisdictional competence and then held *substantively* in South Africa's favor, as in fact the South African ad hoc judge, J. T. van Wyk, argued in his separate opinion in the *South West Africa Cases (Second Phase)*, *supra* note 30 of chapter 1, at 62–213.

as to how the World Court should handle various aspects of the big case. This uncertainty needs to be stressed because we want to support an attitude toward judicial function that sees the Court as neither oblivious to the structure of the state system nor as intimidated by it.

Part of the reason why the 1966 judgment was so poorly received was the widely shared conviction that the Court's reliance on a jurisdictional rationale was either incomprehensible or devious. Either the law was an ass, or the judges were covert racists who wanted to help South Africa without admitting what they were doing. In this respect, a comment by Leo Gross guides us from the concern with recourse to the Court in this chapter to the concern of the next chapter with substantive response by the Court: "Nothing could be more fatal to the Court than a reputation of excessive formalism."[53]

[53]Gross, *supra* note 19, at 433.

CHAPTER III

The Issue of Judicial
Style in the Big Case

With one's principles one wants to bully one's habits, or
justify, honor, scold, or conceal them: two men with the
same principles probably aim with them at something basically different.

FRIEDRICH NIETZSCHE, "Epigrams and Interludes,"
Beyond Good and Evil.

Once the big case is presented to the Court, the Court must
respond. This response is in itself a self-appraisal of judicial
function by the principal officers of the Court and discloses
their outlook on its proper relationship with the United Nations and with the realm of sovereign states. As the *South West
Africa* litigation moved from the initial request for an Advisory
Opinion in 1949 to the *Namibia* opinion of 1971, the judges
manifested a diversity of views on critical questions, generally
framed as technical discussions of interpretative canons or private law analogies. It is never possible to know the degree to
which *manifest judicial style is a professional posture* or is actually
an accurate portrayal of the grounds of decision. This uncertainty relates to the latent content of adjudication—the unacknowledged and perhaps unrealized foundations of consciousness that support and explain an affinity for some lines of
legal argument and an antipathy towards others.[1]

The technical character of judicial controversy is a disadvantage in the big case because it gives the outcome, especially
in an unpopular decision, an arbitrary and artificial quality.
Both sides in any controversy can be made to sound reason-

[1]Lyndell Prott shows a comparable concern with latent content by indicating that
her investigation of the World Court "is a very delicate one because it demands to
some extent the exposure of hidden tensions and concealed motivations within the
Court." Dr. Prott has in mind mainly the influence of professional training and
political culture on judicial behavior. Her book is stimulating, original in its focus. L.
PROTT, THE LATENT POWER OF CULTURE AND THE INTERNATIONAL JUDGE xix (1979).

able and convincing. Several conclusions *seem* to be technically possible. In addition, there is some sense that values and free choice often are smuggled into the judicial process in technical disguise, particularly if a judge's political profile seems to correspond with the way in which he or she resolves a technical controversy. This impression is especially strong in the big case, such as *South West Africa,* where the racial dimension dominates all other considerations and where sympathy for the policy of the South African government never could be directly acknowledged. These considerations are not generally discussed in scholarly commentary on judicial behavior. Noting such personal ingredients of a court decision is regarded as demeaning, conjectural, and deniable. Nevertheless, it is a part of the international setting, particularly because many Third World contries regard unacceptable judicial determinations as rationalizations for unacceptable values and interests. The angry General Assembly response to the 1966 decision in the *South West Africa* dispute illustrates this outlook and its strength.

Despite the question of hidden motives, it remains useful to pay heed to the manifest level of judicial behavior. How do judges on the Court explain and justify their decisions and their differences? Do they alter their style to accommodate or to foreclose the big case? Admitting that there exist multiple lines of plausible technical argument, is one side more convincing than the other?

In the last chapter, we focused on whether *recourse* to the World Court would be constructive under certain circumstances. In this chapter our concern is with *response*—what the Court has done (and should do) once a moving party has decided on recourse to the Court in a big case. Dual procedures of access make the distinction important between access by a United Nations organization through an advisory proceeding and access by a state or states by way of contentious proceedings. The dispute over South West Africa illustrates both settings for adjudication.

The 1950 Foretaste

During the League period South Africa had put forward proposals at various times for the incorporation of South West Africa into its own territory as a fifth province. This approach became a serious goal of the South African government at the San Francisco conference planning for the future United Nations. There South Africa argued for the incorporation of South West Africa on several grounds: the de facto pattern of administration that already made the territory an integral part of South Africa, its geographical proximity, the comparable ethnic structures of mandatory and mandate, and the legal situation consequent upon the dissolution of the League.[2]

The trusteeship system of the United Nations failed to make any definitive arrangement for assimilating former mandates, although the general assumption was made and expressed that mandatory states would accept a new United Nations system of international supervision as an acceptable substitute for the mandate system. South Africa refused to take the trusteeship path, although at the outset it did not repudiate altogether its link to the United Nations. In 1964 it pushed ahead with its preference for incorporation by "consulting" the wishes of the inhabitants of the territory, a procedure that predictably, given South African control of the process, yielded a strong show of support by both white and tribal peoples for incorporation. Armed with the results of the consultation, South Africa pressed its case for incorporation within the United Nations. On December 14, 1946, the General Assembly by a 37–0–9 vote in Resolution 65(I) rejected incorporation and instead invited South Africa to propose a trusteeship arrangement for South West Africa. In response, South Africa agreed not to incorporate South West Africa, but refused to accept the recommendation of trusteeship, contending that it would maintain the status quo by upholding the Mandate. Here again it is important to note that the language of the resolution was restrained. 65(I) could have declared that it was obligatory for South Africa to proceed immediately to negotiate a trusteeship agreement with the General Assembly. Instead, it merely "recommend[ed]" that South West Africa "be placed under international trusteeship and invite[d] the Government of the Union of South Africa to propose for consideration of the General Assembly a trusteeship agreement." Of course, whatever the language relied upon by the General Assembly, its resolutions remain, technically, nonbinding recommendations by virtue of its competence under the Charter, although the respon-

[2]See J. DUGARD, ed., *supra* note 29 of chapter 2, at 89–91.

sibility and authority of the Assembly might be greater in a fiduciary circumstance of this sort.

During this period, even after Resolution 65(I), South Africa continued to submit annual reports to the United Nations on the discharge of its responsibility as mandatory. In 1948, however, there was a political change of government in South Africa, bringing the Nationalist party to power with a more nationalistic outlook and with a new leadership that was more explicit about its commitment to racial hierarchy as the party's basic social policy. In 1949 the new government in Pretoria announced that it would no longer submit reports to the United Nations. At the same time, it proceeded to work out an even closer association between South Africa and South West Africa, producing a situation that one expert South African observer, John Dugard, describes as "close to annexation."[3] The new South African leadership believed the way to handle the United Nations was to create a fait accompli by moving toward de facto annexation, making it practically impossible to demand that South West Africa be split off from South African control. By General Assembly Resolution 337(IV), the United Nations indicated that it "regretted" South Africa's approach, especially its refusal to continue to submit reports.

Then in December 1949, the General Assembly, stymied diplomatically asked in Resolution 339(IV), by a vote of 40–7–4, for an advisory opinion from the World Court on the following general question:

> What is the international status of the territory of South West Africa and what are the international obligations of the Union of South Africa arising therefrom . . . .

This general question was particularized in three parts:

(a)   Does the Union of South Africa continue to have international obligations under the Mandate for South West Africa, and, if so, what are those obligations?

(b)   Are the provisions of Chapter XII of the Charter applicable and, if so, in what manner, to the Territory of South West Africa?

(c)   Has the Union of South West Africa the competence to modify the international status of the Territory of South West

[3] *Id.* at 122.

Africa, or, in the event of a negative reply, where does competence rest to determine or modify the international status of the territory?

It is significant that at this stage South Africa participated voluntarily in the Court proceedings, submitting a written statement and making an oral presentation on behalf of its position.

The Court was unanimous about the character of South West Africa as a mandated territory; it agreed that the chapter XII provisions of the Charter "provide a means" by which the territory "may be brought under the Trusteeship System," that South Africa does not have the unilateral competence to modify the status of the territory, and that modification of this status can validly occur only if South Africa acts with the consent of the United Nations. In effect, the unanimous parts of the Court judgment gave satisfaction to the United Nations position; the General Assembly was supported in its view that the mandate survived sufficiently to preclude the annexation of the territory of South West Africa, at least without the consent of the United Nations. Additionally, the trusteeship system was confirmed as an available alternative to mandatory status. On this agreed foundation, the divergent views of the Court centered on what the character of South Africa's obligations as mandatory power were after the collapse of the League.

Our discussion here will concentrate on two areas of disagreement. Significantly, both questions, the question of administrative supervision and the question of trusteeship obligation, relate to the nature of the connection between South Africa, as a surviving mandatory power, and the United Nations, as successor organization. In contrast, there was unanimous agreement on the status question that the mandate, as such, survived and that neither South Africa nor the United Nations had acquired any greater rights than they had possessed during the League period. Thus, South Africa could not modify the mandate without the assent of the General Assembly (relevant to its incorporation plan), and the General Assembly could not increase the level of its own supervisory authority over that held by the League Council. In effect, the Court was agreed at the level of principle on the nonlegislative character of the dissolution of the League. The sacred-trust aspect of the earlier League relationship sustained the status quo, while the sovereignty aspect of the earlier relationship rested on the mandate as an agreed-upon treaty, restraining any expansion of the claim of the United Nations to supervise the promotion of the well-being of the inhabitants of the territory. How to effectuate this reconciliation in practical terms was what divided the judges.

In 1950 the conflict over apartheid was comparatively muted. The request for an advisory opinion did not cause a great stir. There was a definite political interest and moral concern by United Nations member states, but the relationship between South Africa and the United Nations, although strained by the Nationalist party victory, was still well within the domain of normal diplomacy. It was not yet a big case, and therefore, the referral of the dispute or case to the Court in 1949 seemed like an appropriate step for a dispute in which some complicated and controverted issues of status and obligations resulted from the transition to the new organization of the United Nations. The issues raised did bear more generally on the way the Court should specify its role within the United Nations framework, but the request did not relate directly to the *substance* of apartheid. In such circumstances, the Court was under no great pressure to decide in any particular way. I suppose it is correct to say that had the Court validated South Africa's basic contention that the mandate had lapsed and that the option of incorporation was thereby permissible, some sort of backlash against the Court as colonialist and racist would have occurred even back in 1950. Inevitably, given the general international preference for resolving disputes by negotiation, the request for an Advisory Opinion was an expression of some measure of political frustration arising out of South Africa's resistance to trusteeship and its refusal even to continue supplying annual reports.

Yet, despite the apparent normalcy of the adjudication, the seeds of the future split on the Court were apparent even then. With respect to administrative supervision, the majority opinion argued that "[t]he obligation incumbent on a mandatory State to accept international supervision and to submit reports is an important part of the Mandates System" that directly relates to "the effective performance of the sacred trust of civilization."[4] The Court acknowledged that "some

---

[4]*The International Status of South West Africa, supra* note 25 of chapter 2, at 136.

doubts might arise" because the mandated territories "were neither expressly transferred to the United Nations nor expressly assumed by that organization."[5] The opinion stressed the importance of the rights of the peoples in the mandated territory, as well as the rights of states, and concluded that despite some rather indefinite language in chapter XII of the Charter, including article 80(1), "[t]he purpose must have been to provide a real protection for those rights [of the inhabitants]; but no such rights of the peoples could be effectively safeguarded without international supervision and a duty to render reports to a supervisory organ."[6] The Court also invoked article 10 to endorse the competence of the General Assembly to discuss and make recommendations on any questions within the scope of the Charter to validate its concern with South West Africa. The majority opinion crucially emphasized that "[t]he degree of supervision to be exercised by the General Assembly should not therefore exceed that which applied under the Mandates System, and should conform as far as possible to the procedure followed in this respect by the Council of the League of Nations."[7] In effect, the UN was empowered to sustain League arrangements, but not to expand standards of international accountability or even to alter its form.

The essence of the majority logic was that the "sacred trust" obligations must be read into the United Nations context to whatever extent necessary to sustain the kind of relationship that had existed during the League period. As a practical matter, this meant at minimum, administrative succession by the General Assembly to the role of the Permanent Mandates Commission. For some members of the majority, as we note below, it meant more than this—it meant that the territory became subject to a trusteeship arrangement as well.

The minority on the issue of administrative supervision consisted of two white Commonwealth judges—Read from Canada and McNair from the United Kingdom.[8] Their separate concurring opinions exerted much influence on the legal reception of the case, especially in the crucially relevant Anglo-

---

[5]Id.
[6]Id. at 136, 137.
[7]Id. at 138.
[8]See comments on McNair and Read in L. Prott, supra note 1, at 225.

American community.[9] McNair's opinion has received at least
as much attention as the opinion of the majority has. It was
divided into two parts: in the first, he presented a way to
account more satisfactorily and legally for the survival of the
mandate after the dissolution of the League, and in the second, he gave his argument on the impropriety of conferring
competence on the General Assembly with respect to administrative supervision. It is worth our taking special note of the
McNair/Read position on this second issue.

McNair argued that with the dissolution of the League "the
obligations owed to the League itself have come to an end,"
whereas "[t]he obligations owed to former Members of the
League . . . subsist."[10] Thus, reliance is placed on former members of the League to supply judicial supervision of the mandate by way of recourse to the International Court of Justice, as
prescribed by the compromissary clause in article 7 of the mandate. From McNair, it followed then that administrative supervision had lapsed. Why? Because "the League and its Council
and Permanent Mandates Commission . . . no longer exist, so
that it has become impossible to perform this obligation.[11]

But why does the United Nations *not* succeed to the obligations of the League? Here is where the disagreement centers.
McNair's frequently quoted contention is that to attribute succession to the United Nations "is pure inference, as the
Charter contains no provision for a succession such as exists in
Article 37 of the Statute of the International Court" with respect to "the compulsory jurisdiction of the Permanent Court
in regard to Mandates."[12] McNair examines other evidence of
the succession associated with the alleged intentions of the
League, as well as with South Africa's statement of apparent
acquiescence in this shift in supervisory authority, *and* the language of articles 77 and 80 in the Charter which transfer by
implication the administrative functions of the League to the
United Nations. He concludes:

> I cannot find any legal ground on which the Court would be
> justified in replacing the Council of the League by the United

[9]Their opinions are treated as concurring opinions, evidently because they share
the majority views on the issues of status and trusteeship, although on the implications
of status—re: administrative supervision—their position is definitely one of dissent.
[10]*The International Status of South West Africa, supra* note 25 of chapter 2, at 158.
[11]*Id.* at 159.
[12]*Id.*

Nations for the purposes of exercising the administrative supervision of the Mandate and the receipt and examination of reports. It would amount to imposing a new obligation upon the Union Government and would be a piece of judicial legislation.[13]

Read emphasized in his separate dissenting opinion that, given the nature of the legal situation, only a three-sided agreement between the mandatory, the League, and the United Nations could result in the continuation of administrative supervision, and no such agreement was ever forthcoming.[14] The whole mandate relationship was a unified whole that was founded on treaties and explicit agreements, one in which the "consent" of the parties was crucial for any new arrangement.[15]

What is this confrontation really about? Twelve of the judges pointed their underlying analysis toward "the sacred trust" imperative, seeking to imply a subsidiary intention of the League and the United Nations for making it effective. In this majority view, the mandate cannot be maintained as operative unless administrative supervision of the sort contemplated by the League is maintained; judicial supervision is, in contrast, uncertain, discontinuous, marginal, and insufficient. At the same time, the importance of sovereignty is acknowledged to the extent that the level of United Nations supervision is not to be allowed to exceed that level that South Africa and the League had agreed upon in the treatylike text of the Mandate agreement. Given the character of the League's actual supervision and given the colonial environment that prevailed at the time of the Permanent Mandates Commission, it is difficult to believe that the League approach, if intended seriously, could have been an adequate basis for upholding what even in 1950 the membership of the United Nations understood to be minimally necessary by way of supervision for assuring the well-being of the inhabitants.[16] In this respect, the majority on the

[13]*Id.* at 161, 162.

[14]*Id.* at 172.

[15]Read argues that the General Assembly itself has set guidelines for transfer of functions that depend on an initiating request by South Africa as the mandatory power. *Id.*

[16]Dugard gives an excerpt from a debate in the South African House of Assembly in which Mr. Eric Louw, prominent diplomat and specialist in South-West African affairs, directed the following remark to the Prime Minister:

I can speak from personal experience, having on two occasions had the honour of submitting the South-West Africa report to the League of Nations Mandates Commission. And, Mr. Speaker, let me say this, that the Mandates Commission of those days was a body of sympathetic affable gentlemen. . . . The examination of the

Court handed down a compromise of sorts between the McNair/ Read view of a diminished mandate in the United Nations period and the view of De Visscher (and others) that South Africa must negotiate toward a trusteeship agreement.

Turning to the trusteeship issue, a bare majority of the judges construed the language of chapter XII literally to conclude that the failure of the Charter to obligate the mandatory in any explicit way to come to a trusteeship agreement must be respected and that acceptance of the Trusteeship System by the mandatory, while desirable, must be entirely voluntary. The advisory opinion confirmed the view that "the normal course indicated by the Charter" would be for the mandatory to conclude a trusteeship agreement, but goes on to say that nothing supports the existence of "any legal obligation for mandatory States to conclude or to negotiate such agreements."[17]

Judge Charles De Visscher, supported by five other judges' opinions (including the separate dissenting opinions of Judges Alvarez and Krylov), argued from "the clear intent of the authors of the Charter to substitute the Trusteeship System for the Mandates System."[18] This reading of the intention of the Charter is reinforced by the view that the Charter must be construed so that "the entire régime contemplated and regulated by the Charter" (namely, the Trusteeship System) could not be frustrated by "individualistic concepts which are generally adequate in the interpretation of ordinary treaties. . . ."[19] The Charter, as "a great international constitutional instrument," must be read so as to give effect to its principal purposes, at least to the extent of obligating a mandatory state to cooperate with the United Nations by negotiating "with a view to concluding a Trusteeship Agreement," although, it should be noted, "without thereby jeopardizing its freedom to accept or refuse the terms of such an Agreement."[20]

Union by UNO Trusteeship Committee will be very different from what it was in the days of the old League of Nations, because the old League, with possibly a half a dozen exceptions, was a white organisation, an organisation of predominatly European powers . . . . [T]he UNO is a horse of a different colour, because the UNO is predominantly coloured. . . . And the position is going to be very different when our representative—I pity the poor man—turns up to submit his report on South-West Africa, to UNO as at present constituted.

J. DUGARD, ed., *supra* note 29 of chapter 2, at 118–119.

    [17]*The International Status of South West Africa, supra* note 25 of chapter 2, at 140.

    [18]*Id.* at 188.

    [19]*Id.* at 189.

    [20]*Id.* at 190.

Judge Alvarez, the visionary jurist from Chile, went further than the other dissenters. He regarded the entire legal controversy in this case (as he has in other cases in which he participated), as being subject to the broad requirement that "*the new international law*" be established by the Court to support "*social interdependence* which is taking the place of traditional *individualism.*"[21] He argued that most discussions about South-West Africa "have been complicated and even made obscure" by attempts to solve problems by reference to the old sovereignty-weighted (individualistic) international law. Alvarez concluded that "[i]n fact, the question is an entirely new one and comes under the new international law."[22] Without benefit of much technical apparatus, he reached the conclusion that South Africa "is under the legal obligation not only to negotiate this agreement [on Trusteeship], but also to conclude it. This obligation derives from the spirit of the Charter, which leaves no place for the future co-existence of the Mandates System and the Trusteeship System."[23] Of all the judges, Alvarez alone talked about the competence of the General Assembly under article 10 of the Charter to terminate the mandate, especially should South Africa breach its obligation to conclude a trusteeship agreement.[24]

Judge Alvarez virtually set aside the sovereign rights of South Africa. He placed the question of the mandate in the general perspective of what the Charter seeks to achieve and what is necessary to make the idea of a "sacred trust" work in the context of the United Nations. Several observations are important with regard to this singular dissenting opinion:

—Judge Alvarez stood alone on the Court;
—his opinion has generally been neglected, although occasionally criticized in the extensive scholarly commentary on the case;[25]

[21]Italics in original, *id.* at 174–75.

[22]*Id.* at 175.

[23]*Id.* at 193.

[24]"The Assembly having the faculty to confer that trust has also the faculty to revoke it." *Id.* at 183. *See also id.* at 185.

[25]A typical reaction of scorn is that of the South African jurist Ellison Kahn, who at least notices the Alvarez opinion: "With all due respect to so eminent a jurist as M. Alvarez, it is not surprising that inconsistencies appear in his Opinion, when regard be had to his unorthodox approach to problems of international law. . . . With the aid of what rules of construction does M. Alvarez propose to create, or if you will, expound the new international law?" 4 INT'L L. Q. 78, 93 (1951). For an extended excerpt of

—Judge Alvarez puts forward the only set of views on the future of the mandate that holds out some genuine prospect for effective fulfillment from the viewpoints of the inhabitants of the sacred trust;

—by 1966 his views prevailed in the political arena, with the passage of General Assembly Resolution 2145 (XXI), revoking the mandate;

—his views prefigured the disposition of the case in the legal arena by means of the determination by the World Court in its 1971 *Namibia* advisory opinion;

—interestingly, his *applied views relating specifically to the South West Africa dispute proved far more prophetic and realistic than his general* insistence on the adoption of a new international law.[26]

This is a remarkable set of propositions, especially when placed in the context of the decline in the fortunes and reputation of the Court. It suggests, first of all, that the range of relevant controversy on the Court may not relate significantly to its treatment of the big case. Neither the majority nor the minority opinions (except possibly the opinion of Alvarez) entailed any adequate conception of how to make the mandate effective. McNair and Read, despite their *legal* acumen, propose something transparently ineffectual, namely, reliance on judicial supervision by means of recourse to the Court. The majority does not do much better by limiting supervision to the transmission of self-serving reports (and the receipt of petitions). Even the minority of five judges that supports the De Visscher argument that South Africa is obliged to negotiate a trusteeship agreement, while South Africa's right of refusal is also preserved, provides no reasonable and assured way to obtain such an agreement. Without providing a means to this end, the United Nations supervisory role must remain nominal, or else be continually improvised on an ad hoc basis. Of course, there are gradations of policy in each of these posi-

Kahn's view, see *id.* at 78–99. The main inconsistency that Kahn notes is the assertion by Judge Alvarez near the end of his opinion (p. 184) that "[e]ven admitting that there is no legal obligation to conclude an agreement, there is, at least, a political obligation, a duty which derives from social inter-dependence and which can be sanctioned by the Assembly of the UN." I find nothing inconsistent here. Alvarez seems to be saying that even if one grants the majority position on trusteeship, still the General Assembly can act under article 10 to fulfill Charter intentions if no agreement is forthcoming.

[26]Although it can be argued that overall Third World pressure for a new international economic order is, in part, a call for "a new international law" based on the sort of considerations Alvarez emphasized.

tions, but all these positions adhere largely to the sovereignty side of the controversy, thereby preserving South Africa's capacity to nullify United Nations supervision. In this regard, only Alvarez is clearheaded about what is required to make the mandate work, despite the fact that all fourteen judges unanimously agree that the mandate status did survive the collapse of the League and that the sacred-trust dimension is its most vital element.

We can summarize the legal situation as of 1950 by comparing the operative positions of disagreement in relation to the mandate (see table 1):

This range of positions on the Court was promoted, in part, by an ambiguous legal situation. For one thing, the League never clearly specified its intentions regarding a transfer of functions to the United Nations. For another, the United Nations Charter never clearly indicated an obligation of mandatory states to work within the trusteeship system. Whether these ambiguities that framed the Court's inquiry were themselves the results of compromises between statism and internationalism that were introduced into the League's final acts and into the United Nations constitutional document remains uncertain. What confronted the Court, however, were the opposed positions of promoting the sacred trust or upholding sovereign rights. There was clearly no disposition on the Court to adopt South Africa's position, which, had it been accepted, would have paved the way for the incorporation of South West Africa into South Africa. Unanimity in the Court in this regard might have had a practical effect. Without such unanimity, South Africa might have felt freer to proceed as it wished. After all, South Africa's preferred position was rejected. South Africa by now has moved away from its claim to the right to incorporate South West Africa and toward some kind of self-determination posture, preferably manipulated under its control.

The General Assembly's position was also rejected, except by Judge Alvarez. The majority of the Court held that South Africa need not submit to trusteeship unless it so decided. Even the minority would not push South Africa beyond a probably meaningless obligation to negotiate the issue.

The result of the compromise is strange. The mandate does not lapse with the dissolution of the League, nor does it get transferred, per se, into the successor arrangements of the

Table 1. Positions of disagreement in relation to the mandate, 1950

	Advocate	Positions
1	South Africa	Mandate lapsed
2	McNair/Read	Mandate survived; obligations to League lapsed and not transferable to the United Nations
3	Majority of International Court	Mandate survived; obligations to League transferable to United Nations
4	De Visscher minority	Mandate survived; South Africa obligated to negotiate trusteeship agreement
5	Alvarez dissent General Assembly majority	Mandate survived; South Africa obligated to conclude trusteeship agreement

United Nations. It lives on *as a mandate,* and the United Nations is assigned the role of acting as much like the League as is possible. The formal obligations were easily enough maintained in roughly equivalent forms, but the contrast in organizational environment between the colonialist League and the anticolonialist United Nations set the stage for the clash that subsequently emerged. The objective situation was untenable in this fundamental regard, no matter what the Court did, and in this respect, it probably would have made little difference had the De Visscher minority prevailed.

The General Assembly in Resolution 449A (V) accepted the 1950 Advisory Opinion and established the ad ad hoc Committee to work with South Africa on its implementation. As John Dugard points out, this action of deference to the outcome in the International Court of Justice was taken despite the Court's rejection of "the main contention of the General Assembly that South Africa was obliged to place South West Africa under trusteeship."[27] At the same time, the General Assembly was not altogether deterred from pursuing its insistence on the trusteeship route as the appropriate form of administrative supervision in the United Nations era. It passed Resolution 449B (V), reiterating its demand to South Africa that South West Africa, as the sole surviving mandate, be included in the trusteeship system.

The dispute was not yet a big case in 1950. The Court's

[27]J. DUGARD, ed., *supra* note 29 of chapter 2, at 162.

disposition of it was generally "acceptable," although it fell politically short of what the General Assembly wanted and juridically short of what some legal commentators thought strictly appropriate, namely, the McNair/Read restrictive view of the judicial function as set forth in their separate opinions, but not adopted by the Court as a whole. South Africa explicitly rejected the advisory opinion on the ground that it failed to consider some newly available evidence that sustained the view that the United Nations did not inherit the supervisory role exercised by the League. Instead, South Africa proposed that it negotiate a new instrument of agreement with the three surviving members of the Principal Allied and Associated Powers (France, the United Kingdom, and the United States) of World War I who had conferred the original mandate.[28] In essence, South Africa changed its position from advocating incorporation to supporting the position taken by the McNair/Read minority.[29]

There were negotiations conducted between South Africa and the United Nations' ad hoc Committee during 1951–53, but they proved fruitless because South Africa would not alter its refusal to accept United Nations administrative supervision or to negotiate a trusteeship agreement. South Africa insisted on its willingness to maintain the mandate as it had been doing, but continued to refuse all accountability to the United Nations. The General Assembly, growing ever more frustrated, continued to press its demand that South Africa be obliged to put the mandate within the Trusteeship System. In the Fourth Committee, the United Nations granted oral hearings to petitioners from South West Africa, over South African objections. By means of Resolution 749A (VIII), a permanent committee on South West Africa was created in 1953, partly expressing the Assembly's realization that no solution for this conflict would come quickly and partly creating a mechanism to regularly inform the General Assembly of changes in the situation in South West Africa. In effect, the General Assembly was moving toward discharging its responsibilities for administrative supervision *without* the cooperation of South Africa. Such actions could be regarded as unilateral

[28]For material on South Africa's position, see *id.* at 164–73.

[29]The South African representative in the Fourth Committee made this explicit (*see id.* at 164, 165); presumably, this endorsement would not extend to their judgment that judicial supervision continued to exist.

implementation of the 1950 Advisory Opinion. The General Assembly also endeavored, at least in form, to limit its role to that played by the Permanent Mandates Commission in the League period. For example, Resolution 794A (VIII) called upon the Committee on South West Africa to:

> (b) Examine, as far as possible in accordance with the procedure of the former mandates system, reports and petitions which may be submitted to the Committee or to the Secretary General;

> (c) Transmit to the General Assembly a report concerning conditions in the territory taking into account, as far as possible, the scope of the reports of the Permanent Mandates commission . . . .

In essence, the political body of the United Nations was content to act within the terms of the 1950 Opinion, even though that Opinion did not altogether support the will of the General Assembly. This action illustrates a phase of relatively harmonious interaction between the legal and political arenas of the United Nations in regard to the South-West Africa dispute.

The future troubles in relations between the judicial and political branches, however, were already discernible in the 1950s. The basic International Court of Justice juridical criterion of equivalence between the United Nations and the League was unworkable. The United Nations' environment simply was not, in fact, equivalent to the environment of the League. South Africa was confronted with the prospect of far more hostile and critical supervision. The reality of such an escalation of supervisory claims was bound to bother those judges who understood the essence of the mandate system to be the balance between the sovereign status of the mandatory and the trust status of the mandate, as construed by means of serious reference to positivist canons of sovereign consent. As developments unfolded, it became clear that there was no meeting ground between what was acceptable to the General Assembly and what was agreeable to South Africa. To fit the mandate into the United Nations was asking that the square peg be somehow fitted into the round hole. The 1950 opinion unwittingly contributed to the ensuing confusion by its pious formulation of an unworkable juridical criterion of equivalence. Should the Court have foreseen this? What else could the Court have done that would have been preferable?

On all of these issues, only Alvarez provided a way out by his insistence upon "a new international law" premised on "social interdependence." But the prevailing traditional jurisprudential paradigm that sets the boundaries for the range of acceptable judicial behavior precluded the Alvarez approach, except as an idealistic and eccentric deviation.[30] The marginality of the Alvarez approach is reinforced by the failure of major scholarly commentators even to notice the substantive relevance of Alvarez's approach in their assessments of the Court or of the *South West Africa Cases*.[31] At the same time, the Court was not so indifferent to its role in the United Nations system or to the trust character of the mandate as to accept South Africa's position on the lapse of the mandate with the demise of the League. Despite wide disparities in their jurisprudential and ideological outlooks, the judges were unanimous in their insistence that the mandate, as a legal and political status, survived in some form and to some extent.

Referring back to table 1, positions 1 and 5 were excluded by the judges from the realm of judicial possibility. The paradigmatic limits on realistic options confined the decision makers to positions 2–4, especially positions 3 and 4. Position 2 was too close to position 1 in practical effect to be acceptable *within* the Court, although its positivistic logic appealed to commentators of this persuasion as "the correct" solution. Positions 3 and 4 were really close to each other in practical effect, as there is little reason to suppose that position 4's support of a duty to negotiate a trusteeship agreement would

[30]On these issues, Prott's book is invaluable, *supra* note 1; on the idea of paradigm shift in international legal studies, see Falk, *A New Paradigm for International Legal Studies: Prospects and Proposals,* 84 YALE L.J. 969 (1975).

[31]*E.g.,* Slonim's references to Alvarez are contained in two footnotes, S. SLONIM, *supra* note 38 of chapter 2, at 111 nn.4, 6; Dugard's references consist of a scornful set of comments contained in a long excerpt from an article by Ellison Kahn, *reprinted in part in* J. DUGARD, ed., *supra* note 29 of chapter 2, at 145–51; Kahn, *The International Court's Advisory Opinion on the International Status of South West Africa,* 4 INT'L L. Q. 28 (1951). There are some brief appreciative references to Alvarez's approach, although without reference to the South-West Africa dispute, in H. LAUTERPACHT, *supra* note 33 of chapter 1, at 125, 134; Jenks, who also has some brief references to his position in several cases not including his *South-West Africa* dissent, lists Alvarez as one "of the outstanding international lawyers of the last fifty years" and elsewhere praises his "dauntless enthusiasm," but nowhere is there a genuine discussion of his approach. C. W. JENKS, *supra* note 7 of chapter 1, at 430, 773; and Franck never mentions his name in the course of his long study of third-party procedures. T. FRANCK *supra* note 19 of chapter 1; other examples could be added, but the neglect seems beyond reasonable doubt—the Alvarez approach has hardly even been considered worth refuting!

have led anywhere, even on the plane of legal posture. The Court was divided over nuance—how to draw the boundary between South Africa's mandatory obligations and its sovereign rights.

Within the United Nations, all attempts to implement the 1950 Advisory Opinion were resisted by South Africa. The South West Africa Committee proceeded to prepare reports and propose procedures that would enable the General Assembly to exercise its supervisory role, subject to the guidelines of the 1950 Opinion. In these efforts the Committee attempted to apply the main juridical criterion of equivalence between the League and the United Nations. An initial problem concerned voting rules. The Council of the League had operated according to a unanimity rule, whereas according to article 18, the General Assembly, by a majority vote, can make any issue into an important question, which is then to be resolved by a two-thirds majority vote. The Committee proposed to the General Assembly that it adopt so-called Rule F, by which matters relating to petitions and reports relevant to South West Africa would be treated as important questions requiring a two-thirds vote. The Committee *urged* that the Assembly adopt Rule F with the concurrence of South Africa, or if this concurrence were withheld, that it seek legal clarification by way of a request for an advisory opinion from the Court. South Africa strenuously refused to concur with these actions, arguing that the General Assembly, by substituting Rule F for unanimity, would be exceeding the degree of supervision exercised by the League and thereby violating the guidelines set forth in the 1950 opinion. The Fourth Committee of the General Assembly initially voted to accept Rule F and to delete the condition that either South Africa concur with its adoption or the Court be requested to evaluate the legality of the proposed voting procedure.

At this stage, the United States was joined by several important states (Mexico, Sweden, Norway) in demanding that this legal situation be clarified by the Court. Otherwise, these states threatened to withdraw altogether from further participation in the Committee. In response to these developments, the General Assembly reconsidered its earlier vote, and a new proposal requesting an advisory opinion on Rule F passed by a vote of 25–11–21.[32]

---

[32]For a careful account of this parliamentary process, see S. SLONIM, *supra* note 38 of chapter 2, at 144–48.

Several interesting developments are noteworthy here. First, the more conservative approach toward the South-West Africa question was taken by the United States and consisted of trying to slow down, or at least to legitimate, the dynamic operating in the political arena of the General Assembly by accepting as plausible South Africa's objections to Assembly procedures and by insisting that the Court alone was competent to resolve such objections.[33] Recourse to the Court, *at this stage,* seemed motivated by an intention to delay the political processes of the General Assembly. Second, the more militant majority, although only a bare majority in 1954, seemed impatient with and distrustful of any further judicial scrutiny of the political process.[34] The Court was perceived as a potential impediment to the just resolution of the dispute with South Africa. That dispute seemed to the General Assembly majority to require coercion, not legal affirmation. As a steadily growing majority of the member states came to this conclusion, there also grew a corresponding conviction that worrying about legal proprieties constituted a diversion of energies and resources. Third, South Africa refused even to participate in the proceedings before the Court, contending that the request presupposed the validity of the 1950 advisory opinion. South Africa insisted on its right to treat the outcome of any such request as merely "advisory" in relation to its obligations. This stand later added to the incentive to bring about a contentious proceeding that would cut this last thread of legal plausibility associated with South Africa's defiance in regard to the General Assembly's entitlement to supervise compliance with the mandate.

Slonim concludes that the decision to submit the question of voting procedure to the Court "was not motivated by a really objective concern with the international law on the subject— for the majority of the members entertained no doubts on that score. . . . It was practical necessity, not legal niceties, which had dictated recourse to the Court."[35] It seems relevant to note that, if there had been *no* doubts as to the propriety of the action, there would have been no occasion for "objective concern." Because of this split between the perceived need for and the perceived undesirability of recourse to the Court,

[33]It should be acknowledged that the United States submitted a detailed statement to the Court in support of the legality of Rule F.

[34]The original vote in the Fourth Committee rejecting recourse to the Court was 18–18–16.

[35]S. SLONIM, *supra* note 38 of chapter 2, at 148.

there was an unwillingness to altogether suspend operations in
the political arena while the Court deliberated on the question. The Assembly was willing to defer resolutions on receiving petitions pertaining to South West Africa, but voted to
endorse a report of the South West Africa Committee that
condemned South Africa's administration.[36]

As it turned out, the Court was unanimous on the basic
compatibility between the voting procedures of Rule F and the
guidelines of the 1950 Opinion.[37] In that sense, the view of
those who felt it unnecessary to obtain judicial clarification was
vindicated. The majority opinion (and the three separate
opinions) concentrated on determining whether the Rule F
voting procedure was inconsistent with the juridical criterion
of equivalence between League and United Nations. Their
opinion proceeded in a complicated way to argue that the
degree of supervision was not in question because that guideline was concerned with the substance of supervision and voting procedure was not a matter of substance. It also argued
that Rule F conformed "as far as possible" to League procedures, given the juridical setup of the United Nations that,
according to article 18, restricted voting procedures in specific
ways, thereby preventing the adoption of a rule of unanimity.

The separate opinions (by Judges Basdevant, Klaestead, and
Lauterpacht) argued, in whole or in part, against the rationale
of the majority. Lauterpacht's opinion has been the most influential and is the most interesting for our purposes. He
argues at great length that the majority rationale is one of
"mere construction" that does not dispose of the substance of
South Africa's contention that a two-thirds voting procedure
involves an increase in the supervisory role.[38] He agrees that it
does involve such an increase in one respect, although he concludes that Rule F is nevertheless acceptable because the
League Council never really acted on the basis of unanimity
(the mandatory was never vested with a veto) and, more importantly, because the Council could reach binding decisions
whereas the Assembly can only make recommendations. This
latter point proved to be decisive for each of the three judges
dissatisfied with the majority approach. It is a significant issue

[36]*Id.* at 148–49.
[37]*Voting Procedure on Questions Relating to Reports and Petitions Concerning the Territory
of South-West Africa,* 1955 I.C.J. 67 (Advisory Opinion of June 7).
[38]*Id.*

because it prefigures the later split of the Court on how to regard formal acts of the General Assembly in interpreting the mandate's basic substantive provision concerning the well-being of the inhabitants. In this case, it was their *depreciation* of the status of General Assembly resolutions that enabled these judges to go along with the Assembly on its voting procedure for South West Africa. As of 1955, these separate opinions, especially that of Judge Lauterpacht, were important mainly as contributions to the development of international law and not for their bearing on the settlement of the South West Africa dispute.

For one conservative commentator, R. Y. Jennings, then a jurist and now a judge on the Court, the *Voting Procedure Opinion* was so unconvincing that it "seems to me to demonstrate the soundness and wisdom of the 1950 dissents."[39] These dissents could be convincing only if the Court were to be seen as separate altogether from the United Nations system. Presumably, "soundness and wisdom" for Jennings involves finding modes of equivalence that pass positivist canons of legal technicality vis-à-vis South Africa's sovereign right not to have the actual impact of supervision exceed in any way that it had agreed to in the original 1920 Mandate agreement. Such a purist view of equivalence was rejected by *all* judges on the Court—its acceptance would have amounted to a virtual endorsement of South Africa's basic claim that with the dissolution of the League it was entitled either to incorporate South West Africa or to maintain, on its own, its duties as mandatory.

The same sort of issue in relation to voting procedure arose again, this time involving the right of the General Assembly to receive *oral* petitions on the status of South West Africa.[40] The controversy basically posed the equivalence issue again because the League had received only written petitions. The question

[39]Jennings, *The International Court's Advisory Opinion on the Voting Procedure on Questions Concerning South-West Africa*, in 42 TRANSACT. GROT. SOC'Y 94, 97 (1956). From the context it is clear that the reference is to the McNair/Read dissents that are based on the impossibility of regarding the United Nations as capable of generating a type of supervision equivalent to that which existed in the League period. On this, Professor Jennings adds the point that the Permanent Mandates Commission was the real administering authority for the League (consisting of "disinterested, expert, and cogent advice"), and was not at all reproducible in the United Nations context; the Trusteeship Council and the Fourth Committee of the General Assembly both are composed of political representatives of member states.

[40]On the background of judicial recourse, see S. SLONIM, *supra* note 38 of chapter 2.

put to the Court by the General Assembly was whether the United Nations' receipt of oral petitions was consistent with its 1950 Opinion.[41] By so framing the inquiry, as with the earlier voting procedure question, the Assembly both constrained the scope of judicial inquiry within narrow limits and, as it turned out, divided the Court. In contrast to the previous question of voting procedure, where it was necessary for the General Assembly to adopt some voting arrangement to carry out its supervisory functions, the issue of oral petitions was a discretionary aspect of the supervisory role. Since oral petitions were not *received* in the League period, their reception could easily be perceived as something *additional,* and therefore they could be perceived as being not really authorized by the injunction of the 1950 Opinion to maintain the pre–United Nations status quo vis-à-vis the mandate. On this question, it is significant that a majority of the South West Africa Committee and of the Fourth Committee believed that granting oral petitions was inconsistent with the 1950 Opinion.[42]

As it turned out, five judges argued that the 1950 Opinion should be read restrictively to mean that only those elements of supervision that were actually exercised in the League period could be equivalently reproduced in the United Nations context. The majority, consisting of the other eight participating judges, stressed the principle of effectiveness regarding the sacred trust, taking due account of the added difficulties created by South Africa's refusal to cooperate with the General Assembly by way of reports and the forwarding of written petitions.[43] Hence, for the Assembly to exercise "equivalent" supervisory authority, it needed to evolve alternative methods for obtaining information. Listening to oral petitions was held to be a reasonable way to achieve this degree of effectiveness.

The split on the Court in the 1956 advisory opinion can be interpreted in different ways. First of all, it can be taken, in whole or in part, at face value as a technical disagreement over the proper mode of construction of the 1950 Advisory Opinion. The presence of several Third World judges among the five dissenters, however, suggests that something more may have been at stake, although this something was not ac-

---

[41]*Admissibility of Hearings of Petitioners by the Committee on South-West Africa,* 1956 I.C.J. 23, 24 (Majority Opinion of June 1).

[42]For more general discussion, see S. SLONIM, *supra* note 38 of chapter 2, at 156–57.

[43]*See,* especially, Lauterpacht's Separate Opinion, *supra* note 41, at 35–59.

knowledged. A second line of argument regarding this split suggests that the dissenters were eager to discourage recourse to the Court for a controversy that had assumed by now such a manifestly political character.[44] Whether the 1956 split also portended the more significant division that emerged in the context of the contentious proceedings, as Slonim suggests, remains ambiguous.[45] The later split, although comparable in its explicit concerns, arose *after* the threshold of the big case had been crossed. It is not surprising, therefore, that the ideological alignments relating to the appropriate scope of *judicial function* and to the proper way for the Court to draw the *legal/political boundaries* of the case were reversed. The dispute took on a different character after 1956 that altered dramatically the way the Court's judicial behavior regarding it was perceived.

Of course, it is interesting to speculate, as has *not* been done, what the effect might have been if the 1956 minority had prevailed. It might have caused some minor immediate surprise but have had the desired longer-term effect of weighting the political balance in the United Nations, especially among African countries, against the 1960 decision taken at Addis Ababa to urge Ethiopia and Liberia to initiate contentious proceedings in the Court. Would the opposite result in 1956 have further eroded the United States' attempt to couple political initiatives taken in the United Nations with their validation by the Court? Perhaps a different outcome in 1956 would have reduced the pressure on having recourse to the Court in 1960 to the point that this option might not have been taken. The decision of 1956 was the third recourse to the Court in the dispute, and by then, it was clear both that juridical coercion was not about to persuade South Africa to change its position and that South Africa's recalcitrance was not going to deter the General Assembly from taking its own actions. Why then were the judges not more sensitive to the future vulnerability of the Court, especially the jurisprudentially conservative ones? One explanation in line with my overall argument is

[44]S. SLONIM, *supra* note 38 of chapter 2, at 163, writes: "By 1956, then, a clear division had developed in the Court over the proper role of the judicial organ in the South West Africa crisis and the degree to which the 1950 opinion could provide all the answers to that sore problem. A significant group of judges (mostly from non-aligned states) looked to the General Assembly itself to find a solution to this problem, which they considered basically political."

[45]*Id.*

that, as long as the dispute was a small case, the overriding interest of all concerned was in building up the role of the Court by its acting "constructively," and this encompassed seizing opportunities for the development of international law.[46]

It seems reasonable after thirty years to conclude that, however the Court had drawn the line between South Africa's mandatory obligations and its sovereign rights, it would have been impossible to avoid the escalation of the importance of the dispute between South Africa and the United Nations. South Africa was unwilling either to renounce its position as mandatory (although it has moved far closer to a posture of renunciation in the wake of the Portuguese collapse) or to renounce its racist policies of administration. The United Nations had become increasingly insistent on its view that South Africa as mandatory was unacceptable per se, a colonialist anachronism aggravated by an undeniably racist system of administration. In such a situation, with one side holding the territory and the other side determined to displace it, a power struggle was bound to ensue. In such circumstances, "law," in general, is marginalized, possessing, at most, tactical importance. To place the Court in the middle of such a situation, especially when political expectations run high and enforcement prospects are low, is to assign it a no-win role.[47] This is what happened when the South West Africa dispute was returned to the Court in 1960 in the guise of a dispute between Ethiopia and Liberia and South Africa.[48]

THE 1962 RESULT

After the 1956 advisory opinion, widespread confusion surfaced in the United Nations about what to do next. Resolving legal doubts about United Nations actions by means of the Court's advisory opinions seemed of limited further value. South Africa did not even participate in the 1955 and 1956 proceedings and refused to consider anything flowing from the 1950 advisory opinion as authoritative, so far as its own legal position was concerned. A relatively conciliatory mood

[46]A view of the Court's prime mission held by such influential figures as Hersch Lauterpacht and Leo Gross. See chapter 1.

[47]However, from some perspectives, as arued in chapter 2, it was appropriate to do this.

[48]For discussion of recourse issues, see chapter 2.

surprisingly persisted in the United Nations. The Fourth Committee of the General Assembly agreed to the appointment in 1957 of the Good Offices Committee (made up of the United States, Britain, and Brazil) to seek a negotiated solution for the dispute. The composition of this committee moved implictly toward South Africa's position that the three remaining Principal Allied and Associated Powers of World War I possessed the best reversionary claim to act in relation to the mandate since the demise of the League. The only departure from this position was to appoint Brazil rather than France to the Good Offices Committee. South Africa responded favorably to the formation of this committee by agreeing to hold discussions with the committee relating to the future of South West Africa. The committee considered various alternatives and finally worked out what was described as a compromise in the form of a partition plan. The economically valuable parts of South West Africa, where the whites lived, were to be incorporated into South Africa, while the remainder, the tribal homelands, were to be placed under the Trusteeship System as called for by Chapter XII of the Charter. It was a true compromise only in the functionally minor sense that it combined South Africa's preference for incorporation with the United Nations preference for trusteeship. The proposed partition was overwhelmingly rejected in October 1958 (by a vote of 61–8–7) by the Fourth Committee as an unacceptable outcome of negotiations. The Good Offices Committee was instructed to put aside partition and explore instead the possibility of negotiating an acceptable arrangement for the entire territory. It did so without success in the ensuing year, demonstrating that a negotiated agreement on the whole of the territory was not possible.[49]

As a consequence of these negotiations, each side hardened its position. South Africa moved openly to implement its long-expressed desire to incorporate the territory, while the organizations of the United Nations moved toward a coercive position by declaring in a series of resolutions that the situation in South West Africa constituted a threat to international peace, thereby enabling Security Council action. This polarization was widened still further as a result of the explosive impact on

[49]For account of these negotiations, see S. SLONIM, *supra* note 38 of chapter 2, at 173–75; J. DUGARD, ed., *supra* note 29 of chapter 2, at 198–215; and G. COCKRAM, *supra* note 31 of chapter 2, at 269–73.

world public opinion of the Sharpesville incident in March 1960, in which a large number of unarmed demonstrators in South Africa were shot in the back and killed by security forces. An increasing polarizing influence came from the greater numbers of African (and Asian) members who led the United Nations toward a greatly increased concern and militancy vis-à-vis apartheid.[50] The struggle over the future of southern Africa was moved off the back burner in international relations, where it had long been left to stew. In 1961 South Africa declared itself a republic and withdrew from the British Commonwealth, and hardened still further its laager mentality of self-reliance at home and nonaccountability abroad.[51]

It is against this general background of developments that the South-West Africa dispute was returned to the Court in 1960 in a momentous contentious proceeding.[52] This time, significantly, South Africa participated vigorously in its own defense, sending an excellent legal team to The Hague, in order to contest the jurisdiction of the Court. Some South African political leaders, including the leader of the opposition, Sir De Villiers Graaff, expressed concern about the international effects of an adverse outcome in the case, which they regarded, given the climate of opinion and the history of prior Court determinations, as a foregone conclusion.[53]

In 1960 the Court was faced with an application from Ethiopia and Liberia that centered on confirming in a binding form the 1950 advisory opinion regarding both the survival of the mandate and South Africa's duty to accept a transfer of administrative supervision from the League Council to the United Nations General Assembly. In addition, the Court

[50]On the latter point, see G. COCKRAM, *supra* note 31 of chapter 2, at 274–78; Cockram quotes Foreign Minister Eric Louw's comments in 1963 to the South African House of Assembly, including the following conclusions: "The Afro-Asian bloc is today in control of the United Nations, and there you have the explanation for the increase in hostility towards South Africa . . . ."

[51]J. DUGARD, ed., *supra* note 29 of chapter 2, at 216, also emphasizes these three critical factors as setting the stage for the contentious proceedings; for greater detail on whether South Africa's rights as Mandatory were affected by its decision to become a republic, see *id.* at 231–36.

[52]On the importance vis-à-vis judicial orientation see Leo Gross's important discussion of the clear difference between the approach taken by the Court in its advisory and contentious roles—stressing progressive notions of effectiveness in advisory settings and positivist canons of caution in contentious settings—see Gross, *supra* note 19 of chapter 2, at 385–404.

[53]*See* G. COCKRAM, *supra* note 31 of chapter 2, at 294–95.

was asked, crucially, to determine that the extension of apartheid to South West Africa constituted a flagrant violation of the basic obligation of the mandatory contained in article 2 of the mandate to "promote to the utmost the material and moral well-being and the social progress of the inhabitants of the territory." The application to the Court rested upon the compromissary clause in article 7 of the mandate, which stated "if any dispute whatever should arise between the Mandatory and another Member of the League of Nations relating to the interpretation and application of the provisions of the Mandate, such dispute, if it cannot be settled by negotiation, shall be submitted to the Permanent Court of International Justice . . . ."

With respect to the Court's jurisdiction, the applicant states contended that article 80 (1) of the United Nations Charter preserved the rights of members of the League concerning the operation of any surviving mandate, including the right to take a dispute to the World Court. Furthermore, article 37 of the Court's Statute specifically provided that "[w]henever a treaty or convention in force provided for reference of a matter to a tribunal . . . or to the Permanent Court of International Justice, the matter shall, as between the parties to the present Statute, be referred to the International Court of Justice." Ethiopia and Liberia therefore argued that the article 7 provision of compulsory jurisdiction was covered by the Court's own Statute, despite the nonexistence in 1960 of the League tribunal originally named.

South Africa was participating in the case at this stage *only* to challenge the jurisdictional foundation of the case. It certainly did not welcome the shift to the judicial forum of the Court as an opportunity to demonstrate its faithful discharge of its obligations as mandatory.

South Africa's four preliminary objections structured the jurisdictional phase of the controversy. South Africa contended, in general, that Ethiopia and Liberia lacked *standing* and that the court, therefore, had no jurisdictional basis on which to consider the merits of their arguments. In particular, South Africa claimed:

1. By reason of the dissolution of the League, the mandate is no longer a "treaty or convention in force" within the meaning of article 37 of the Court's Statute;

2. Neither Ethiopia nor Liberia is "another Member of the League of Nations," as is required in order to invoke article 7 of the Mandate;

3. The conflict or disagreement alleged by Ethiopia and Liberia to exist between them and South Africa is by its character not a "dispute" as envisaged by article 7, as no material interest of either Ethiopia or Liberia are at stake;

4. The conflict or disagreement is not one that "cannot be settled by negotiations," a condition of article 7, and there is thus no proper basis for compulsory jurisdiction.[54]

None of these objections was without some serious legal force. Not only did South Africa's ad-hoc appointee, Judge van Wyk, uphold all four of South Africa's Preliminary Objections but, more significantly, so did Judges Spender and Fitzmaurice in their Joint Dissenting Opinion. Of course, jurisdiction in the World Court must be well-grounded; in effect it must be grounded beyond a reasonable doubt. Any substantial jurisdictional objection, if not overcome, is sufficient to prevent the Court from reaching any discussion of the substance of the controversy. The burden of persuasion is on the state invoking the Court's jurisdiction. In this respect, assuring the Court's jurisdiction, if it is contested, is an aspect of protecting sovereign rights and includes the discretion to refuse a third-party settlement. Even if jurisdiction is not challenged by the respondent state, it still must be established by the Court to its own satisfaction as an aspect of the proper delimitation of judicial function. Our concern here is not with the subtleties of legal standing, but rather with the dynamics of the South-West Africa dispute as revelatory of disagreements within the Court about such broad matters as "judicial function," "law," and the interaction between the Court and the General Assembly. More specifically, the focus in this chapter is judicial style and approach. The 1962 phase of the case foreshadows the 1966 outcome of the contentious proceedings; for this reason, it seems appropriate to concentrate our attention upon the differences between the majority opinion (including that opinion as it was elaborated in Judge Jessup's long separate opinion) and the Spender/Fitzmaurice joint dissent, and

[54] For exact formulation of these Preliminary Objections, see *South-West Africa Cases* (Ethiopia v. S. Afr.; Liberia v. S. Afr.), 1962 I.C.J. 319, 326–27 (Judgment of December 21).

in addition, to give special attention to the Court's treatment of the third Preliminary Objection on requisite legal interest, which in 1966 became the basis for eventually refusing access to the Court to Ethiopia and Liberia.

The majority opinion viewed the questions submitted for adjudication as normal legal issues and examined the Preliminary Objections from the broad perspectives of the 1950 advisory opinion and in light of the principle of effectiveness. As the Court said: "the rights of the Mandatory . . . are . . . mere tools given to enable it to fulfill its obligations," and must be subsumed beneath "the primary, overriding purpose" of the Mandate which is "to promote 'the well-being and development' of the people of the territory under Mandate."[55] The orientation of the Court is conditioned by a stress on *institutional effectiveness* rather than on *contractual rights*. Once this orientation is adopted, it is rather an easy matter to rely selectively on analysis and evidence to dispose of the technical questions: Is there a dispute? Is the mandate a treaty or a convention? Is the agreement in force? Does the compromissary clause extend to "former Members of the League" when it reads "another Member of the League" and to the International Court when it refers to the Permanent Court? Does "any dispute whatever" extend to disputes that do not relate to material interests? Have negotiations occurred such that it can be concluded that the dispute "cannot be settled by negotiations?" All these questions, in order to sustain jurisdiction, had to be answered in the affirmative,[56] an outcome that Wilfred Jenks aptly characterized as resting "essentially upon far-reaching considerations of international public policy."[57] Some of these links in the majority's jurisdictional chain of reasoning are weak.[58]

[55]*Id.* at 328.

[56]"In order to assume jurisdiction, the Court had not only to reject *all* the objections formally presented by the Respondent but also certain others." Spender/Fitzmaurice Joint Dissenting Opinion, *South-West Africa Cases (Second Phase), supra* note 30 of chapter 1, at 465.

[57]C. W. JENKS, *supra* note 12 of chapter 1, at 491.

[58]In this regard, see the one-page Declaration of Judge Spiropoulos:

It appears to me that any attempt to give an affirmative answer to these questions, and they are not the only ones that arise, must be based on arguments which, from the standpoint of law, do not seem to me to have sufficient weight. . . . To be upheld, the Court's jurisdiction must be very clearly and unequivocally established, and that does not seem to me to be the case here.

South-West Africa Cases (Preliminary Objections), supra note 54, at 348. Spiropoulos refrains from elaborating any rationale, or from linking his views to that of any other

The other foundation of the majority opinion is the weight of the 1950 advisory opinion, including its "unanimous holding" in support of "the survival and continuing effect of Article 7 of the Mandate. . . . Nothing has since occurred which would warrant the Court reconsidering it."[59] This affirmation of the 1950 decision is reinforced in 1962 by the simple finding that South Africa's decision to join the United Nations operated as a conferral of consent to the transfer of the compulsory jurisdictional obligation to the International Court of Justice as it was embodied in article 37 of the Court Statute.[60]

Sir Percy Spender and Sir Gerald Fitzmaurice in their joint dissent reject this method of construction in toto. They contend that the approach of the majority is one that proceeded backwards from the conclusion that "compulsory adjudication" was an aspect of the mandate as an institution to the end that this "should not be held to have become inoperative merely on account of a change of circumstances." They charge that "[i]t is evident that once a tribunal has adopted an approach of this nature, its main task will be to discover reasons for rejecting the various objections or contra-indications that may exist, or arise." These judges go on to say that they are "unable to adopt this approach. In our opinion, the only correct method of procedure is to begin by an examination of the legal elements . . . to consider what are the correct conclusions which, as a matter of law, should be drawn from them."[61] Their use of the words *law* and *legal* is polemical, intended to suggest that the majority in contrast acted in a "political," and hence, a "nonlegal," "nonjudicial" manner.

This interpretation is made clearer by Spender and Fitzmaurice in their often-noted passage on fundamental outlook:

> We are not unmindful of, nor are we insensible to, the various considerations of a non-juridical character, social, humanitarian and other, which underlie this case; but these are matters for the political rather than for the legal arena. They cannot be allowed

---

dissent; it is enough for him to conclude that Ethiopia and Liberia have not sustained their jurisdictional burden—there is no necessity, especially in dissent, to show why.

[59]*South-West Africa Cases (Second Phase), supra* note 30 of chapter 1, at 334.

[60]The logic here is straightforward: The Charter as treaty makes members automatically parties to the International Court of Justice Statute in article 93.

[61]All references in this paragraph are to *South-West Africa Cases (Second Phase), supra* note 30 of chapter 1, at 465–66.

to deflect us from our duty of reaching a conclusion strictly on the basis of what we believe to be the correct legal view.[62]

Their conclusion is buttressed by the related argument that Ethiopia and Liberia are principally concerned with article 2 and the physical and moral well-being aspect of the charges they are bringing against South Africa. Spender and Fitzmaurice argue that such an issue is inherently incapable of judicial resolution because objective criteria do not exist by which to test the mandatory's conduct. To assess the "well-being" of the inhabitants involves "questions of appreciation rather than of objective determination," questions whose "proper forum . . . is unquestionably a technical or political one" such as was formerly provided by the Permanent Mandates Commission League Council and is currently provided by the Trusteeship Council and the General Assembly.[63] According to these judges the practical lack of a proper forum for making such determinations is no basis for asking the Court to perform a nonjudicial task. Their attitudes toward the proper forum for assessing the well-being of the inhabitants of the mandate also "strongly reinforce" their central conclusion that compulsory jurisdiction *never* could have been intended to include disputes about the conduct of the mandate in its sacred-trust aspect (as distinct from its material-interests aspects). For this reason alone, the third Preliminary Objection should have been sustained.

Their ninety-nine page opinion investigated in agonizing detail the various technical implications that flow from their point of view. In this respect, their conclusions are scrupulously sustained. Indeed, they are quite convincing *if one disregards* what Jenks referred to as the international public policy aspects of the dispute and takes a very restrictive view of sovereign consent. It is significant that never in the League period was the compromissary clause ever invoked to enforce a conduct provision and that the only litigation it ever generated, the *Mavrommatis* cases, dealt with questions of material interest of a member. Furthermore, the mandate system in the League period did seem to stress the notion of sovereign rights more than sacred trust, and, in this sense, it can be

[62]*Id.* at 466.
[63]*Id.* at 467.

argued that those rights provide a truer measure of what
South Africa in retrospect can have and should have been
held to have accepted as of 1920. Spender and Fitzmaurice
argued that

> [t]he scope of any consent given, must necessarily be assessed in
> the light of the circumstances as known and existing at the time
> when the consent was given; . . . [i]t is almost conclusively demon-
> strable that the Mandatory, in 1920, could not have been contem-
> plating the eventual dissolution of the League, and that if it had
> done so, it would certainly have refused to agree to any adjudica-
> tory obligations continuing after such an occurence.[64]

This contractual outlook also governed their interpretative approach—especially their interpretation of whether the language of article 7 can be construed functionally so as to substitute former members (for a nonexistent League) for members, or whether the International Court is able to be substi-
tuted for the Permanent Court. In both cases, they stress the
literal interpretation as the boundary for what was agreed
upon. However, when they considered "any dispute whatever," the plain meaning of the phrase gave way before their
functional construction of what this provision in the mandate
for judicial supervision must have meant, given their reading
of its legislative history. If there is any consistency here, it lies
in their attempt to assess the contractual relationship embodied in the mandate in terms deferential to the sovereign
rights of South Africa circa 1920.

The Spender/Fitzmaurice argument rests on two principal
grounds:

> First, the issues submitted for resolution are not able to be de-
> cided by judicial means and belong exclusively in the political
> arenas of the United Nations;

> Second, South Africa never consented to compulsory jurisdiction
> in the Mandate contract for *this* kind of case (that is, involving the
> content of "well-being").

The majority opinion did not attempt to meet the Spender/
Fitzmaurice critique on its own terms of legal analysis. Judge
Jessup in his Separate Opinion sought to demonstrate that
someone as concerned about proper judicial function and

---

[64]Both quotations, *id.* at 567.

positivist legal criteria as Spender and Fitzmaurice could arrive at the opposite conclusions with respect to the Court's jurisdiction. He relied heavily, perhaps excessively, on Judge McNair's separate opinion in 1950 to substantiate his view, especially the argument that the compromissary clause survives the dissolution of the League.[65] Compared to the majority, Judge Jessup is far more technical in his approach as he explores the relevant legal history and invokes legal experts and past judicial decisions to support his general construction that the compromissary clause was an essential element of the mandate that was intended to reinforce the sacred-trust character of the arrangement. Jessup's efforts to construe South African consent are more detailed than those of the majority, but they are not really more convincing. He gives a distinctly "American" (that is, an idealistic) view of the mandates system as of 1920 (as "one of at least four great manifestations in 1919–1920 of the recognition of the interest of all States in matters happening in any quarter of the globe") and of appropriate international judicial function as extending to the appreciation of generalized phrases like *well-being*, and he cites explicit references to the judicial practices of the United States Supreme Court.[66] There is no way to circumvent the ambiguity of the jurisdictional situation if *sovereign rights* is understood as Spender and Fitzmaurice understand it, nor of the ambiguity of the judicial function if *dispute* is understood as several of the dissenting opinions understand it.[67]

The same difficulties pertained to *negotiations*. In no real sense did either Ethiopia or Liberia or both enter into any distinct negotiations with South Africa. The majority and Jes-

---

[65]*E.g., id.* at 406, 412–17, 418. *Cf.* also Spender/Fitzmaurice treatment of McNair's earlier tangential remarks: "It is, naturally, with diffidence that we feel bound, for reasons which will appear, to differ from this distinguished Judge," *id.* at 508; such an allusion is rare, and betokens the degree to which McNair's authority is relevant for these opposing views that both seek to establish their conclusions as expressive of the basic mission of the Court; it is also worth noting that Judge van Wyk, eager to offset any impression of partisanship, despite supporting South Africa in all aspects of its argument, repeatedly invokes the authority of McNair, especially in terms of his authority on treaty aspects, *e.g., id.* at 517, 580, 583, 588, 590; this preoccupation with McNair's authority along with the neglect of Alvarez's approach is indicative of the influence of the dominance of positivist approaches to "law" and "adjudication" in the Court; note, however, Fitzmaurice's surprisingly sympathetic comment about Alvarez in his essay on McNair's views about the topic "judicial innovation." Fitzmaurice, *supra* note 4 of chapter 2, at 39.

[66]*South-West Africa Cases (Second Phase), supra* note 30 of chapter 1, at 428–29.

[67]*E.g.,* Judges Basdevant, Winiarski, and Morelli, as well as Spender/Fitzmaurice.

sup treat the conference diplomacy of the United Nations as satisfying, in this context, the negotiations preconditions of article 7, whereas the dissenters, in considering the Fourth Preliminary Objection, argue that the absence of any specific negotiations negates the inference of a legal dispute between the parties and also shows that a "dispute" in the relevant sense never genuinely existed.

Who is right? Is it merely a case of Tweedledee versus Tweedledum? I would argue that, despite the legal polemics of Spender/Fitzmaurice (or for that matter the more muted yet no more compelling Jessup counterarguments), no authoritative resolution of the jurisdictional controversy was possible upon any agreed plane of law. In that respect, the majority and some of the minor dissents were more revelatory of the truth, because in these opinions less effort was made to hide the *legally* arbitrary character of the international policy conclusion.

To keep the mandate effective, if this was at all possible, would have required supervision at the international level, especially in view of South Africa's racism and its policy of noncooperation. Judicial supervision is, or can be, an aspect of such effective supervision, and there is a plausible basis for asserting its applicability in the United Nations period via the compromissary clause in combination with the saving clauses of the Charter and Statute. The Court, as the principal judicial organ of the United Nations, should not minimize its role by taking an unnecessarily restrictive view of its jurisdiction, especially, as here, where what is at stake is the abuse of a "sacred trust" toward a dependent people, one of the few shared goals that unites, on principle, the members of the United Nations.

To maintain the supremacy of sovereign rights, on the other hand, it is desirable to construe consent restrictively, especially with regard to the jurisdiction of the Court. From the *Lotus* case onward, this deference to sovereign rights has seemed to be an essential element in building confidence in the Court. To coerce South Africa to defend its administration of the mandate in the Court against its will is almost certainly to engage in an activity that is and shows itself to be "political." Besides, neither the United Nations nor South Africa is at all likely to comply with an adverse finding on the merits. Thus, no matter what happened in the outcome, the Court would have been made to look impotent. For those for whom this consideration is primary, it would clearly be better in this respect to deny jurisdiction at the outset than to look foolish later on.[68]

I would argue that a metalegal, a metajudicial, even a metaconstitutional perspective is what is actually required in order to assess this jurisprudential clash, if that is, in fact, what it is. There is always the possibility, and certainly the suspicion has been voiced, that the conservative jurisprudential stance is "a cover" for moral and political convictions; that those dissenting judges wanted, consciously or not, to shield white South Africa from a nonwhite headhunt being conducted by the General Assembly. Such a suspicion is not out of place, even though Spender and Fitzmaurice seem to suggest in their "not unmindful" passage noted above that they were forced as professional judges to reach legal conclusions that were uncongenial to their humanitarian sympathies. Conversely, Judge Bustamante reinforces his projurisdiction position in a Separate Opinion by such phrasing as "the most categoric legal *and moral* conviction emerges from this examination"—in this instance, of the Fourth Preliminary Objection on negotiations.[69]

There are two concluding observations about the 1962 judgment that bear on this metalegal perspective. The first one has to do with the composition of the Court. If the Court had been substantially in agreement, as it was in 1950, then the resulting consensus of views would of itself have created a stronger impression as to the proper resolution of questions about judicial function in this kind of case. If the consensus outcome had collided with the point of view of the General Assembly, then it would have provoked an angry rejection of the Court as an institution or at minimum it would have raised a call for its substantial reform. If the outcome had conformed with the view of the General Assembly resolutions, then there

---

[68]Such observation applies with especial force if it could have been anticipated, which I do not believe it could reasonably have been, that the 1966 judgment, after much time and turmoil, would, in effect, uphold the third Preliminary Objection, barely rejected in 1962 by a vote of 8–7; note the hint of trouble ahead, however, in the unnoticed remark in Judge Basdevant's dissent: "It is possible that the third objection could be upheld or overruled and hence a decision taken on the jurisdiction of the Court only after discussion of the merits of the dispute referred to the Court." *South-West Africa Cases (Preliminary Objections), supra* note 54, at 464.

[69]*Id.* at 385 (emphasis added).

would have been a perception of the naturalness of this decision, except in conservative circles. In any event, the consensus *on* the Court would have minimized the perception of legal arguments being used as political and moral rationalizations.

There is one further point here. The controversy in the Court was carried on in such elaborate technical detail as to render the arguments inaccessible to nonprofessionals. For a World Court this incomprehensibility represents a failure, on all sides, of adequate judicial style. To succeed, the Court must have the capacity to *educate,* and this requires it to convey its legal analysis, especially in the big case, in clear terms.

Furthermore, in my view, the 1962 Court badly needed a judge with the Alvarez approach connecting international public policy with the articulation of judicial function in the big case. It would have been desirable to make the normative foundations of the judicial response manifest, and to have taken on Spender and Fitzmaurice directly, rather than the way Judge Jessup did, as a technical challenge. The Alvarez element in the Majority Opinion would have generalized its mode of response, making it rest on a wider conception of law and adjudication. The split in the Court would then have been understood more or less for what it was. Judge Bustamante of Peru came closest to providing this perspective, but his approach lacked the clarity of insight and understanding of the Alvarez position.

Of course, it must be acknowledged that Alvarez's view has been ignored, even by progressive jurists from the Third World. Its potential impact depends on the development of an appreciation that this kind of jurisprudence provides a way out of the legal/cultural hegemony implicit in the acquiescence in the international legal technique of the positivist tradition. Another, comparable way out of this traditional postivist hegemony, which is also totally spurned by the dominant legal thinkers thus far associated with the World Court, is suggested by the Yale approach to world public order, as pioneered by Myres McDougal and his principal associates.[70] My point, even

---

[70] I have discussed elsewhere the Yale approach as regenerative of international law in the current world political setting. Falk, *A New Paradigm for International Legal Studies,* 84 YALE L.J. 969 (1975); Falk, *The Role of Law in World Society: Present Crisis and Future Prospects,* in TOWARD WORLD ORDER AND HUMAN DIGNITY 132 (W. Reisman & B. Weston eds. 1975); and see typical comment on Third World participation by an American lawyer formerly associated with the State Department: "[T]he misguided application of this legal philosophy of ethical relativism to

aside from the substance of the matter, is that the application of legal technique to the resolution of conflict in the big case by the World Court cannot succeed if it isolates "legal elements" in a *cordon sanitaire* in the manner of the 1962 Judgment. The attempt to meet the dissenters on their own technical grounds, or to oppose them by underplaying, as the 1962 majority did, the normative content of their interpretation of the mandate based on the principle of effectiveness, only served to cloak political realities and intentions in the guise of formal legal rationales.[71]

In some ironic sense Judges Spender and Fitzmaurice were the only participants in the 1962 Judgment who acknowledged that they were enmeshed in the logic of a big case.

In the Anglo-Saxon legal tradition there is a well-known saying that "hard cases make bad law," which might be paraphrased to the effect that the end however good in itself does not justify the means, where the means, considered as legal means, are of such a character as to be inadmissible.[72]

Such a statement, of course, is self-serving. It is written as if clarity exists with respect to admissible and inadmissible "legal means." The achievement of the Jessup separate opinion is at the very least to negate such purported clarity.[73] Judge Jes-

---

the fragile structure of international law has been generally pernicious. By according the community expectations of Idi Amin's Uganda and Muammar el-Qaddafi's Libya equal value with those of the advanced states of the West, a powerful acid has been poured on the most hallowed premises of international law." Maechling, *supra* note 21 of chapter 2, at 114. Maechling, in reverse, makes my point perfectly about the cultural hegemony of the West. To portray Amin, and even Qaddafi, as representative of the Third World is as polemical as it would be to define the West by reference to Hitler or Vervoerd. It overlooks the changed composition and priorities of international life, especially as these are specified within the United Nations.

[71]In this respect, the position taken here is broader even than the contention, so well articulated by Lyndell Prott, that the adoption of the positivist or legalist frame of reference is consistent with a range of alternative outcomes that encompassed the main antagonistic positions of the judges toward the South-West African dispute, *i.e.,* neither opposed "legal" construction can be objectively declared "the winner." Prott, *Some Aspects of the Judicial Reasoning on the South West Africa Case of 1962*, REVUE BELGE DE DROIT INTERNATIONAL 37 (1967); relevant excerpt in J. DUGARD, ed., *supra* note 29 of chapter 2, at 271–75. To claim the mantle of objectivity, then, as Spender and Fitzmaurice do, is "polemical" in the sense suggested in the text.

[72]*South-West Africa Cases (Preliminary Objections), supra* note 54, at 468, see also the passages discussed above at the outset of their Joint Dissent, at 465–67.

[73]However, to negate clarity is to confirm ambiguity in a jurisdictional setting, and this ambiguity throws one back on the positivist correctness of Judge Spiropoulos' bare insistence that the Court must deny its jurisdiction unless it has been *clearly* established.

sup's approach, however, proves insufficient because of its "silence" about what is at stake *today* (not only when the mandate was established), especially as regards these issues of "law" and "judicial function." Judge Alvarez would almost certainly have given this kind of analysis in 1962 had he remained a member of the Court.[74]

A final point: the legal training and the culture it reflects, which dominated the decision process, given the composition of the Court, confined its operable goals within limits that were unacceptable and incomprehensible to world public opinion. It is not only a matter of regional and ideological affiliation that is at stake here. This incomprehensibility and incompatibility of judicial style are predominantly a consequence of a virtually unacknowledged cultural hegemony with respect to the nature of "law" and "courts." Lyndell Prott's work is important because it brings this element into clear view, even for purposes and with conclusions somewhat different from my own.[75] Non-Western and nonpositivist approaches remain on the distinct defensive in the work *of* and *about* the Court. This is both unfortunate in relation to "international public policy," to borrow Jenks's phrase, and distinctly ahistorical, given the character of international society.

An appropriate conclusion for this discussion is a statement by Hersch Lauterpacht, a jurist who, like Philip Jessup, sought to turn legal technique toward normative ends while still retaining a mainstream Western jurisprudential identity. In 1933 Lauterpacht wrote as follows:

> [P]ositivism in the domain of international law has become unscientific by being driven, through its own exaggerations, to disregard the very practice of States which it professes to regard as the only source of law, so the desire of generations of international lawyers to confine their activity to a registration of the practice of States has discouraged any determined attempt at relating it to higher legal principle, or to the conception of international law as a whole. The latter function can—effectively, it is submitted—be performed by means of the legitimate methods of juridical criticism and analysis.[76]

[74]And see, here, the important efforts of Judge Dillard, *e.g.*, in his Separate Opinion in the *Advisory Opinion on the Western Sahara*, 1975 I.C.J. 12, 125–26 (Judgment of October 16).

[75]*See* L. PROTT, *supra* note 1.

[76]H. LAUTERPACHT, *supra* note 5 of chapter 1, at 438; *cf. also* Fitzmaurice, *Hersch Lauterpacht: The Scholar as Judge* (pts. 1–3) 37, 38, 39 BRIT. Y.B. INT'L L. (1961, 1962, 1963).

More than fifty years after those words were written, their pertinence unfortunately remains undiminished. I doubt whether Lauterpacht's laudable intention is capable of being realized entirely through the application of "legitimate methods," at last if one takes note of the highly technical, often erudite and esoteric, elaboration of legal issues that was so characteristic of Lauterpacht's later career as a World Court judge. The *radical* break needed encompasses method and redefines *legitimacy* in explicitly value-laden terms. Therefore, Alvarez, McDougal, and to some extent Dillard—much more than Lauterpacht, Jessup, or Jenks—point the way toward the proper appreciation of law and judicial function in world society. I believe the confusion of the 1962 result in the Court, not to mention the 1966 aftermath, amply demonstrates this need for a variety of jurisprudential "openings" within the context of the Court. These openings are needed to liberate the court from a conception if its role that seems to reject its wider participation in international political and moral life.

CHAPTER IV

The Problematic Outcome in the Big Case Against South Africa

THE 1966 JUDGMENT: CLIMAX AND ANTICLIMAX

As suggested in the preceding chapter, the judicial maneuvering of the 1966 decision occurred against a backdrop of escalating political concern. South Africa continued to operate in world political arenas to maintain the basic status quo (that is, administering the mandate as *it* saw fit without accepting international supervision) while not openly defying the authority of the United Nations in all aspects of the controversy. Rejecting the sub judice argument, the Committee on South West Africa was instructed by the General Assembly in a resolution passed on April 7, 1961, to visit South West Africa, with or without Pretoria's consent, and to determine whether conditions there constituted a threat to the peace.[1] Access to the territory was denied by South Africa, but the Committee interviewed petitioners from South West Africa in Dar-es-Salaam and Cairo and produced a report that went well beyond prior United Nations recommendations, urging the creation of a United Nations presence in the territory, the revocation of the mandate, and the transfer of governing power either to the United Nations or to the inhabitants of the territory, and calling on the Security Council to enter the conflict by providing implementing measures for these operations. South Africa ignored the report, but invited the past three presidents of the General Assembly to visit South-West Africa in their personal capacity and issue a report. This offer was not accepted.

Instead, the General Assembly formed a new committee, the United Nations Special Committee for South West Africa,

[1] G.A. Res. 1596 (XV), 15 U.N. GAOR Supp. (No. 16A) at 7, U.N. Doc. A/4684/Add. 1 (1961).

with a mandate to enter South West Africa by May 1, 1962, and to implement United Nations policy—to secure evacuation of South African military personnel from the territory, to repeal all apartheid rules and regulations, to release all political prisoners, and to organize elections based on universal suffrage.[2] The South African government actually entered into negotiations with the chairman of the committee, Dr. Carpio, to enable him to visit South Africa and South West Africa in order, apparently, to move the discussion of the dispute toward resolution. Carpio and the vice-chairman of the committee, Dr. De Alva of Mexico, accepted the South African invitation, arriving in South Africa on May 5, 1962. A bizarre series of events occurred: Carpio became sick in the course of the trip, a joint communiqué was issued by the Carpio group generally favorable to South Africa's contention that there was no militarization or threat to the peace in the territory, and the South African government noted a common agreement on both sides on the need to speed the development of the inhabitants.[3] There was great dismay at these developments at the United Nations, and a dispute arose as to whether Carpio had actually endorsed the communiqué that was drafted in Pretoria. Evidently reacting to pressure, Carpio tried to dissociate himself from the joint communiqué. The committee issued a report that altogether ignored the communiqué and called on the United Nations to directly administer the territory as soon as possible in order to rescue the African population from the cruelties of apartheid. This solution was also declared to be overwhelmingly desired by the nonwhite inhabitants.[4] South Africa was bitter about this outcome, claiming that its efforts toward improving the situation were ignored and that the report was irresponsible because it made charges that directly contravened the findings of the committee president and vice president.[5]

United Nations activity continued in high gear. In 1962 the Special Committee on South Africa was dissolved, and the General Assembly transferred the question of South West Af-

[2]G.A. Res. 1702 (XVI), 16 U.N. GAOR Supp. (No. 17) at 39, U.N. Doc. A/5100 (1961).

[3]For convenient text, see J. DUGARD, ed., *supra* note 29 of chapter 2, at 229–30.

[4]For conclusions of Report, see *id.* at 230–31.

[5]The entire complex sequence surrounding the Carpio visit and report is related in detail, although in a spirit sympathetic to South Africa, in G. COCKRAM, *supra* note 31 of chapter 2, at 278–94.

rica to the Special Committee of 24, a Third World—oriented body charged with implementing the Declaration on the Granting of Independence to Colonial Countries and Peoples.[6] The General Assembly in subsequent resolutions sought to increase pressure on South Africa by calling on all states to refrain from supplying arms and oil to South Africa and by requesting that the Security Council act in relation to the critical situation in South West Africa.[7]

In 1961, two indigenous political and military organizations committed to nationalism and liberation were formed in South West Africa: the South West Africa's People's Organization (SWAPO) and the South West Africa National Union (SWANU).[8]

South Africa was also active. Supposedly in response to its commitment to speed the process of self-determination for the nonwhite population in South West Africa, a special governmental commission, the so-called Odendaal Commission of Enquiry, was created in 1962. The Odendaal Report was issued in 1964, and self-determination, South African style, was recommended. The economically valuable lands in the territory were to be preserved for the whites and to be administratively integrated even more closely with South Africa, while ten homelands on marginal lands were to be established for the various distinct nonwhite groups. Increased investment in economic development by means of a five-year plan was also urged. As expected, the Committee of 24 and the General Assembly denounced the Odendaal Report. The report also posed a new legal issue, to the extent that its recommendations were to be actually implemented, namely, a modification of the mandate, which, according to article 7(1), requires "the consent of the Council of the League." After objections to this report were raised in the Hague court proceedings, the South African government indicated that, although it accepted the recommendations of the report, its implementation would be maliciously interpreted as interfer-

---

[6]That is, the historic General Assembly Resolution Declaration of the granting of independence to colonial countries and peoples. G.A. Res. 1514 (XV), 15 U.N. GAOR Supp. (No. 16) at 66, U.N. Doc. A/4684 (1960).

[7]G.A. Res. 1899 (XVIII), 18 U.N. GAOR Supp. (No. 15) at 46, U.N. Doc. A/5515 (1963); G.A. Res. 1979 (XVIII), 18 U.N. GAOR Supp. (No. 15), at 51, U.N. Doc. A/5515 (1963).

[8]See J. DUGARD, ed., supra note 29 of chapter 2, at 216–26.

ence with the ongoing litigation. Therefore, Pretoria agreed to defer action until after the Court handed down its decision on the merits of the case.[9]

What is most relevant to notice is that action on the political track overtook the contemplated relief sought in the Court on the legal track. Already, as of the passing of General Assembly Resolution 1702 (XVI) in 1961, it was clear that the dispute could not be resolved within the mandate framework, and the main effort toward a solution in the United Nations consisted of building a case for Security Council action to back the General Assembly demand that South Africa renounce its role administering the territory and transfer its functions to the mandatory. The Carpio escapade suggests that some ambivalence persisted in this period on both sides as to whether to continue to search for some kind of negotiated solution in tandem with the South African government. The repudiation of the joint communiqué (by Carpio and the relevant United Nations committee) intensified the political character of the struggle.

What could the Court do? The submissions at The Hague went no further than an interpretation of the mandate that might, at best, determine that the extension of apartheid to the territory was a serious violation of the obligation of South Africa as mandatory power. Yet the United Nations' bodies, convinced that South Africa would not desist, already presupposed the need to revoke the mandate and to institute in its stead a pattern of direct supervision that would carry out the sacred trust and lead rapidly to self-determination under the auspices of the nonwhite majority. Similarly, from South Africa's point of view, whatever might happen in the Court seemed, by this point in time, insufficient to check the hostile momentum gathering in the United Nations.

The South African Prime Minister, H. F. Vervoerd, in reacting to the 1962 judgment, made the following statement in January 1963:

> The International Court has, by the closest margin in the history of the Court—indeed by the narrowest margin possible—decided that it is competent . . . and unless South Africa files counter-memori-

---

[9]For consideration of the Odendaal Report, see G. COCKRAM, *supra* note 31 of chapter 2, at 301–16, and map at 307; see also J. DUGARD, ed., *supra* note 29 of chapter 2, at 236–38.

als, its case will go by default. The South African Government, being satisfied that the Republic is administering South West Africa in the spirit of and in keeping with the intentions of the original mandate, has decided to enter into the second phase of the case. . . . The Government's decision should, however, not be construed as implying a change in the attitude which it has consistently held in regard to the South West Africa issue, namely that the International Court has no jurisdiction—a matter on which the present members of the Court are themselves so sharply divided.[10]

Vervoerd seemed to be announcing a *tactical* decision by South Africa to participate on the legal track, but without suggesting any genuine duty on its part to respect an adverse judgment should it occur. If the *jurisdictional* foundation of the case had been so closely contested by the Court itself, why should South Africa be expected to go along in the event of an adverse *substantive* ruling? All along, South Africa had *used* its legal participation to discourage pressure on the political track via the sub judice argument. This tactic, as we have seen, had not discouraged the Afro-Asian majority in the Assembly and its subsidiary bodies from pursuing their purposes, but it may have exerted a certain influence on the leverage countries, the United Kingdom and the United States.

The discussion of the South-West Africa dispute in the early 1960s by American representatives in the United Nations stressed the fact that action against South Africa should proceed on a strong legal footing and that a favorable Court decision could accomplish this and, in so doing, would engender widespread international respect for the General Assembly position.[11] Taken at face value, the U.S./U.K. position was that validation of the position on the legal track was a precondition for effective action on the political track.[12] The motivations for this legalist emphasis have never been made public, but it seems evident that it reflected the tension between moral and political pressures moving these countries to

[10]For a convenient text of the full statement to the South African Parliament, see J. DUGARD, ed., *supra* note 29 of chapter 2, at 275.

[11]For some examples of these sentiments, see G. COCKRAM, *supra* note 31 of chapter 2, at 317–18.

[12]There is reason to question the sincerity of the American position here, given later revelations that Washington's *actual* policy goals were to slow the political track and maintain the status quo; when the Department of State anticipated an anti–South Africa outcome in 1966, its advance planning was directed toward slowing down its expected impact on the political track.

proceed against South Africa and geopolitical and geoeco-
nomic interests moving them to reach an accommodation with
the existing South African leadership.[13] Under these circumstances, the best possible U.S./U.K. position would be one that
seemed to be supportive of the moral mandate, but failed in
fact to mount any *effective* pressure for change. Hence, the
attractiveness of the legal track.

There is one final consideration preliminary to assessing the
judicial outcome itself—whether the pleadings and oral arguments made the Court wary of its capacity to perform on the
legal level of the dispute. Slonim argues extensively that "it is
only by seeing how the case evolved and what was asked of the
Court that one can gain proper perspective on the refusal of
the Court to make any determination on the merits."[14] There is
no doubt that the explosive nature of the issues posed, given
the judicial setting, led to adjustments in tactics in the Ethiopia/
Liberia case to emphasize the legal way of considering the underlying conflict as to racial policy. South Africa, with *great
resources and ingenuity,* sought to overwhelm the Court with
pleadings, witnesses, and arguments that it was acting in good
faith as mandatory and that its judgments as to what constituted the well-being of the inhabitants did not unreasonably
exceed its discretion under the mandate. After all, article 2(1)
did give the mandatory "full power of administration and legislation" to govern the territory "as integral portion of the Union
of South Africa," including the explicit option to "apply the
laws of the Union of South Africa to the territory." How was
the Court to sift through all the evidence thus presented, especially in the context of a deference to the sovereign rights of a
defendant state that placed few limits on that state's assertions
of purely procedural objections or its presentation of evidence?[15] Attempting an undertaking of such magnitude would

[13]A. Lake, The "Tar Baby" Option: American Policy Toward Southern
Rhodesia (1976).

[14]S. Slonim, *supra* note 38 of chapter 2, at 213; full discussion, at 213–77. Slonim's
main thesis is that the shift in strategy by the applicant states converted the proceeding from a Nuremberg-type case to a Brown v. Board of Education–type case, and
that the latter called for a dubious extension of a formal criterion of prohibition—the
norm of nondiscrimination. Slonim's analysis, although careful, remains somewhat
obscure because of his failure to clarify what he means by a Nuremberg-type case;
presumably, this refers to a massive *factual* documentation of the barbaric character of
apartheid.

[15]These tendencies of the Court to lean over backwards to reassure a defendant
state that its sovereign rights are being upheld, is a bar to an efficient adjudicative

invite a series of nonjudicial appreciations of the legal issues that would vindicate the forebodings of the Spender/Fitzmaurice Joint Dissent of 1962. The Applicant states were not sufficiently alert to this quagmire early on in the proceedings.

It is true that the applicants' *emphasis* shifted in the course of the proceeding toward the insistence that the Court should resolve the well-being controversy by a norm or standard that would provide a *legal* criterion for well-being. The character of apartheid was implicit in the formal laws and acts of South Africa. The United Nations condemnation of this set of laws and policies was nearly unanimous, and it was unambiguous and authoritative, especially in a Mandate context; no further inquiry by the Court was necessary. The application of the legal criterion was a standard exercise of judicial function in a treaty construction controversy to decide, What does "well-being" mean?[16] In my view, there is no indication that this change in litigating strategy by the applicants influenced the judicial responses of the Court. Either type of approach to the merits could have been adopted by members of the Court. In fact, the different dissenting judges took a variety of approaches for dealing with the well-being issue.[17] Changes in litigation strategy do not seem relevant to our assessment of respective judicial styles, the main concern of this chapter. Our discussion here can be kept relatively brief, as the assessment of the 1962 Judgment anticipates many of the issues raised by the 1966 split, and because we are primarily interested in conceptions of "law" and "judicial function" in the big case.

Only the Mexican member of the 1966 Court, Judge Padilla Nervo, explicitly acknowledges the overall political and moral context of the case in his Dissenting Opinion:

> The present case is not an ordinary one, it is a *sui generis* case with far-reaching implications of juridical, social, and political nature.

---

process. At the same time, the jurisdiction of the Court depends on confidence by governments that these sovereign rights will be upheld. There is an inevitable dilemma, then, in working for effective adjudication that arises from the essentially voluntary character of both the Court's jurisdiction and enforcement.

[16]I will not repeat here the argument on these issues developed elsewhere. R. FALK, *supra* note 33 of chapter 2, at 126–84.

[17]For instance, compare the *factual* approach of the two African judges, Forster and Mbanefo, *Southwest Africa Cases (Second Phase)*, *supra* note 30 of chapter 1, at 472–82, 483–505, with the *norm/standard* approach of Jessup and Tanaka, at 248–322, 323–442.

It has been, since its inception, a complex, difficult and controversial one, as can be seen, by the fact that the present decision of the Court, to which I am in fundamental disagreement, rests on a *technical* or *statutory* majority . . . .[18]

By "technical or statutory majority" Padilla Nervo is referring to a decision resulting from the vote of the president, authorized by article 55(2) of the Court Statute, which happens in the event that the judges are evenly divided. Accordingly, the president, who happened to be Sir Percy Spender, had a second, swing vote, assuring that judicial history would be written in one way rather than another.[19]

Dissenting Judge Koretsky of the Soviet Union had a different sense of *technical* in mind in his opinion. He argued that the Court in 1966 "reverts in essence" to the 1962 Judgment, revising it without following the appropriate procedures.[20] He charged in effect that the Majority engaged in double-talk when it distinguished between the legal interest it affirmed in 1962 to satisfy questions of jurisdiction and that same interest it denied it 1966 because it appertained to substance or merits.[21]

And thus the "door" to the Court which was opened in 1962 to decide the dispute . . . which would have been of vital importance for the peoples of South West Africa and to peoples of other countries where an official policy of racial discrimination still exists, was locked by the Court with the same key which had opened it in 1962.[22]

In less direct language, he also acknowledged the extralegal importance of this case, but only in a phrase. Unlike several

---

[18]*Id.* at 443.

[19]For reasons detailed in chapter 2, the 1966 outcome was probably more consequential for the Court than for the dispute over South-West Africa.

[20]*Id.* at 239; as set forth in Article 61 of the Statute and Article 78 of the Rules of Court.

[21]Here is how the Majority described its undertaking and approach in the 1966 Judgment:

[T]here was one matter that appertained to the merits of the case but which had an antecedent character, namely the question of the Applicants' standing in the present phase of the proceedings—not, that is to say, of their standing before the Court itself, which was the subject of the Court's decision in 1962, but the question as a matter of the merits of the case of their legal right or interest regarding the subject-matter of their claims, as set out in their final submissions.

Id. at 18. Of course, there was nothing different in 1966 or hidden in 1962 that altered the rationale for disposing of Preliminary Objection No. 3, which had apparently been accepted earlier.

[22]*Id.* at 240.

other dissenters, Judge Koretsky made no effort to move beyond his reaffirmation of the jurisdictional premise to a consideration of the merits of the case. There is also no Marxist-Leninist content in his analysis of the issues, not even in his critique of the majority. In many ways his dissent parallels in tone that of Judge Jessup, although it lacks the detailed presentation and stops short of dealing with the substantive claims. In passing, we must wonder why, given the degree to which Soviet judges on the Court have been such faithful executees of Soviet foreign policy, they have been so jurisprudentially and ideologically docile.[23]

The majority in 1966 reproduced the reasoning and conclusion of the Spender/Fitzmaurice 1962 Joint Dissent. Its basic line of argument was that there was only one *legally* correct approach available to judges who accepted the professional criteria of their roles. The dissenters who disagreed with the 1966 outcome were motivated by *nonlegal* considerations:

> that humanitarian considerations are sufficient in themselves to generate legal rights and obligations, and that the Court can and should proceed accordingly. The Court does not think so. It is a court of law and can take account of moral principles only in so far as these are given a sufficient expression in legal form. Law exists, it is said, to serve a social need; but precisely for that reason it can do so only through and within the limits of its own discipline.[24]

As is made evident by the efforts of several of the dissenters to demonstrate the existence of the requisite legal interests, there proved to be no agreement even among the positivists on the Court that the "discipline" of law was at all dispositive of the issues here. The majority's insistence on clarity was, at best, polemical. Reasonable jurists of comparable intelligence, professional competence, and concern for firming up the boundaries between the "legal" and the "political" could and did confidently take opposite tacks.

[23]In my view, the Court would have become a more lively, relevant arena if Marxist jurisprudential perspectives, especially in the setting of the big case, had been developed to a greater extent by Soviet and East European judges; there are some pallid intimations of a Marxist-Leninist approach to the World Court in Arkadyev and Yakovlev, *International Court of Justice Against International Law*, 12 INT'L AFF. (Moscow) 967 (1966).

[24]*South-West Africa Cases (Second Phase), supra* note 30 of chapter 1, at 34. Later on, the majority opinion makes clear that "legal form" in the Mandate context means exclusively "the legal rights and obligations . . . provided by the relevant texts."

Judge Jessup's dissent in 1966 is interesting in this regard. His reliance on positivist sources and procedures of inquiry and his frequent invocation of the authority of McNair, Lauterpacht, Manly Hudson, and even Spender and Fitzmaurice, were all part of a strenuous effort to demonstrate that he was as sensitive to legal professionalism in the Western, indeed Anglo-American, style as his adversaries were. In this respect, Jessup's primary audience seems to be his colleagues on and off the bench in the mainstream of international law practice. The technical character of his rationale and discussion makes few, if any, *explicit* concessions to those humanitarian considerations central to the disagreements splitting the Court. To some extent, Jessup's originality consists mainly in commending an image of judicial function borrowed from the practice of the American Supreme Court, a practice that has the complete sanction of one, but only one, important domestic legal system.[25] In this ambitious effort Jessup seems to have been no more successful than Alvarez was. His views on judicial function have not exerted any discernible influence on the Court's subsequent technique or rationale, which has not been the case with his learned inquiries into the historical background of a dispute or his interpretations of a treaty text. Nor do these views of his on judicial function seem appropriate to the context of the World Court. The analogy between American society and world society is not generally useful, nor is the related one between the Supreme Court and the World Court. Furthermore, reliance on a United States' conception of "law" and "judicial function" is not culturally acceptable in virtually *any* part of the world at this stage of history. Judges Tanaka and Padilla Nervo, then, especially with Judge Alvarez in the shadows, contribute more to the formation of an acceptable orientation for the Court than does Judge Jessup.

Without, I hope, belaboring the point, it is fascinating to consider the opening page of Jessup's Dissenting Opinion. He alone of the judges does not deal at the outset with the actual dispute, nor does he castigate the majority for its de facto reversal of the 1966 decision. Instead he devotes his attention mainly to his sense of the Court as a legal institution. Jessup begins as follows: "Having very great respect for the Court, it is for me a matter of profound regret to find it necessary to

[25]*See, e.g., id.* at 385–86, 416, 435–38.

record the fact that I consider the Judgment which the Court
has just rendered by the casting vote of the President. . . .
completely unfounded in law."[26] The phrase *unfounded in law*
is the essence of Jessup's controversy with the majority and
also refers to his contention that "the Court is not legally justified in stopping at the threshold of the case," thereby "avoiding a decision on the fundamental question" of apartheid.
Because he finds the majority opinion "unfounded in law,"
Jessup refuses to be confined, as Judge Koretsky was in his
dissent, to arguing again about whether the compromissary
clause in the mandate confers compulsory jurisdiction in a
dispute involving a conduct provision. Judge Jessup asserts
that it is "his judicial duty" to deal with the question of
whether the extension of apartheid to South West Africa violates article 2(2) of the mandate. With undoubted irony considering Fitzmaurice's elaborate praise of the judicial achievement of Lauterpacht, Jessup defends his conception of the
scope of dissenting and separate opinions: "I am in complete
agreement with the views of a great judge, a former member
of this Court—the late Sir Hersch Lauterpacht—who so often
and so brilliantly contributed to the cause of international law
and justice his own concurring or dissenting opinions."[27] Jessup is obliquely defending himself against the blistering attack
by the Court's president, Sir Percy Spender, upon those who
insist on extending their dissent beyond the jurisdictional
domain.[28]

The same constraints on judicial inquiry allegedly pertain to
the central issues of construction of the mandate as basic text.
The majority proceeds from a central premise: "The Court
must have regard to the situation as it was at that time [when

[26]*Id.* at 325; the evident intent to emphasize the slenderness of the majority is
softened by a long textual footnote on the same page in which he remarks that "I do
not consider it justifiable or proper to disparage opinions or judgments of the Court
by stressing the size of the majority."

[27]*Id.*; Jessup goes on to cite approvingly a passage in H. LAUTERPACHT, *supra* note
33 of chapter 1, at 66–70, to invoke, appropriately given his overall stance, the
authority of Charles Evans Hughes as to the role of dissents, and to mention that
Hughes's views were explicitly endorsed by Lauterpacht. My point here is to emphasize the Anglo-American context of jurisprudential debate.

[28]Spender Declaration, *South West Africa Cases (Second Phase)*, *supra* note 30 of
chapter 1, at 51–57; one notices that, here alone in the contentious proceedings,
Judge Fitzmaurice has not joined his Commonwealth colleague. Also nowhere does
Spender deal with Lauterpacht's conceptions or practice. *But see* what could be taken
as a disparaging reference in paragraph 34 of his Declaration, *id.* at 57.

the mandate was framed]. . . . and to the intentions of those concerned as they appear to have existed, or are reasonably to be inferred, in the light of that situation."[29] On the other hand, Jessup along with some of his dissenting colleagues insists that the textual intentions of those concerned can be accurately construed only by means of a full inquiry into the actual behavior of the parties in relation to their treaty obligations before and after inception of the mandate. Jessup's method involves exhaustive legal research to satisfy positivist canons of consent. Padilla Nervo is more appealing, and I think more convincing, when he proceeds by a chain of normative reasoning from a single assertion—"The world of 1920 is gone."[30]

When Padilla Nervo comes to the issue of apartheid, he also emphasizes the evolving character of international law: "the moral and legal conscience of the world, and the acts, decisions and attitudes of the organized international community, have created principles, and evolved rules of law which in 1920 were not so developed . . . ."[31] Padilla Nervo rejects the dichotomizing of law and morality so characteristic of Anglo-American positivism. He sees the mandate system as part of an effort "to help in the organization of a new world order, in which backward people, on all continents, would have a chance to be free from the former traditional chains of slavery, forced labour, and preys of greedy masters."[32] The entire controversy is lifted out of the *contractual* matrix concentrating on agreements and consent, and even out of the *institutional* matrix of questions of effectiveness. The mandate derives its essential character, for Padilla Nervo, from its relevance to the historic struggle for self-determination carried on by the peoples of the Third World—no matter that this was not un-

[29]*Id.* at 23.

[30]*Id.* at 463; and further from Spender's Declaration, also at 463:

The interpretation of the Mandate and the obligations of the Respondent, is to be made, taking into account, besides the text and spirit of relevant instruments, the circumstances existing now in 1966, not only those which prevailed in 1920. The arms, the convictions, the needs of the peoples and States for the maintenance of peace, in the closely interdependent world of our days is, and should be a fundamental consideration in the mind of this Court.

This passage suggests a widening of judicial function beyond the confines of the strictly legal. Does it mean becoming "political" in the sense of deciding what the law "is" by reference to what the General Assembly wants it to be? Not necessarily at all; see text below for further consideration.

[31]*Id.* at 467.

[32]*Id.* at 465.

ambiguous at the outset of the mandatory relationship in
1920. What counts now in forming a legal position is the clear
moral imperative with respect to dependent peoples.

This imperative is shaped, in part, by the role of the General Assembly. The Court is identified by Padilla Nervo as "an
organ of the United Nations" whose role is conditioned by the
Charter, which includes the obligation to cooperate with other
United Nations organs. The well-being obligation in article
2(2) of the mandate:

> is a sociological fact which has to be measured and interpreted by
> the current principles, rules and standards generally accepted by
> the overwhelming Majority of States Members of the United Na-
> tions, as they were continuously expressed through a great num-
> ber of years, in the relevant resolutions and declarations of the
> General Assembly and other organs of the international commu-
> nity, in accordance with the binding treaty provisions of the
> Charter.[33]

There is a kind of acknowledgment of positivist criteria here—
the General Assembly authoritatively interprets the Charter;
the members consented to the Charter and its procedures.[34]
Yet, the essence of Padilla Nervo's approach in the big case is
to articulate in clear terms what is at stake for the parties and
then to resolve the central issue by reference to sociological
considerations (the will of the international community) that
enable a confident and acceptable interpretation by the Court
of the legal situation.[35] There is no need for an elaborate
technical exegesis that neither can, nor should provide the
Court with a substitute for its own moral/legal commitment in
a case like this.

In some ways Judge Forster from Senegal was even more
overt than Padilla Nervo in his insistence that the law must be
construed by the Court in such a way as to take account of

[33]*Id.* at 468–69.

[34]*Id.* at 469; "The Court should also recognize those decisions [of the General
Assembly] as embodying reasonable and just interpretations of the Charter . . . ."; *id.*
at 469, also at 470.

[35]In the context of this chapter, the will of the community as legal criterion can be
understood in the minimum sense of the views held in common by the overwhelming
majority of governments, as conveniently expressed in widely supported resolutions
of the General Assembly. In a more theoretical sense, this conception of the will of the
community is not adequate, as it is dubious whether their support for General Assembly action is to be taken as a serious manifestation of political will to achieve a given
result.

humanitarian considerations. Forster, more concretely even than Padilla Nervo, does not argue—as Jessup does and to some extent as Judge Tanaka does—that a purely legal orientation to judicial function could uphold the applicant's case. As Forster puts it at the outset of his dissent, "[h]owever learned the reasoning of the majority Judgment... I am unable to subscribe to it."[36] To be "learned" is not the most relevant criterion for this judgment, nor does the value of learnedness delimit the scope of judicial discretion. "It is not playing politics or taking into account only ethical or humanitarian ideals to ascertain whether the Mandatory's policies are a breach of the provisions of the Mandate...."[37] There is a legal anchor in the mandate; the Court is not just embarking on a normative voyage of its own invention. More specifically, the rationalization given by the majority, although learned, is misleading to the extent that it conveys the impression of necessity. Judge Forster shows that the technical notion of legal interest is at best "vague" and "many-sided." The majority could have been equally learned (as was Jessup, although Forster does not say this), had it proceeded to the merits.[38]

The Court had the duty, according to Judge Forster, to declare whether or not South Africa had abused the inhabitants of the mandate territory in breach of its obligations as mandatory, and "not merely" the duty to engage in "arid scrutiny and relentless analysis" of the legal interests of Ethiopia and Liberia to raise the question.[39] More important in this context is the duty of the Court to protect "African peoples who have no access to the Court because they do not yet constitute a State."[40] Judge Forster asserted that if the Court had cast aside its hypertechnicality, "it would have found the multiplicity of impediments put in the way of coloured people in all fields of social life."[41]

From the viewpoint of substantive jurisprudence, Judge Tanaka's dissenting opinion is very significant. He builds bridges from the sociopolitical analysis of Alvarez (and a few other Third World judges, such as Bustamante, Azevedo, and less

---

[36]*Id.* at 474.
[37]*Id.* at 481.
[38]See his discussion, *id.* at 481–82.
[39]*Id.* at 482.
[40]*Id.* at 481.
[41]*Id.* at 482.

insistently, Padilla Nervo) and Alvarez's contention that the
Court should contribute to the declaration and formation of a
new international law to the self-denying positivist ordinances
of Spender and Fitzmaurice. Tanaka acknowledges that it is
acceptable for the Court to reconsider jurisdictional type questions at any stage in the adjudication process, if it is necessary
proprio motu, but concludes "that there are not sufficient reasons to overrule on this point the 1962 judgment" and that the
Court should proceed to decide the questions of the "ultimate" merits of the dispute.[42] He also justifies considering the
ultimate merits, the apartheid question, in his dissent, disa-
greeing with the Spender Declaration on the issue and asserting the right of a dissenting judge at the merits stage "to deal
with all matters on the merits entirely irrespective of the content of the majority opinion."[43] In this regard, Judge Tanaka
is quite correct in noting that "[d]isagreement between the
dissenting view and the majority view is not limited to the
matter of legal right or interest, but it is concerned with the
whole attitude *vis-à-vis* all questions on the merits."[44] He
presumably intends to refer to the Spender/Fitzmaurice 1962
contention that the conduct provisions of the mandate are not
justiciable because no legal criteria for their interpretation exist or were ever intended to exist, considering the discretion
vested by Article 2(1) in the mandate and the consensual
mode by which the League Council operated. The issue was
less directly considered by the 1966 majority, except in their
tangential contention that the mandates system never intended a *legal process* to operate as a check upon the discretion
of the mandatory with respect to the conduct provisions.[45]

It is interesting here to compare Tanaka's and Jessup's styles
on these jurisdictional matters and also in regard to the ultimate merits of the case. Tanaka makes scant use of Anglo-
American authorities, especially for making general points,
whereas Jessup relies mainly upon those very authorities who
would normally be treated as most authoritative for the majority position. The issue of judicial style is not trivial in a big
case. Jessup's approach implies that a humanistic potential is
built into the mainstream positivist tradition, if that tradition is

[42]*Id.* at 250.
[43]*Id.* at 263.
[44]*Id.* at 262.
[45]*Id.* at 46–47.

correctly construed. Tanaka is more radical, resting his argument on universalistic considerations of common sense and reason.

This divergence is even more evident in relation to the article 2 question of apartheid. Tanaka is persuaded by the attitude adopted by Judge Bustamante toward the mandates system in his 1962 separate opinion, namely, that the responsibilities of the mandatory take precedence over its rights and that the mandate's institutional character is more critical than its contractual character.[46] Tanaka's orientation, drawing its central inspiration from a Third World judge, is nevertheless more legally disciplined than the simple assertions to the same effect by Judge Padilla Nervo. Judge Tanaka in the latter part of his dissent characterizes this approach as representing:

> a scientific method of interpretation . . . in which the consideration of spirit and objectives as well as social reality of this [Mandate] system play important roles. This method of interpretation may be called sociological or teleological, in contrast with strict juristic formalism . . . [r]elying on the concept of the Mandate as an institution of a sociological nature, we take a *step forward out of traditional conceptional* [sic] *jurisprudence,* which would easily assert the lapse of the Mandate on the dissolution of the League.[47]

Significantly, for Tanaka, as for Alvarez and others, the task before the Court is to supplant the old legal paradigm with a new one, and not, as Jessup argues, merely to suggest that the old one has been misused. He asserts essentially the reverse of what the 1966 majority contended.

In the critical questions of the links between law, morality, and politics, Judge Tanaka also takes a more subtle position than that of the majority, the Jessup dissent, or the dissents of Judges Padilla Nervo, Forster, or Mbanefo:

> Politics, law, morality, religion, education, strategy, economy and history are intermingled with one another in inseparable complexity. From the point of view of the Court the question is how to draw the line of demarcation between what is law and what is extra-legal matter, particularly politics which must be kept outside of justiciability . . . .[48]

[46]*Id.* at 267, also at 266; reinforced by a technical reference to McNair's views, *id.* at 268.

[47]*Id.* at 276.

[48]*Id.* at 265.

The Court assuredly requires a method to define its autonomous province, but it cannot properly delimit the judicial function by some artificial concept of "law" isolated from the political, moral, and historical context.

The most creative aspect of Judge Tanaka's dissent comes with his sophisticated effort to interpret the sources of law in such a way as to endow them with a natural law content, especially in a setting where human rights are at issue. He accepts the view that the mandatory's discretion, as laid down in article 2(1) of the Mandate, is nonjusticiable except to the extent that its embodiment by the Mandatory violates an applicable legal criterion as measured by article 38 of the Court's Statute.[49] "Here we are concerned with the existence of a legal norm or standards regarding non-discrimination. It is a question which is concerned with the sources of international law . . . ."[50] In this respect, Judge Tanaka regards the activity of international organizations, especially the General Assembly, as providing a collective and accelerated procedure for the *creation* of customary international law, within the meaning of article 38(1)(b).[51]

Even more radically, Judge Tanaka suggests that article 38(1)(c) dealing with "general principles of international law" is helpful to the proof in the World Court of the claim that apartheid violates the mandate by way of a norm or standard of nondiscrimination. In a strong antipositivist statement Tanaka observes:

> [t]he principle of the protection of human rights is derived from the concept of man as a *person* and his relationship with society which cannot be separated from universal human nature. The existence of human rights does not depend on the will of a State . . . . A State or States are not capable of creating human rights by law or by convention; they can only confirm their existence and give them protection.[52]

[49]*Id.* at 285–86.

[50]*Id.* at 287.

[51]*Id.* at 291–92, also at 294; Tanaka notes that the validation of "parliamentary diplomacy" in the 1962 opinion properly implies a parallel rethinking of the formation of customary international law.

[52]*Id.* at 297; he links human rights here explicitly both to natural law, *id.* at 296, and to the notion of *jus cogens, id.* at 298; Tanaka asserts openly that Article 38(1)(c) went "beyond the limit" of legal positivism and that it is "undeniable that . . . some natural law elements are inherent," *id.* at 298.

In this way the norm of nondiscrimination is declared by Judge Tanaka to exist by way of the traditional sources of international law "cumulatively functioning" in this context.[53]

What Judge Tanaka has done, perhaps in too abstract and philosophical a manner to gain any substantial following, is to specify a method of judicial inquiry and discourse appropriate for the big case—one that relates values to law in an integral way and yet stops well short of supposing that a court is merely a conduit for political action. More concretely, he suggests that the World Court needs to adapt its conceptions of "law" and "judicial function" to its role in the world system, thereby according weight to the international community's collective processes of norm-formation. There is nothing provincial or casual about this approach; it carries forward and deepens the intentions and meanings of Judge Alvarez. Parenthetically, although he cites the inspirational relevance of secondary sources authored by Jenks and Jessup, Tanaka nowhere mentions the relevance of Alvarez's earlier and similar views, even though they are expressed in opinions of the World Court, including specifically his opinion in the initial judicial stage of 1950 in the South West Africa disputes.

What we find, then, in several of the 1966 dissents, especially those of Judges Tanaka and Padilla Nervo, is a new adjudicative paradigm struggling to come into being. This struggle is far from resolved and the validity of the process and its fruits have remained almost invisible in the world community. The need to disparage the Court and the old paradigm of law because of the 1966 outcome has cast a dark shadow over the political imagination of the international community since then. The decline in the judicial activity and the status of the Court, despite the presently more responsive character of the majority of Court judges, has confused this issue. Indeed, it is remarkable that McNair's views are cited, often repeatedly, by practically every judge in the minority, while not a single reference to Alvarez's 1950 dissent is to be found in the 505 pages of the 1966 opinions.

My argument is that the 1962/1966 splits were most fundamentally about competing paradigms of judicial function. In

---

[53]*Id.* at 300; Judge Tanaka also regards the human rights provision of the Charter as an Article 38(1)(a) treaty source, *see id.* at 287–91.

this respect, the crucial split in the Court during the contentious proceedings was not between the majority and the dissenters, but between the majority and that subset of judges drawn from the dissenters committed to a new jurisprudential and cultural foundation for the World Court.[54] The cultural dimension of this new undertaking is the least frequently noticed—that is, freeing the authority of "law" from Anglo-American (and European) interpreters and interpretative style, *relying on or building up non-Western judicial authorities*, and appealing to universal and collective considerations.[55] Of course, there is a paucity of non-Western authorities on many questions of international law, but a judge so inclined could simply admit this and go on to assess whether the Western authorities are sufficiently representative of non-Western perspectives on a given question as to be entitled to respect.

John Dugard suggested that studies of the *South West Africa Cases* would "soon proliferate like mushrooms in the legal journals of the world."[56] He might have added books. The decision has attracted unusually extensive commentary, polarized in a manner comparable to the split in the Court itself, but in a ratio corresponding more closely to the antiapartheid consensus of world public opinion. In effect, the critics of the Court have particularly attacked the refusal of the grounds of the decision to be moved beyond those of 1962 and the refusal of the Court to deal with the ultimate merits, while the apologists have said in various ways that the outcome was professionally solid, and if blame existed, it should be directed toward the United Nations or the applicant states for the manner in which they developed their arguments or for having presented a nonjusticiable challenge before the Court. Because of the popular furor aroused by the decision, the professional debate seemed reduced to a single question: Was the Court in 1966 a goat or scapegoat?[57]

[54]I disagree, for instance, with the characterization of the split made by John Dugard (and to a degree with my own earlier writing on the case): "[T]he majority in 1966 can be associated with the precepts of legal positivism whereas the minority may be associated with functional jurisprudence, sometimes called sociological jurisprudence." J. DUGARD, ed., *supra* note 29 of chapter 2, at 366; R. FALK, *supra* note 33 of chapter 2, at 378–402.

[55]It may be apt to recall references to the site, architecture, working languages, and staff, to emphasize its decidedly European character.

[56]J. DUGARD, ed., *supra* note 29 of chapter 2, at 332.

[57]For a convenient and balanced review of this scholarly literature, see *id.* at 332–75.

Of course, the issue of the proper attitude to be taken toward "law" and judicial function was central, if often only implicit, in this literature. It was raised most clearly perhaps by Michael Reisman in his important critique of the majority's handling of the case from beginning to end: "The July 18th Judgment brings out, with stunning clarity, that the theories *about* law held by judges are a highly significant, if not decisive, determinant of judicial outcomes."[58]

THE 1971 SEQUEL

There is no need to recount the story of the dismay in the United Nations, especially among Third World delegations, after the 1966 judgment was announced. As far as I can tell, not a single government altered its stand on the issues as a consequence of the Court decision, except possibly to reconsider whether it had ever been sensible to entrust a dispute of this magnitude to the World Court. As discussed earlier, the immediate effects of the judgment included some small efforts to punish the Court financially and to assure that, to whatever extent possible, the judges who voted with the majority or ones with similar views would not get elected to the Court.[59]

In emotionally charged debates at the next session of the General Assembly, the Court as an issue generated much embittered and strong language. In one characteristic statement, Mr. Achkar from Guinea told the General Assembly that the Court decision was "indeed the alliance of colonial and racist forces with the illegitimate interests of an obsolete world," and that Judge Spender's role made him "guilty of the attempted murder of the International Court of Justice."[60]

The essence of the General Assembly reaction, however, was an insistence on movement along the political track. Mr. Kallon of Sierra Leone expressed the more considered African mood and the overwhelming consensus of the General Assembly:

[i]ndeed, some delegations clearly stated years ago that the path was more political than legal and that the General Assembly should have taken necessary action. Now we know that the last six years at the International Court of Justice were wasted . . . . For

[58]Reisman, *Revision of the South West Africa Cases,* 7 VA. J. INT'L L. 87 (1966).
[59]See chapter 2.
[60]21 U.N. GAOR (1414 plen. mtg.) at 1, U.N. Doc. A/PV. 1414 (1966).

too long we have sat at the sides and waited on the Court for the signal for our own political action. The Court has given that signal and we must have the courage and the determination to take unified and concerted action to ensure that the Mandate which was placed in the unworthy hands of the Government of South Africa is exercised by the United Nations itself.[61]

Action on the political level now could increase its velocity without anticipating any contention from the moderate states that legal validation was needed for it. If the Court would not cooperate even to the modest extent asked for at The Hague, then it had proved itself irrelevant to the overall process of mobilizing pressure against South Africa. It thus became possible to put forward the real political demand that was building up in the United Nations—to shift the administering authority for the mandate from South Africa to the United Nations and to prepare the people of the territory for a normal postcolonial situation of national independence. In one respect, then, the Court's "failure" was itself a contribution to the political process.

The culmination of the General Assembly debate was the famous Resolution 2145 (XXI), passed by a vote of 114–2(South Africa and Portugal)–3(France, United Kingdom, and Malawi) on October 12, 1966. This resolution terminated the mandate, shifted South Africa's former administrative responsibilities to the United Nations, and established the Ad Hoc Committee for South West Africa to recommend "practical means" by which South West Africa should be administered so that the people of the territory could be enabled to exercise their right of self-determination. The Court's actions had become part of the political background against which these actions were taken. The advisory opinions of the Court of 1950, 1955, and 1956, as well as the judgment of 1962, were specifically recalled in order to affirm that South Africa's obligations as mandatory persisted after the dissolution of the League and that supervisory jurisdiction then extended to the United Nations. The resolution also indicated that its supporters were "[g]ravely concerned at the situation in the Mandated Territory, which has deteriorated following the judgment of the International Court of Justice of 18 July 1966."

From a juridical viewpoint, what is most significant about

[61]21 U.N. GAOR (1419 plen. mtg.) at 1, U.N. Doc. A/PV. 1419 (1966).

resolution 2145 is the shift it establishes from treating South West Africa as a Mandate dispute to insisting upon regarding it as an issue of self-determination and anticolonialism. Such an interpretation was implicit in earlier Assembly actions, but never had this position won such wide approval in a setting where a fundamentally new course of action was being proposed.

The fourteen-members of the Ad Hoc Committee set up by the resolution could not agree on a positive role for the Security Council. For different reasons, the United States, the Soviet Union, and some Third World countries, especially those from Latin America, were unwilling at this stage to move beyond the formal revocation of the mandate.[62] In a sense, only the language of response was changed. The African states, it will be recalled, originally went to the Court in 1960, partly in order to find a way to involve the Security Council in an enforcement procedure, especially in the face of the expectation that South Africa would refuse to comply with what was assumed would be a decision adverse to its interests. Nevertheless, in 1967 the African states were being effectively told that they could *say* what they liked in the General Assembly as long as they didn't try to *do* anything in the Security Council (even the Soviet Union advised recourse to the Organization of African Unity rather than the Security Council).

Nevertheless, the political momentum proved irresistible. An eleven-member United Nations Council for South West Africa was created in 1967 with the impossible task of administering the territory.[63] South Africa successfully refused to allow the Council to establish any presence whatsoever in the territory. The Third World countries continued to push hard, contending that the situation was a prime threat to international peace and security. The territory was renamed Namibia to symbolize its change of status, and the Council on Namibia was empowered to issue passports to Namibians and to engage in training programs.[64] In any case, the same living situation for the people of the territory persisted, because no coercive means existed to effect the imposition of the United Nations position or even to generate pressure in that direction.

[62]*See* S. SLONIM *supra* note 38 of chapter 2, at 319–20.

[63]G.A. Res. 2248 (S-V), 5th Special Sess., U.N. GAOR Supp. (No. 1) at 1, U.N. Doc. A/6657 (1967).

[64]G.A. Res. 2372 (XXII), 22 U.N. GAOR Supp. (No. 16A) at 1, U.N. Doc. A/6716/Add.1 (1968).

Some changes did occur in the ensuing period. South Africa extended the application of its domestic Terrorism Act to South West Africa and proceeded to arrest and try thirty-seven leading Namibians. For many reasons including human rights grounds, this trial aroused a worldwide protest that resulted in a Security Council resolution of condemnation in January 1968 that took specific note of the termination of the mandate in 1966 by General Assembly resolution 2145.[65] The argument of the new resolution was that to prosecute Namibians in 1968 presupposed a valid South African authority, but that on the contrary since 1966, regardless of what the situation might have been earlier, South Africa had been "illegally" extending its law and its government over the territory in defiance of the United Nations. After the Namibian defendants were convicted and sentenced, a second Security Council resolution was passed that condemned the trial as "illegal" and criticized South Africa's refusal to heed the United Nations.[66] Also in this period, South Africa began taking steps to implement the recommendations of the Odendall Commission, including its plans for self-government in a series of African Bantustans. Such actions, involving substantial moves toward annexation, further engaged the Security Council in a confrontational role increasingly parallel to that played earlier by the General Assembly. In a series of subsequent Security Council actions, the revocation of the mandate was specifically endorsed and South Africa was instructed by Resolution 269 to abandon its administration of the territory by October 4, 1969. Slonim remarks, consistent with his scornful view of the United Nations role throughout, "[n]ot unexpectedly, the target date set by the Security Council resolution . . . came and went, with South Africa doing nothing to loosen its hold on South West Africa, and with the Security Council taking none of the threatened 'effective measures.' "[67]

After South Africa's failure to heed the United Nations' insistence on its withdrawal from Namibia, resort was had by the Security Council to what Dugard calls "more cautious and

[65]S.C. Res. 245, 23 U.N. SCOR at 1, U.N. Doc. S/INF/23/Rev. 1 (1968).
[66]S.C. Res. 246, 23 U.N. SCOR at 2, U.N. Doc. S/INF/23/Rev. 1 (1968).
[67]S. SLONIM, *supra* note 38 of chapter 2, at 327.

realistic action" in the form of Resolution 276.[68] The Security Council, by a vote of 13−0 with France and Britain abstaining, condemned South Africa, declared that "the continued presence of the South African authorities in Namibia is illegal," and established an ad hoc subcommittee to explore "ways and means" to implement the relevant resolutions of the Council in view of "the flagrant refusal" of South Africa to withdraw from Namibia.[69]

Once again the political track seemed blocked. The major powers were unwilling to implement their support for the United Nations position, and South Africa was as recalcitrant as ever. In this situation, almost out of desperation, recourse was had to the Court again. Partly it was a matter of motivating those states with leverage, Britain and the United States, to take action in support of the United Nations position. The legal context also had been established by a typically comprehensive South African exposition, written to explain its refusal to carry out Security Council Resolution 269 and attacking the legal grounds of all United Nations actions stemming from the revocation of the mandate.

Accordingly, the Security Council met on July 29, 1970, and passed two resolutions that were responsive to the report of their subcommittee. The first set forth the proper attitude for states to take toward the disputed territory in view of South Africa's refusal to get out of Namibia.[70] The second requested an advisory opinion from the Court on the question of the "legal consequences of the continued presence of South Africa in South West Africa (Namibia) notwithstanding Security Council Resolution 276.[71] The question put to the Court was deliberately cast in somewhat limited terms; evidently, its sponsors were hoping to confine the Court's inquiry to the question of the appropriate means for the United Nations to adopt, vis-à-vis the illegal South African presence in Namibia. Its sponsors were not interested in directing the Court to consider the broader question of

[68]J. DUGARD, ed., *supra* note 29 of chapter 2, at 441.
[69]S.C. Res. 276, 25 U.N. SCOR Supp. (No. 34) at 2, U.N. Doc. S/INF/25 (1970).
[70]S.C. Res. 283, 25 U.N. SCOR Supp. (No. 34) at 2, U.N. Doc. S/INF/25 (1970).
[71]S.C. Res. 284, adopted 12−0, with Poland, the Soviet Union, and Britain abstaining. 25 U.N. SCOR Supp. (No. 34) at 4, U.N. Doc. S/INF/25 (1970). On the political background of recourse to the Court, see J. DUGARD, ed., *supra* note 29 of chapter 2, at 376−446; S. SLONIM, *supra* note 38 of chapter 2, at 313−39.

whether the General Assembly possessed the authority in
1966 to revoke the mandate.

Slonim, for one, is convinced "[t]hat this resort to the
Court's advisory function was not motivated by any genuine
doubts regarding the legality of United Nations action."[72]
While I agree with the substance of Slonim's contention, I
disagree with his tone, which suggests impropriety. Law is not
a game to be played by actors necessarily holding "genuine
doubts." Especially after 1966 there were solid reasons for
clearing the legal air, even if the outcome was reasonably assured in advance. Besides, a positive response by the Court
might have helped the General Assembly and Security Council
to be more effective in pursuing their objectives. Such effectiveness was, or should have been, the main concern of United
Nations policy-makers. They needed to decide how to use a
variety of strategies and arenas to give the values and concerns
professed by the overwhelming majority of states a greater
prospect of realization, especially in this case where the consensus was strong, the defiance blatant, and the challenge to
United Nations authority central.

The sponsors of this move were fundamentally interested in
resolving the underlying concerns about judicial recourse in
this case.[73] An affirmation of legality by the Court could not
be expected to alter either South Africa's recalcitrance or the
attitude of the Great Powers towards Namibia. In this respect,
the clearer the basis for United Nations action becomes, the
plainer the weakness of the organization also becomes. And
when it comes to the question of enforcing or not enforcing
United Nations sanctions against South Africa, not only the
states with material and geopolitical interests at stake, such as
France, the United Kingdom, and the United States, but
others as well, such as the Soviet Union, take stands showing
that they do not want to endow the United Nations with an
enforcement role or capability. Such reluctance is partly the
result of a dogmatic allegiance to sovereign rights associated
with the domestic jurisdiction provisions of the Charter and
partly a reflection of the adverse internal politics of the
United Nations on such past occasions as the Korean War and
the Congo Operation. Yet these potential problems of respect

[72]*Id.* at 329; see his reasoning at 330–32.
[73]*See* chapter 2.

for the authority of the Court were not as great in 1970 as they had been before and after the 1966 decision. The Court was being asked to assess the legal consequences of South Africa's continued presence in Namibia. This question sought legal clarification (or reinforcement) in a situation in which no significant split existed on the political plane. The situation thus greatly contrasted with a comparable request for clarification by way of the Court in *Certain Expenses*.[74]

Our concern in this chapter is primarily with style rather than substance. The issues presented to the Court in 1970 were interpreted by the majority as involving an inquiry into the validity of Resolution 2145 by which in 1966 the General Assembly had originally purported to revoke the mandate. The Court rejected the approach that had helped shape the way the question to the Court had been framed in the Security Council. That is, the Court rejected the view that it should proceed from the premise of regarding the revocation as a given, and that it should only examine the legal consequences that flow from Resolution 276, which called upon states to take various steps designed to put pressure on South Africa for its failure to vacate the territory as demanded by the United Nations.

The Court gave its opinion by a vote of 11–2 (Judges Fitzmaurice and Gros dissenting) that South Africa's continued presence in Namibia was illegal and that it was under an obligation to withdraw immediately. By a vote of 11–4 (Judges Fitzmaurice, Gros, Dillard and Onyeama dissenting) the Court gave its opinion that member states of the United Nations are under the obligation to recognize the illegality of South Africa's presence in Namibia and to refrain from acts that might imply any legality for South Africa's presence in or administration of the territory. By the same 11–4 vote the Court declared that even states that are not members should cooperate with the United Nations' efforts to end South Africa's illegal presence in the territory.

In style, the majority opinion is a conservative response to the Security Council question. It was narrowly conceived, perhaps for the tactical reasons of wanting to build a strong judicial majority or as a way of making its conclusions most persuasive to the juridical sensibilities of the least politically committed

---

[74]*See* chapter 5.

states (especially France, the United Kingdom, and the United States). By calling the response conservative, I mean to point to the Court's refusal to place the controversy squarely in its moral, humanitarian, and historical context, or to conceptualize the Court's role in less positivist terms.

In some ways the 1971 Advisory Opinion was exceedingly positivist in style. The earlier legal guidelines that had been set forth by the Court, especially in 1950, were given great weight and were frequently cited. The difficulty for the Court was to get around the consensual and contractual nature of the mandate, especially the requirement of consent from both sides for any modification of the mandate. To uphold the United Nations position in 1971 it was necessary for the Court to confer upon the organization the power of unilateral revocation. The Court had to imply that there had been some real ambiguity as to the intentions of the parties to the mandate in 1920.

It is in relation to this requirement that John Dugard speaks of "the triumph of teleological interpretation" to denote the shift from 1966 to 1971. My point is that this shift took place *within* the positivist paradigm, rendering the substance of the decision more consonant with the jurisprudential needs of the global system, but still failing to move toward the new kind of orientation that Judge Alvarez called for so clearly in 1950 and that Judge Padilla Nervo and others seemed to support in 1966.

To be sure, the Court in 1971 did call attention to the development of international law relative to the anticolonial movement of dependent peoples towards self-determination, citing General Assembly Resolution 1514 with approval. It proceeded to interpret the mandates system in this wider historical context. The central idea of sacred trust was asserted as "not static," but "by definition evolutionary."[75] And the Court added:

> viewing the institutions of 1919, the Court must take into consideration the changes which have occurred in the supervening half-century, and its interpretation cannot remain unaffected by the subsequent development of law . . . ; [t]hese developments leave

[75]*Legal Consequences for States of the Continued Presence of South Africa in Namibia (South West Africa) Notwithstanding Security Council Resolution 276 (1970)*, 1971 I.C.J. 16, 31 (Advisory Opinion) [hereinafter referred to as *Legal Consequences for States of the Continued Presence of South Africa in Namibia*].

little doubt that the ultimate objective of the sacred trust was self-determination and independence of the peoples concerned.[76]

This understanding, taken in combination with the earlier actions of the Court, is used to confirm the survival of the mandate and the transfer of the League functions to the United Nations. Some attempt is even made in the formation of the judgment to build an argument for South African acquiescence in these developments.[77]

The General Assembly action also is placed in the wider historical context of the past twenty years, in which the General Assembly had been persistently rebuffed in its attempts to carry out its supervisory role and to negotiate some satisfactory arrangement with South Africa. The issue this history poses, then, is whether the General Assembly can, with or without the Security Council, revoke the mandate and substitute its own authority for that of South Africa in the territory. This question raises the underlying issue of the judicial review by the Court of actions taken by other principal organs of the United Nations. The Court rejects the view that it is precluded from inquiry by the narrow terms of the question submitted, which restricts the Court to the consideration of Resolution 276. Instead, the Court, rather confusingly, disavows judicial review and yet, at the same time, declares that it will consider the objections that have been directed at the validity of General Assembly Resolution 2145.[78] By reference to general principles of international law applicable to a treaty relationship, the Court concludes that a material breach of contract has occurred as a consequence of South Africa's persistent violation of the mandate, especially by its refusal to submit reports and to accept the Assembly's administrative supervision, obligations confirmed by the 1950 advisory opinion.

The most dubious positivist link in the Court's chain of legal reasoning has to do with the Assembly's capacity to transcend its normal recommendatory role. The essence of the position taken by the majority in a confusingly concise form is that the Assembly's action in Resolution 2145 followed from its competence to declare the mandate to be terminated—the Court asserts that "[t]his is not a finding on facts, but the formula-

[76]Id.
[77]Id. at 41–43.
[78]Id. at 45.

tion of a legal situation."[79] More centrally, the Court concludes that the Assembly "in specific cases within the framework of its competence" is able to pass resolutions "which
make determinations or have operative design."[80] In effect,
the Court is saying that the General Assembly, as the successor
to the League Council, needs to have the competence to assure that the sacred trust is not nullified by the failure of the
mandatory to comply with its terms. The kind of failure that
might supply a basis for such General Assembly action needs
to be "non-factual" (that is, not requiring a judgment about
South Africa's performance), and therefore exclusive emphasis is placed by the Court on South Africa's refusal to submit
to Assembly supervision, including its refusal to submit reports. The Court regards the declaration of the legal situation
as contained in Resolution 2145 as being based on its earlier
"findings" concerning South West Africa—"the Court adheres
to its own jurisprudence."[81]

Subsequent Security Council endorsements of Resolution
2145 impart a binding character to the decisions of the Assembly, especially in relation to those states that voted against
Resolution 2145 or did not endorse it. These Security Council
resolutions, including Resolution 276, are binding on the entire membership of the United Nations.[82]

There is a clearer consideration of these matters in Judge
Dillard's important separate opinion. Dillard suggests that the
majority approach, based mainly on the idea that General Assembly actions "*vis-à-vis* non-consenting States fall into the
category of recommendations" that need to be converted by
the Security Council into "a binding decision operative as
against non-consenting States," is not the only way to validate
Resolution 2145. He favors an approach that confers on the
Assembly a "decision-making power" in the context of terminating the mandate, a competence that is derived from the
logic of United Nations Charter article 80 and that involves
"no invasion of national sovereignty," since Assembly action is

[79]*Id.* at 50; as such, this is a response to South Africa's contention that a factual
investigation was needed before the Assembly could make any declaration about the
fulfillment of the mandate.
[80]*Id.*
[81]*Id; but see* Judge Fitzmaurice's exhaustive contentions in his dissent that the prior
findings of the Court were, at most, advisory, and hence nonbinding.
[82]The extent of legal effect of Security Council resolutions under Article 25 is a
controversial aspect of the majority opinion.

confined to "a territory and regime with an international status.[83]

The political backlash from the 1966 majority outcome forms the backdrop for these judgments. Judge Dillard argues that if the judicial arena is unavailable to decide in a binding form whether substantive violations of the mandate have taken place, then such violations must be authoritatively assessed by the supervisory organ for the mandate in the post-League period. He quotes, no doubt with ironic satisfaction, that passage in the Court's 1966 judgment in which the Court suggests that "any divergence of view concerning the conduct of a mandate were regarded as being matters that had their place in the political field, the settlement of which lay between the mandatory and the competent organs of the League."[84] Hence, to turn around now and suggest that the Assembly cannot act without a judicial foundation of a binding character "would amount to a complete denial of remedies available against fundamental breaches of an international undertaking."[85]

We are thrown in this case back to the limits of legal positivism in order to deal with a claim that rests, above all, on the special authority of the organized international community to act on behalf of a dependent people in a territory that is not itself a sovereign state. The absence of "consent" by South Africa or of explicit authority on the part of the General Assembly is overcome by the use of extensive implied powers. That is, the General Assembly is understood to have the competence that is required to do whatever is necessary under evolving conditions to protect the well-being of the inhabitants of the mandated territory. South Africa's version of "well-being" is unacceptable and amounts to a breach of such a fundamental character in the mandate that the mandate can be revoked and South Africa required to leave the territory. This collective process, in order to be effective, must be binding on the entire membership of the United Nations, indeed on all states.

Note the two special features of this judicial endeavor, which combines liberal ethics with positivist method. First, the essence of South Africa's breach is declared to be a technical

[83]Id. at 163.
[84]Quoted at 48; South West Africa Cases (Second Phase), supra note 30 of chapter 1, at 45.
[85]Id. at 49.

one—a refusal to report to and to accept General Assembly
supervision—rather than the substantive inhumane treatment
of the inhabitants by way of severe racial discrimination. Second, the Court validates a General Assembly role by means of
the termination of the mandate and validates the United Nations substitution of itself as administering authority in the
territory in a way that goes far beyond the degree of supervision contemplated in the League period. These United Nations actions exceed the equivalence guideline that seemed so
crucial to the Court in its 1950, 1955, and 1956 advisory opinions. Of course, because South Africa has repeatedly frustrated all attainment of equivalence by its refusal to cooperate
with the United Nations (either via reporting or by negotiating
a trusteeship arrangement), there was no way to avoid non-
equivalence either by acquiescing in South Africa's posture or
by terminating its effective role.[86] Yet nowhere does the Court
clearly connect its earlier consensual view of how to modify
the mandate with its 1971 approval of a unilateral approach.

Therefore, for those who take the trouble—Slonim for instance—the 1971 outcome is exceedingly vulnerable to the
kind of positivist assault mounted against it in Judge Fitzmaurice's extended dissent.[87] Characteristically, Fitzmaurice initi-
ates his extended inquiry by suggesting that "[a]lthough I respect the humanitarian sentiments and the avowed concern
for the welfare of the peoples of South West Africa which so
clearly underlie the Opinion of the Court in this case, I cannot
as a jurist accept the reasoning on which it is based."[88] He

[86]Note the suggestion by Judge Gros in his dissent that the entire case for termination of the mandate could be properly built, within the confines of the 1950 advisory
opinion, around South Africa's refusal to negotiate with the United Nations in good
faith a new arrangement for South West Africa. *Id.* at 341–45.

[87]Slonim concludes that "[t]his dissent, despite the fact that it represents the view
of a solitary judge, must be regarded as a formidable challenge to the majority opinion, since it highlights mercilessly the omissions of that opinion, and the extent to
which it merely assumes or glosses over what it should establish," S. SLONIM, *supra*
note 38 of chapter 2, at 342; *see also id.* at 343–44. The "formidable challenge" is *only
relevant* with respect to those that operate within the positivist paradigm, that is, it
should have been a formidable challenge to those judges who drafted the majority
opinion and let it rest on positivist grounds; for those who reject such a paradigm in
the big case, a different persuasive path of reasoning existed premised on values,
human rights, and the authority of the United Nations to promote self-determination
by reference to the law-creating capacity of the will of the organized international
community.

[88]*Legal Consequences for States of the Continued Presence of South Africa in Namibia,*
supra note 75, at 220.

rejects as unfounded the major premise of the majority that a breach by South Africa of its obligations under the mandate has been established by an acceptable legal method. His view of what the mandate required of South Africa has to be read in contractual terms:

> My reading of the situation is based—in orthodox fashion—on what appears to have been the intentions of those concerned at the time. The Court's view, the outcome of a different, and to me alien philosophy, is based on what has become the intentions of new and different entities and organs fifty years later. This is not a legally valid criterion, and those thinking of having recourse to the international judicial process at the present time must pay close attention to the elaborate explanation of its attitude on this kind of matter which the Court itself gives in its Opinion.[89]

This criticism overstates its jurisprudential basis, because there exists no such agreement on how to proceed positivistically in a situation in which the underlying instrument of agreement has a constitutional character. Who is to say, going back to 1950, that Judge De Visscher used less legally valid criteria of interpretation than did Fitzmaurice, even if we grant the latter's broader position that positivism (ambiguously reinforced by natural law) reflects what mainstream Euro-American professional lawyers understand by "law" and "judicial function."[90] Fitzmaurice is correct to point out that a government resting its claims on outmoded vested rights that collide with deeply felt human rights would do well to pay "close attention" to what the Court did in 1971.[91]

Fitzmaurice believes that the mandatory's failure to carry out the sacred trust aspects of its obligation because of the inability of the United Nations to take over the role of the League is one of those legal realities that must be accepted at "the present stage" of the development of international law:

[89]*Id.* at 223.

[90]Incidentally, Fitzmaurice's jurisprudential bravado with respect to his colleagues on the Court rests on totally unexamined and undemonstrated assumptions, the very sin he most consistently charges, and as Dugard contends, *supra* note 29 of chapter 2, at 412–33, the Court had consistently followed the teleological approach prior to 1966; Fitzmaurice's views, not those of the 1971 majority, represented the deviant position on the proper "legal" approach to judicial interpretation.

[91]As will be argued in chapter 6, the International Court of Justice should not base its future on securing the confidence of governments with a conservative view of the international legal order; building their confidence will destroy the real potential for growth that I believe the Court possesses.

"This is precisely what that system itself in large measure is, and will, pending changes not at present foreseeable, continue to be. It is not by ignoring this situation that the law will be advanced."[92] In effect he insists that we are dealing with a sovereignty-determined system of rights and duties. To the extent that we neglect this feature of the world political and legal structure, we undermine the role of law as an instrument of international coordination. Judicial determinations will then be unenforceable and scorned by those governments called to account. The mandates context does not establish any exception to these rules. It arose out of a voluntary contractual arrangement. To make modifications in that arrangement, South Africa's consent is required.

In an uncharacteristic "Postscriptum," Judge Fitzmaurice argues that South Africa might have incorporated South West Africa in the 1945–56 period and so confronted the United Nations with a fait accompli. It did not do so, and accordingly, there should be "a reciprocal and corresponding realization" that the United Nations cannot unilaterally convert the territory into "the sovereign independent State of Namibia." He ends on a practical note: "Clearly therefore, in a situation in which no useful purpose can be served by launching the irresistible force against the immovable object, statesmanship should seek a *modus vivendi*—while there is yet time."[93] But what is a modus vivendi in the late twentieth century on an issue of self-determination that is perceived so clearly and one-sidedly by international society? Judge Fitzmaurice appears to mean by his phrase "while there is yet time" some means short of armed struggle. But again, the anticolonial movement overwhelmingly regards its most glorious victories as those achieved through force of arms, and it does not look upon these issues, especially with regard to South Africa, as negotiable. In any case, years of "negotiations" have demonstrated that South Africa is not willing to remove the objectionable features of racist rule from South West Africa, much less move toward an acceptable form of self-determination for its peoples.[94]

[92]*Legal Consequences for States of the Continued Presence of South Africa in Namibia, supra* note 75, at 224.

[93]*Id.* at 298; revealingly, Slonim ends his long book with this quotation, which he says "remains pertinent," that is, a path to solution by way of diplomatic negotiations; S. SLONIM, *supra* note 38 of chapter 2, at 365.

[94]Compare in this regard the deft conclusion of Judge Dillard's separate opinion, which combines sweeter words than Fitzmaurice's with a more internationally acceptable orientation:

Judge Fitzmaurice, despite his writing in the context of an advisory opinion, seems to assume no accountability in relation to the views of the situation held by the members of the United Nations. After the international reception accorded the 1966 majority opinion, it should have been evident to him, at a minimum, that the Court, in order to survive as an institution, had to steer a middle course in the big case between upholding sovereign rights and executing the political will of the United Nations. The Court, through both the electoral and the appropriations processes, is subject to political checks that are built into the positivist conception of the United Nations.[95] Following his line of legal reasoning may win plaudits from some legal advisers in the more industrial countries, but it represents no way at all to take legal account of the geopolitical structure of the present world system.

Neither, however, does the majority approach. It is too technical, too uninspiring, and it fails to give aid and comfort by actually resolving positivist doubts.[96] Because of the evolution of the history of the mandate, its complexity and its ambiguity, and because of the uncertain foundations of General Assembly authority in relation to the mandate system, it is impossible to remove these doubts in the technical way the Court attempted to do so. To the extent that the attempt is made within such boundaries, it will always be vulnerable to the Spenders, Fitzmaurices, Slonims, and Johnsons. It is true that as a matter of craft, the technical case of the 1971 opinion

It may be hoped that South Africa, as a great nation, will respect the judicial pronouncement of this Court and the almost unanimously held view in the United Nations that its administration of Namibia must come to an end. It may be hoped, also, that in the delicate and difficult era that lies ahead, especially in the period of transition, a spirit of mutual goodwill may, in time, displace one based on mutual misunderstanding.

Legal Consequences for States of the Continued Presence of South Africa in Namibia, supra note 75, at 168–69. In effect, Judge Dillard suggests that South Africa go along with the United Nations position, but that the United Nations proceed in a cool way. Whether it is feasible to heed such a suggestion at this time, when the label *great nation* is attached to South Africa, home and base of apartheid, is doubtful. It ignores the pain and hurt of the leadership in ex-colonies that dominate international institutions—no matter how badly that leadership treats its own populations once independence is achieved.

[95]Indeed, his isolation in 1971, compared to 1966 and even 1962, suggests the operation of this process.

[96]On this I agree with Slonim's conclusion, *supra* note 38 of chapter 2, at 343, that [i]f the purpose of requesting the advisory opinion was to dispel, once and for all, any doubts regarding the validity and legal force of the United Nations action in purporting to terminate the mandate, then it would seem that the Court, by refusing to address itself to the central legal problems involved, has done very little to remove these doubts.

could have been improved by much better legal research and reasoning. This would have neutralized some of the influence of the Fitzmaurice dissent. It would not have altered one iota the United Nations acceptance of or South Africa's rejection of the 1971 opinion.[97]

Of the 1971 judges, only the vice president of the Court, Judge Ammoun of Lebanon, strikes the correct note in acknowledging the moral-historical essence of the controversy and taking sides in a manner that is forthright. As he observes close to the beginning of his separate opinion, the Security Council request to the Court seeks "for the first time" clarification with regard to

> certain fundamental principles of international law. These are . . . the sovereignty of dependent peoples, the mandate institution, its nature and its objects, the right of peoples to self-determination and decolonization, equality between nations and between individuals, racial discrimination as expressed in the doctrine of *apartheid* . . . and, in sum, the whole body of human rights and their imperative universal character . . . [a]ll these notions are the outward expression of a new body of international law, the consequence of an irreversible social and political evolution of the modern world.

Most significantly, from the perspective of judicial style, he adds that the Court has "not overlooked" this evolution, but "it has not always gone far enough in spelling out the legal conclusions to which they [*sic*] point."[98]

Judge Ammoun discusses with unusual candor the legitimacy of the struggle of the Namibian people as something that "cannot be in any doubt." More specifically, Ammoun says, "I could therefore have wished that the Court, like the General Assembly and the Security Council, had mentioned in its Opinion the legitimate struggle of the Namibian people."[99] He asserts that the opinion would have had more "persuasive force . . . . if it had retraced the path whereby this right of peoples has made its entry into positive international law and had determined exactly what were the factors which have gone into its making."[100]

[97]*See* J. DUGARD, ed., *supra* note 29 of chapter 2, at 490–91, for text of Prime Minister Forster's negative response.

[98]All quotations in this paragraph from *Legal Consequences for States of the Continued Presence of South Africa in Namibia, supra* note 75, at 67.

[99]*Id.* at 70.

[100]*Id.* at 74; also at 75, where he talks of "a page of history which needs turning that must be seen in attachment to an outdated law which denies resolutions of the

This approach by Judge Ammoun, overlooked by commentators and not even referred to by Slonim or Dugard, points the only way to the rehabilitation of the Court in the big case. The role of the World Court needs to be conceived in inspirational as well as technical terms. This understanding accepts the law-forming quality of the will of the international community expressed through the activities of the organ of the United Nations. It acknowledges that this approach may bring about some marginal increase in the alienation of non-Communist more industrial states, but it enlists the Court in the overriding struggle of the majority of United Nations members to achieve a more just world order. The Court could likely become a more important arena for solving international controversies if its identity were to be redefined in these terms. Such a change might lead to more "big cases" being referred to the Court by way of requests for advisory opinions. In any case, it could hardly diminish today's modest caseload of contentious proceedings.

CONCLUSION

We know that the Court's Advisory Opinion did not change very much of anything. South Africa remained steadfast in its refusal to accede to the United Nations' position. The Security Council could not get across the enforcement threshold to implement its purposes. The sovereign rights of South Africa, regardless of the legal situation, governed the de facto situation in Namibia. Perhaps it is true that the Court's role, excepting the 1966 decision, did help to dissuade South Africa from taking the ultimate confrontational action of incorporation in relation to the United Nations. It seems likely, however, that this level of deference to world public opinion and authority was dictated by practical considerations, especially by the apprehension that incorporation would shift the antiapartheid campaign directly against South Africa itself. In a way, the United Nations preoccupation with South West Africa/ Namibia has served as a lightning rod. South Africa has attempted at all stages to keep

United Nations the authority with which the Charter has invested them, which authority has been reinforced by the almost unanimous will of the peoples of the world. That will is incomparably more decisive than that of the five or six Powers which have asserted an opposite conception while relying on a claim to representativity whose lack of legal basis they must confess."

expectations alive that the central issue could be resolved peacefully and successfully, provided that its own domestic jurisdiction be respected, as a quid pro quo for agreement. Particularly since 1971, the South African Government has moved toward embracing some more acceptable form of self-determination for Namibia, perhaps reacting to the heightened political awareness that the inhabitants have exhibited, to the growing strength of the Namibia liberation movements, and to the evidence of greater and greater labor unrest, especially among the Ovambo people, as well as bipartisan pressure from the United States for a negotiated diplomatic settlement.

The record of the Court is a mixed one. Its main feature has involved an outdated intrapositivist struggle for jurisprudential ascendency. Only a scattering of judges, most significantly from the Third World, have moved toward the articulation of a needed jurisprudence outside the positivist paradigm for this kind of big case.[101] The pioneering contributions of Judges Alvarez, Tanaka, Padilla Nervo, and Ammoun in conceptualizing this sort of jurisprudence have been so far mainly ignored even by academic commentators, including those from the Third World; yet, this work points the most acceptable way to the future. This new jurisprudence needs to be value oriented, ideologically representative of the international majority, responsive to and articulate about the historical tendencies of the age. It should draw its support from "authorities" outside the Euro-American fraternity of legal experts. The formulation of legal opinions in a big case needs to be careful in relation to technical considerations, but it should not convey its conclusions in a heavy jargon loaded down by citations that are not accessible to nonlawyers, and it must not ignore the underlying moral and political concerns that give rise to the importance and prominence of the controversy in the first place.

Such a new global jurisprudence needs to be championed by articulate individuals who are known and respected. I would hope that the nomination and election procedures of the Court take increasing account of the opportunity that now exists to revive the Court and to make it serve the specific needs of our time.

[101]Judge Onyeama of Nigeria demonstrated in his separate opinion in 1971 that even an African member of the Court can adopt a strictly positivist approach, *id.* at 126–49; whereas Judge Tanaka's dissent in 1966 illustrates the potentiality to evolve a global perspective despite a developed-country background.

CHAPTER V

The Iran Hostage Case
Marginalized Recourse

WITH JACK SANDERSON

The legal event, the *United States of America v. Iran*, decided by the Court in May 1980, illustrates a distinctive kind of failure in a big case.[1] Here, as in the South African case, recourse to the Court was sought, with only the most minimal expectations of compliance by Iran in the event of the expected favorable outcome. Beyond this, the United States itself simultaneously pursued non-third-party approaches and did not even hold off on the use of force until after the judicial outcome had been rejected by Iran. Finally, when the Court confirmed the American position, which already had been unanimously supported in the Security Council, the United States failed to pursue its judicial victory through that organ, not even seeking sanctions and enforcement procedures as it is entitled to do under article 94 of the United Nations Charter.[2]

Procedurally, the Court had little difficulty establishing jurisdiction in this case. This is often the most contentious part of proceedings before the International Court of Justice. Substantively, the Court was in complete unanimity in finding Iran in violation of conventions governing diplomatic relations among nations and was in almost complete unanimity in holding that the Iranian government violated certain bilateral agreements with the United States (only Justices Morozov and

[1]*Case Concerning United States Diplomatic and Consular Staff in Tehran, United States of America v. Iran* (1980), in *World Court Renders Final Judgment on Hostage Case*, 17 DEP'T STATE BUREAU PUB. AFF. (1980) [hereinafter cited as U.S. v. Iran].

[2]Among useful assessments of the Court's role in the Hostages Case, unfortunately unavailable at the time this chapter was written, see Stein, *Contempt, Crisis, and the Court: The World Court and the Hostage Rescue Attempt*, 76 AM. J. INT'L L. 499 (1982); E. Gordon & P. Youngblood, *The Role of the International Court in the Hostages Crisis—A Rejoinder*, 13 CONN. L. REV. 429 (1981); Rubin, *The Hostages Incident: The United States and Iran*, in 36 YEARBOOK OF WORLD AFFAIRS 213 (1982); Wegen, *Discontinuance of International Proceedings: The Hostages Case*, 76 AM. J. INT'L L. 717 (1982).

Tarazi dissented).[3] Because of prior actions taken in the
United Nations, as embodied in Security Council Resolutions
457 and 461, which called on the Iranian government to release the American hostages immediately, the task of the
Court seemed almost preordained[4]—to confirm the violation
of the legal principles involved and to leave any inquiry into
potentially mitigating circumstances in the political realm to be
handled by the political organs of the United Nations. A wider
conception of the dispute pertained, for instance, to the five-
member Commission of inquiry established by the Secretary
General, Kurt Waldheim, to investigate the encounter between the United States and Iran as a whole, including Iranian claims against the United States and the Shah.

Iran's refusal to take part in the proceedings before the
Court—was an outcome of both the Iranian belief that the
decision was, in large measure, a foregone conclusion and the
rejection by the Islamic leadership of the whole United Nations / International Court of Justice structure and of Western
institutions more generally. As a result, the special mitigating
circumstances noted by then Iranian Foreign Minister Sadegh
Ghotbzadeh in two letters to the Court,[5] while considered, did
not enjoy the benefit of a forceful presentation to the judges.
The Iranian leadership perceived the entire legal proceedings
and arena as inherently hostile and anti-Islamic. From the
Iranian perspective any participation in the process could only
serve to legitimize an institution conceived at the time to be
antithetical to the goals of the Islamic Revolution. By refusing
to take part in the proceedings, however, the Iranian leadership allowed the United States to define the scope of the judicial inquiry and passed up the opportunity to present its case
against the United States' abuses of Iranian sovereignty before
an international audience.

Thus, the proceedings before the Court, in terms of both
substantive jurisprudence and legal advocacy, were remarka-
bly one-sided. The formal legal issues before the Court concerning alleged Iranian violations of international legal principles governing diplomatic relations remained uncomplicated
by any politically mitigating considerations. In any case, the

[3]*See supra* note 1, at 21.
[4]S.C. RES. 457, 34 U.N. SCOR Supp. (No. 1) at 24, U.N. Doc. S/INF/35 (1979);
and S.C. RES. 461, 34 U.N. SCOR Supp. (No. 1) at 24, U.N. Doc. S/INF/35 (1979).
[5]U.S. v. Iran, *supra* note 1, at 6, 7.

United Nations Security Council in the two resolutions noted above and the Court itself in its Preliminary Judgment of December 1979[6] had previously found Iranian conduct, *in and of itself*, to be worthy of condemnation.

As a result of Iran's rejection of these international institutions as necessarily opposed to the Islamic Revolution, the circumstances surrounding the conduct of United States–Iranian relations and these particular events were examined, especially by the Court, in only the most perfunctory manner. In such a one-sided atmosphere, the Court could contribute little to the resolution of the crisis. It could only provide legal validation for United States claims against the Iranian government, perhaps thereby creating a climate within which forcible measures would be more easily accepted. In effect, the Court contributed to the one-sided international perception of the issue, in a context, unlike that underlying the South African cases, in which a moral consensus on the underlying issues at stake did not exist or was the opposite of the narrow legal consensus on the illegality of the hostage seizure. The Court could have better improved the international understanding of the basic issues involved in this conflict by connecting the narrow legal issue with the broader context of mutual grievance instead of confirming the obvious, but restricted, contention that diplomatic immunity is an unconditional right. Whether such a "political" role for the Court would be beneficial to its status as the main judicial organ of the United Nations depends largely on whether its identity is specified by a positivist, neorealist, or postrealist (panhumanistic) jurisprudence. These various jurisprudential conceptions are intellectually (and politically) defensible, although I have been arguing on behalf of a panhumanistic reorientation that includes taking due account of ideological and cultural pluralism.

By taking the case to the Court in the first place, the United States did not expect to endure the ordeal of a comprehensive inquiry into the litany of countercharges being advanced at the time by the Iranians. The American assessment of recourse to the Court probably assumed that it was (1) unlikely that the Iranians would participate in the proceedings before the Court and (2) highly unlikely that the Court would permit

---

[6]*International Court of Justice: Case Concerning United States Diplomatic and Consular Staff in Tehran, Request for the Indication of Provisional Measures, reprinted in* 19 INT'L LEGAL MATERIALS 1 (1980).

a full hearing covering the more "political" claims by Iran that the United States allegedly repeatedly used embassy premises to intervene illegally in the internal affairs of Iran.

Recourse to the Court was invoked by the United States to validate and legitimize its legal case against the Iranian government, as well as to give the appearance of having exhausted all peaceful remedies for resolving the conflict. During the course of the proceedings before the Court, however, the United States was actively engaged in taking a series of unilateral actions, ranging from the deportation of some Iranian nationals in the United States to the freezing of Iranian assets in the United States, and this series of actions culminated in the aborted military rescue mission of April 1980. These policies demonstrated that the United States' appearance before the Court really seemed marginal to the resolution of the dispute in the eyes of leading American policymakers.[7] While the case was still pending before the Court, the United States undertook a military rescue operation in Iran that, in itself, appeared to be a gross violation of international law (despite the United States' attempted justification of this action under Article 51, specifying "self-help" measures). Thus, in spite of the United States' apparent adoption of third-party procedures to resolve the conflict, the Court and international law generally were regarded as so tangential to solving the dispute that the United States government was willing to flaunt the significance of the pending proceeding by acting as if it had already been made and had been repudiated by Iran.

Such a pattern of actions seems difficult to explain except in political terms. The United States' purpose in going to the Court to receive confirmation of its legal claim can best be understood as its having wanted to foster the impression that it would exhaust all possible peaceful remedies before it would

[7]This is how then Secretary of State Cyrus Vance expressed his view of the Court's role in his reflective memoirs. His remarks are relevant, but constitute the sole reference to the Court in the course of a detailed discussion of the hostage diplomacy. Vance's words were as follows: "We were aware that Tehran would probably ignore an order from the World Court to release the hostages, but a ruling that Iran had violated international law would increase world pressure and deepen Iran's isolation." C. VANCE, HARD CHOICES 378 (1983). Even less notice was given to the role of recourse to the Court in Zbigniew Brzezinski's reconstruction of the events. "To be sure, we were encouraged by the unanimous vote of the International Court of Justice in favor of the American position, but how effective that would be in Iran was very problematical." Z. BRZEZINSKI, POWER AND PRINCIPLE 378, 484 (1983).

have recourse to coercive means of solving the conflict. To have anticipated a favorable outcome in the judicial arena of the World Court would have tended to nullify the apparent reason for going there in the first place, but could be justified on the ground of building a basis for recourse to force as a last resort. Such apparent incoherence may reflect bureaucratic politics (that is, different parts of the government taking con-tradictory approaches to the hostage issue) or domestic pres-sures (especially as there was a rising tide of public impatience with the United States government in the early months of 1980, within a setting of impending presidential elections, for not doing enough to rescue the hostages).[8] In any event, the treatment of the Court by both the United States and Iran underscored in quite different ways both its impotence and its low stature.

The Court, in its subsequent decision in mid-May, noted with dismay the unilateral military action taken by the United States. Apart from two dissenting judges, however, the Court failed to place the rescue operation in the context of an ongo-ing abuse of Iranian sovereignty by the United States.[9] The majority seemed inclined to consider the operation more as an affront to the judicial process (which of course it clearly was) than as a violation of Iranian sovereignty and international law.[10]

Beyond this, the United States' response to the Court's deci-sion serves to show that the Court's role in resolving the dis-pute was severely limited. Instead of going back to the United Nations Security Council to seek sanctions against Iran for its failure to comply with the Court's judgment (as specified and allowed under article 94 of the United Nations Charter), the United States government allowed its apparent success with third-party strategies simply to lapse. The purported rationale for the United States' failure to pursue the action in the Secu-rity Council—that further consideration of the issue would

[8]In the days subsequent to the seizure of the embassy, military options were considered and their connection to Carter's reelection prospects noted. For instance, Brzezinski tells of a November 23, 1979, meeting of the National Security Council on what could be done by way of military action and of a debate about political versus military approaches. Brzezinski notes, without comment, that "Ham [Hamilton Jor-dan] whispered to me that Carter simply would not be reelected President if he did not act firmly." *Id.* at 483.

[9]U.S. v. Iran, *supra* note 1 (majority opinion).

[10]*Id.*

only inflame the controversy and contribute to its perpetua-
tion—is unconvincing. The United States apparently felt that
its legal position had been vindicated by the Court and that it
could therefore legitimately pursue more "effective" unilateral
and diplomatic approaches.

Before proceeding further, it is necessary to outline the
chronology of events surrounding the deliberations of the
Court in this case, as well as to summarize the major legal
issues that were put before the Court. Soon after the seizure
of its embassy in Teheran on November 4, 1979, allegedly in
response to the United States decision to allow the Shah to
enter the United States and to refuse Iranian claims that he be
returned to Iran to face trial, the United States government
instituted proceedings before the Court asking it to order Iran
to release the United States hostages immediately.[11] The
United States pursued a similar tack in the Security Council.
According to the State Department spokesman, Hodding
Carter III, the purpose of these efforts was "to put additional
pressure on Iran and to lay the groundwork for future actions
by the Security Council if Iran refused to heed a World Court
decision."[12]

In its brief submitted to the Court on November 29, 1979,
by Roberts B. Owen, legal adviser of the State Department,
the United States asked the Court to find that Iran had "violated its international legal obligations to the United States,"
and that Iran was "under a particular obligation immediately
to secure the release of all United States' nationals."[13] Further,
the Court was asked to declare that Iran should pay reparations to the United States for such violations and should
prosecute those responsible for the crimes committed against
United States Embassy personnel.[14] Specifically, Iran was accused of violating several international agreements: the Vienna Convention on Diplomatic Relations of 1961, the Vienna
Convention on Consular Relations of 1963, the Economic Relations and Consular Rights between the United States and
Iran of 1955, and the Convention on the Prevention and Pun-

---

[11]See supra note 1.

[12]Tribunal of U.N. Is Asked to Order Teheran to Release the 50 Captives, N.Y. Times,
Nov. 11, 1979, at 16.

[13]Request for Interim Measures of Protection, reprinted in 18 INT'L LEGAL MATERIALS
1482 (1979).

[14]Id.

ishment of Crimes Against Internationally Protected Persons Including Diplomatic Agents of 1973. The United States' brief contended that each of these agreements established an adequate basis for the jurisdiction of the Court over the present dispute.[15]

Iran participated in the preliminary phases of recourse to the Court only in the form of the submission by Foreign Minister Ghotbzadeh of a letter acknowledging the proceedings before the Court and arguing that the Court had no jurisdiction to consider separately the "marginal and secondary" aspect of the hostage seizure without examining the "more than 25 years of continual interference by the United States in the internal affairs of Iran, the shameless exploitation of our country, and numerous crimes perpetrated against the Iranian people, contrary to and in conflict with all international and humanitarian norms."[16] The Iranian letter concluded that "the Court cannot examine the American Application divorced from its proper context, namely the whole political dossier of the relations between Iran and the United States over the last 25 years."[17] Despite the recommendations of some Iranian leaders to the contrary, no effort was ever made to put these objections into legal form or to argue their relevance to the dispute by reference, for instance, to Article 41 of the Vienna Convention, which prohibits using embassy premises in a manner inconsistent with the sovereign rights of the host country.[18]

Notwithstanding these Iranian objections to the jurisdiction of the Court to rule on the particular issue framed by the United States' request for provisional measures, the Court

[15]*Id.* at 1482–87.

[16]U.S. v. Iran, *supra* note 1, at 7.

[17]*Id.*

[18]The Court, for example, could have cited Article 41 of the 1961 Vienna Convention on Diplomatic Relations to sustain a formal inquiry into the Iranian charges against United States Embassy personnel. Article 41 states:

1. Without prejudice to their privileges and immunities, it is the duty of all persons enjoying such privileges and immunities to respect the laws and regulations of the receiving State. They also have a duty not to interfere in the internal affairs of that State.

Vienna Convention on Diplomatic Relations. Even in the absence of an Iranian representative at the proceedings, the Court could, on its own initiative, have used this principle to examine charges that the United States had used embassy personnel to interfere with Iranian domestic affairs. For convenient text of Vienna Convention see L. Henkin and others, eds., *Basic Documents Supplement to International Law* 230–35 (1980).

unanimously granted the American request in mid-December, including a directive for prompt release of the hostages, and set early 1980 as the time for hearing full arguments on the merits of the case. Such a quick reaction and disposition was virtually unprecedented and did express the Court's conviction that the hostage crisis was, at its core, a dangerous emergency with an obvious legal response.

The Iranian response to this preliminary decision was stated by Foreign Minister Ghotbzadeh in an interview on December 17, 1979. The deliberations of the Court, according to the Iranian foreign minister, resulted in a "prefabricated verdict" that was "clear to us in advance; for this reason Iran's *Chargé d'Affaires* at The Hague was ordered to officially reject the decision of The Hague Court."[19]

Concurrent with its efforts in the International Court of Justice, the United States was forcefully presenting its case in the United Nations. Soon after the seizure of the United States Embassy on November 9, 1979, Donald McHenry, Permanent United States Representative to the United Nations, requested that the Security Council urgently consider what might be done "to secure the release of the diplomatic personnel being held and to restore the sanctity of diplomatic personnel and establishments."[20] In response, the President of the Security Council, speaking in the Council's name, appealed for the immediate release of the hostages. The President of the General Assembly made a similar appeal.

In late November the Secretary General, under the exercise of his special authority in Article 99 of the United Nations Charter, convoked the Security Council in an effort to find a peaceful solution to the crisis. On December 4, the Security Council unanimously passed Resolution 457 urgently calling upon the government of Iran "to release immediately the personnel of the Embassy . . . ."[21] The Resolution also requested the Secretary General to lend his good offices to assist in implementing the resolution.[22]

At the request of the United States, the Security Council met again in late December to consider possible measures to induce Iran to comply with its international obligations as well

---

[19]Memorial of the Government of the United States of America at 22.
[20]U.N. Off. Rec. (S/13615) (1979).
[21]S.C. RES. 457, *supra* note 4.
[22]*Id.*

as with the provisional measures ordered by the Court and with those directed to it by Security Council Resolution 457. On December 31, the Council adopted Resolution 461, which reiterated most of Resolution 457, deciding additionally to review the situation in early January and, "in the event of noncompliance with the present resolution, to adopt effective measures under Articles 39 and 40 of the Charter of the United Nations."[23]

In connection with the call in both Security Council resolutions for the Secretary General to lend his good offices to aid in overcoming the crisis, Kurt Waldheim visited Teheran in early January, 1980 and reported back to the Security Council on his findings. At least as a partial result of this visit, the Secretary General set up a commission of inquiry to consider the crisis as a whole, including an examination of Iranian charges against the United States and the deposed Shah.[24] While the Commission did fulfill that portion of its mandate that bid it to investigate Iranian grievances against the United States, it was unable to aid in any discernible manner in securing the release of the hostages or in resolving the crisis.

While pursuing these various third-party procedures, the United States also was undertaking a variety of unilateral actions that were definitely linked to the seizure and retention of the American hostages in Teheran. On November 10, 1979, steps were taken to begin to identify all Iranian students in the United States who were not complying with the terms of their entry visas and to commence deportation proceedings against them. President Carter, on November 12, ordered the discontinuation of all oil purchases from Iran. Further, apparently believing that Iran was about to withdraw its considerable funds from United States banks, to refuse to accept payment for oil in dollars, and to repudiate its obligations owed to the United States and its nationals, the President acted to block all official Iranian assets, estimated at around $8 billion, including deposits in banks both in the United States and in foreign branches and subsidiaries. The United States government also informed the Iranian chargé d'affaires in Washington on December 12 that the number of personnel assigned to the Iranian Embassy and to consular posts was to be restricted and

[23]S.C. Res. 461, *supra* note 4.
[24]U.N. Off. Rec. (S/13710) (1980).

reduced (note that all these actions took place prior to the World Court's order governing provisional measures but after the submission of the complaint).[25]

In early January 1980, as per Resolution 461, the Security Council met to consider imposing economic sanctions on Iran for its noncompliance with both the two United Nations Resolutions and the preliminary ruling of the Court. A draft resolution calling for the United Nations to impose economic sanctions against Iran under chapter 7 provisions in the Charter was vetoed by the Soviet Union, the vote being 10 in favor, 2 opposed, and 2 abstentions.[26]

After a period of greater and more hopeful activity on the diplomatic front failed to secure the hostages' release, the United States, on April 7, broke diplomatic relations with the Iranian government and simultaneously prohibited all American exports to Iran. Steps were taken to prepare an inventory of the Iranian assets frozen on November 14, to make a count of outstanding claims of American nationals against the Iranian government, and to design "a program against Iran on behalf of the hostages, the hostage families, and other U.S. claimants."[27] All visas issued to Iranian citizens for entry into the United States were cancelled. On April 17, the United States government announced the imposition of further economic sanctions against Iran, prohibited travel to Iran by United States citizens, and made further plans for reparations to be paid to the hostages and their families out of frozen Iranian assets. Finally on April 24–25, the United States initiated its ill-fated "rescue" mission, an action unconvincingly justified by reference to Article 51 of the United Nations Charter. The mission, according to the United States government, was carried out "in exercise of its inherent right of self-defense with the aim of extricating American nationals who have been and remain the victims of the Iranian armed attack on our Embassy."[28]

Significantly, each of these unilateral actions occurred while the World Court was still reviewing the United States' legal

[25]U.S. v. Iran, *supra* note 1, at 10.
[26]*Draft Resolution Seeking Sanctions Against Iran, reprinted in* 19 INT'L LEGAL MATERIALS 1, 254 (1980).
[27]U.S. v. Iran, *supra* note 1, at 10.
[28]N.Y. Times, May 25, 1980, at 1, col. 5.

claims against Iran.[29] Clearly, the proceedings before the Court as well as any ultimate decision were perceived by the United States as virtually irrelevant to any resolution of the crisis. It is worth observing here that the United States—which had long claimed to be the champion of third-party legal procedures—acted in this instance to undercut the tenuous legitimacy of the Court as a viable institution for settling disputes in today's politically dynamic historical environment. It also acted in a setting that was not shaped by a change of circumstances in the situation of the hostages, such as threats to their lives or even the humiliation and danger of public "spy" trials, an option kept open by the more militant leadership in Iran.

The Court's decision was issued on May 24, 1980. In it, the majority first sought to deal with the absence of any Iranian representative at the proceedings. That absence brought into effect article 53 of the Statute of the Court, under which the Court is required, prior to finding in the applicant's favor, to satisfy itself that the allegations of fact are well founded. The Court concluded that the body of facts in the public record as well as those presented by the United States were sufficient to sustain the allegation of fact upon which the United States based its claim.[30]

Under article 53, the Court was bound to investigate on its own initiative any preliminary question of admissability or jurisdiction that would have arisen had Iran been present. The Court noted the two letters it had received from Iranian Foreign Minister Ghotbzadeh urging that the Court not take cognizance of the United States claims because they represented only "a marginal and secondary aspect of an overall problem,

[29]It should be noted, of course, that an abnormal political situation prevailed in Iran. For one thing, the elected president of the country, as well as the foreign minister, made it evident that they opposed the retention of the hostages, but it also became clear as the crisis unfolded that the Iranian political forces associated with the embassy seizure were trying to destroy the position of these high officials and generally enjoyed the backing of Khomeini, clearly the power center of the Iranian revolution. Such a circumstance—especially given the menacing demonstrations carried on repeatedly outside the embassy and the repeated threats to hold spy trials—created pressures on the United States to act outside a normal diplomatic/legal framework. There was no governing structure in the usual sense in Iran, titular figures could not exercise effective authority, and the main revolutionary leader was clearly not interested at early stages in a law-guided or even a diplomacy-shaped resolution.

[30]U.S. v. Iran, *supra* note 1, at 2.

one that cannot be studied separately . . . ." The overall problem, the foreign minister contended, included

all the crimes perpetrated in Iran by the American Government, in particular the *coup d'état* of 1953 stirred up and carried out by the CIA, the overthrow of the lawful national government of Dr. Mossadegh, the restoration of the Shah and of his regime which was under the control of U.S. interests, and all the social, economic, cultural and political consequences of the direct interventions in our internal affairs, as well as grave, flagrant and continuous violations of all international norms committed by the U.S. in Iran.[31]

The majority rejected the claim that the hostage question was of marginal importance, particularly because of the legal principles involved. Moreover, the majority argued that Iran had failed to demonstrate why the "overall problem" would necessarily preclude the Court from examining the United States' claims. By its absence from the proceedings, Iran had "foregone the opportunities offered to it under the Statutes and Rules of the Court to submit evidence and arguments in support of its contentions . . . ."[32] The majority opinion concluded its discussion of this issue by stating that "never has the view been put forward before that, because a legal dispute submitted to the Court is only one aspect of a political dispute, the Court should decline to resolve for the parties the legal questions at issue between them."[33]

On the additional procedural question of jurisdiction, the majority had little difficulty in finding bases for its judgment in conventions cited in the United States Memorial, namely the two Vienna conventions of 1961 and 1963 on diplomatic and consular relations respectively, and the 1955 Treaty of Amity, Economic Relations and Consular Rights Between the United States and Iran.

In discussing the merits of the United States' claim—that is, whether the acts complained of could be attributable legally to the Iranian state and whether they were compatible or not with Iran's obligations under treaties in force or under other applicable rules of international law—the Court divided the events surrounding the seizure of the United States Embassy

[31]*Id.* at 6, 7.
[32]*Id.* at 11.
[33]*Id.*

into two phases. First, it looked at the events of November 4, 1979, the day of the actual attack on the embassy. The majority, while pointing out that it lacked sufficient evidence to support the claim that the militants were acting on behalf of the Iranian state, did find that the Iranian government failed to uphold its obligations to prevent the attack, to stop it before it reached its completion, or to oblige the militants to withdraw from the premises and release the hostages.[34] This inaction by the Iranian government in the eyes of the Court "constituted clear and serious violation of Iran's obligations to the U.S. . . ."[35] In regard to the events of November 4, then, the Court concluded that the Iranian authorities:

(a) were fully aware of their obligations under the conventions in force to take appropriate steps to protect the premises of the U.S. Embassy and its diplomatic and consular staff from any attack and from any infringement of their inviolability, and to ensure the security of such other persons as might be present on the said premises;

(b) were fully aware, as a result of the appeals for help made by the United States Embassy, of the urgent need for action on their part;

(c) had the means at their disposal to perform their obligations; and

(d) completely failed to comply with these obligations.[36]

Second, the Court examined the events that took place after November 4. The majority found that various organs of the Iranian state had given approval to the embassy seizure and had acted to perpetuate its continuation, thereby transforming acts subsequent to November 4 into "acts of state."[37] The militants accordingly became true agents of the state, which then became internationally responsible for their acts. Thus, the Court concluded that

the Iranian authorities' decision to continue the subjection of the premises of the United States Embassy to occupation by the militants and of the Embassy staff to detention as hostages, clearly gave rise to repeated and multiple breaches of the Vienna Con-

[34]*Id.* at 16.
[35]*Id.*
[36]*Id.* at 16, 17.
[37]*Id.* at 17.

ventions even more serious than those which arose from their failure to take any steps to prevent the attacks on the inviolability of these premises and staff.[38]

Before concluding their judgment, the majority briefly examined both the "special circumstances" alleged by Iran to have justified the seizure of the embassy and the attempted United States military rescue while judicial proceedings were still pending. Concerning the former, the Court argued that even if the alleged criminal activities of the United States in Iran could be considered as having been fully established, it could not accept such reasoning as justification for the Iranian actions. This was so, the Court averred, because diplomatic law constitutes a "self-contained regime," providing the "necessary means of defense against, and sanction for, illicit activities by members of diplomatic or consular missions."[39] Nor could the admission of the deposed Shah into the United States "affect the imperative character of the legal obligations of the Iranian Government . . . ."[40]

On the question of the aborted United States raid to rescue the hostages, the Court expressed "its concern in regard to the United States' incursion into Iran."[41] The Court further observed that the operation, undertaken while judicial proceedings were still pending, "is of a kind calculated to undermine respect for the judicial process in international relations . . . ."[42] Nevertheless, the Court held that neither the question of the legality of the operation nor any responsibility arising from it was before the Court, and thus it could not affect the judgment of the Court on the United States' application.

Because of the foregoing analysis, the Court concluded that "Iran, by committing successive and continuing breaches of the obligations laid upon it . . . has incurred responsibility towards the United States." The Court decided:

1. By thirteen votes to two, that Iran has violated, and is still violating, "obligations owed by it to the United States of America under international conventions in force between the two countries, as well as under long-established rules of general international law";

[38]*Id.* at 18.
[39]*Id.* at 19.
[40]*Id.* at 20.
[41]*Id.* at 21.
[42]*Id.*

2. By thirteen votes to two, that these violations "engage the responsibility" of Iran;

3. Unanimously, that the government of Iran must immediately release the United States nationals held as hostages and place the diplomatic premises in the hands of the protecting power;

4. Unanimously, that "no member of the U.S. diplomatic or consular staff may be kept in Iran to be subjected to any form of judicial proceedings or to participate in them as a witness";

5. By twelve votes to three, that the government of Iran "is under an obligation to make reparation to the Government of the United States of America";

6. By fourteen votes to one, that "the form and amount of such reparation, failing agreement between the parties, shall be settled by Court . . . ."[43]

In the two dissenting opinions, issued by Justices Morozov (Soviet Union) and Tarazi (Syria), much greater emphasis was placed on defining the political context of the Court's ruling. Particularly in regard to points 1 and 2 above—that is, the degree of obligation owed by the Iranian government to the United States—these two dissenting judges broke with the majority in seeking to allow a fuller consideration of the political situation. Justice Tarazi's opinion is especially sensitive to the Iranian charge of a legacy of United States abuse of Iran's national sovereignty as being partially exculpatory for the embassy seizure. Justice Morozov's dissent focuses more on the unilateral United States responses to the seizure while it was "apparently" pursuing third-party procedures for resolution of the conflict. In his opinion, Justice Morozov in essence argued that,

> while declaring its intention to settle this dispute between the United States of America and the Islamic Republic of Iran by peaceful means, and presenting its Application to the Court, the Applicant in fact simultaneously acted contrary to its own declaration, and committed a series of grave violations of the provisions of general international law and the Charter of the United Nations . . . . The Applicant has forfeited the legal right to expect the Court to uphold any claim for reparation.[44]

Justice Morozov went on to cite several instances of what he called "incorrect" or "one-sided" reasoning on the part of the

[43]*Id.*
[44]U.S. v. Iran (Dissenting Opinion of Justice Morozov), *supra* note 1, at 24.

majority. The Court should have more strongly and unequivocally condemned the United States for its aborted military
raid, as well as for the provocative act of admitting the Shah to
the United States for medical treatment.[45]

While Justice Morozov's dissent is a rather polemical attack
on United States activities after the seizure of the embassy,
more or less a faithful reflection of Soviet foreign policy at the
time, Justice Tarazi provides a more balanced and thoughtful
opinion that demonstrates how Iran's "political" complaints
against the United States could and should have been incorporated into the Court's majority opinion. Had it been so incorporated, that opinion could have served as another example
of the kind of enlightened jurisprudence we discussed earlier,
and which is necessary if the Court is to achieve significant
stature in today's dynamic world. Justice Tarazi, while concurring with the majority on the Iranian violation of the Vienna
conventions, nevertheless

> found some difficulty, arising on the one hand from the situation
> that has developed in Iran since the overthrow of the regime of
> which the former Shah was the symbol, and on the other hand
> from the conduct of the applicant State . . . in deciding and de-
> claring only that the Government of the Islamic Republic of Iran
> was responsible *vis-à-vis* that of the United States of America while
> neglecting to point out at the same time the latter had also in-
> curred responsibility . . . .[46]

In his dissent, Justice Tarazi held that the approach of the
Court was "inadequate" because "it is not right to proclaim the
responsibility of the Iranian Government unless [the Court's]
examination is *first* preceded by an appropriate study of the
historical facts antedating the seizure . . . ."[47] In this regard,
the Court's efforts, although "laudable" given Iran's absence
from the proceedings, "remained insufficient."[48] He depicted
the overly legalistic approach of the majority, which viewed
the "political" allegations of Iran as being outside the framework of the Court's powers, as being both politically transpar-
ent and very unhelpful.

After an examination of the "revolutionary context" of the

---

[45]*Id.* at 25.
[46]U.S. v. Iran (Dissenting Opinion of Justice Tarazi), *supra* note 1, at 26.
[47]*Id.*
[48]*Id.*

Iranian situation—quoting, for example, Fereydown Hoveyda's work *The Fall of The Shah* and Henry Kissinger's *The White House Years*[49]—Justice Tarazi moved on to examine the series of United States unilateral responses to the crisis. Justice Tarazi argued that the actions of the United States government not only undercut the legitimacy of the ongoing judicial process, but also mitigated any Iranian responsibility toward the United States and created a United States responsibility toward Iran.

In conclusion, the Tarazi dissent, while concurring with the Majority's findings on Iranian violations of the Vienna conventions, "could not support the idea that the Iranian Government should be declared responsible" unless the Court also found:

(i) that the responsibility in question is relative and not absolute . . . and

(ii) that the Government of the United States of America, by reason of its conduct both before and after the institution of proceedings, has equally incurred responsibility.[50]

The case of the *U.S.A. v. Iran* is representative of the shifting flow of history in the international system today. This flow is symbolized by the Islamic Revolution in particular and by radical Third World nationalism in general, and it runs counter to many Western interests. This flow of history presents a challenge not only to the efficacy of the Court as a viable institution, but also to the continued existence of the international system characterized by European–North American hegemony of which the international legal system is but a part.

The apparent inability and unwillingness of the Court to examine the "political" record of United States–Iranian relations as a special circumstance affecting, not the violation of international law per se, but the degree of obligation incurred by Iran, is yet a further example of the emptiness of objectively formal Anglo-European jurisprudential techniques for resolving conflicts that are inevitably characterized by political demands and dimensions. International legal disputes always have had political bases. Today, however, emergent political realities not only shape the nature of legal controversies, but they also challenge the ability of the present international legal system to adapt itself to new political contexts and, ultimately, to survive. Not since the creation of the Court have the dynamics of political change in the international system so threatened to render it, at best, an anachronistic irrelevancy.

Even the United States, often regarded as the leading international advocate of third-party procedures in resolving international conflict, demonstrated by its various unilateral actions pending the judicial decision its understanding of the real marginality of the Court. The United States' strategy seems clearly to have been to use the Court as an ancillary tool in mobilizing world and domestic public opinion against Iran and in paving the way for potential sanctions to be imposed by the Security Council in the likely event that Iran ignored the Court's ruling. Thus, the Court was perceived and used, as it was in the South African cases, not as an institution for clarifying points of international law, but as an enforcement mechanism to be employed at some future time. It would be interesting to speculate as to whether the United States would have taken its case to the Court if it had expected Iranian participation in the proceedings, or if it could have anticipated a more thorough inquiry by the Court into the conduct of United States–Iranian relations in the period since 1953.

By its refusal to consider the special circumstances noted in Foreign Minister Ghotbzadeh's letters, the Court also demonstrated its lack of sensitivity to the possible resolution of the crisis. Although the claims put forward by the Iranian government against the United States would certainly have benefited from the presence of a forceful advocate, the Court had the power under article 53 of its Statute to examine the charges if it had deemed them germane. The Court, however, viewed them as marginal to the narrow legal issue that was presented in the United States Application—that is, the question of Iranian responsibility for the hostage seizure—and thereby condemned itself to playing a necessarily marginal role in resolving the crisis.

By allowing the United States to define the legal issue, thereby limiting the scope of the inquiry, the Court perpetuated the one-sidedness of the proceedings. Clearly, such a one-sided examination of the issue could not in any way help the process of developing a solution for a crisis so obviously calling at the time for compromise. Indeed, the Court may even have contributed to the worsening of the crisis by strengthening the legal perception of the United States' charges, thereby justifying in the eyes of the United States public opinion at least further self-righteous, unilateral, retributive policies, including the use of military force.

The Iranian case presented a positive opportunity for the Court to engage in the kind of enlightened jurisprudence that would have taken into account not just the narrow legal issue as presented, but the underlying political context and framework. In a world characterized increasingly by a flow of history that runs counter not only to specific Western interests, but also to Western cultural hegemony generally, the Court, if it is ever to become a viable institution, must begin to overcome its provincial jurisprudential outlook. The Court's near-sighted approach to judicial inquiry and international realities, defining its role solely as being to clarify some of the legal issues involved in a dispute, may make the institution even more of an anachronism in the politically volatile 1980s. However, should the Court broaden its approach to reflect the diverse values and ideologies of politics, law, and justice present in the world system today, it could make a positive contribution to the peaceful adaptation of the present international system to the dynamics of fundamental change.

It could be said, in mitigation of the Court's narrowness, that hostage-taking and embassy-seizing were perceived as presenting an emergency situation, an impression reinforced by the December 15 preliminary finding in favor of the basic United States position. The holding of hostages, especially those with diplomatic status, was an act of terrorism, endorsed by the prevailing government in Iran and dangerous for the overall security of relations among sovereign states. In these circumstances, especially given the inflamed atmosphere in Iran, to broaden the inquiry would have given the Court a ridiculous appearance of "fiddling" during a time of acute danger. Such an impression would have been reinforced by the contempt expressed by the main Iranian leader, Ayatollah Khomeini, for the entire United Nations system, as well as the defiant posture taken in response to the December 15 preliminary order of the Court even by "moderates" in the Iranian revolutionary leadership.

In a sense, the Court was faced with a dilemma. To have

broadened the inquiry would have delayed the proceedings and might have resulted in determinations very disturbing to powerful states. To keep it confined to the hostage incident was to confirm the view that the Court is essentially an enforcement agency of advanced industrial states with a Western outlook.

At a minimum, however, it seems reasonable to conclude that it was not responsible for the United States to have recourse to the Court in a big case of this sort if it did not intend to place central reliance on the judicial response in its search for a means to secure release of the hostages, at least in the absence of any deterioration in their condition or prior to Iran's refusal to comply with enforcement orders of the Court as implemented by the Security Council. As it was, it is hardly possible to maintain that the Court played a constructive role or enhanced its reputation, either for effectiveness or for responsiveness to the varying orientations toward law and justice prominent in the world at this time.

CHAPTER VI

A Note on *Certain Expenses*

You utilitarians, you, too, love everything *useful* only as a
vehicle for your inclinations; you, too, really find the noise of
its wheels insufferable?

* * * * *

... we believe that the intention is merely a sign and symptom
that still requires interpretation—moreover, a sign that means too
much and, therefore, taken by itself alone, almost nothing. ...
There is too much charm and sugar in these feelings of "for
others," "*not* for myself," for us not to need to become doubly
suspicious to ask: "are these not perhaps—*seductions?*"

FRIEDRICH NIETZSCHE, *Beyond Good and Evil*

Nietzsche's insistence on probing below the level of preten-
sions, even of conscious intentions, is particularly relevant in
relation to "legal science," especially to its purported objectivity and its technicist mystique of method. It becomes especially
important to grasp these unacknowledged elements if one's
identity as a participant or as an observer happens to coincide
with the interests served by a particular pattern of legal reasoning, or more generally by an underlying and hence "invisible" jurisprudential paradigm.

There is an obvious temptation to extend and test the analysis of the South West Africa litigation to the context of *Certain
Expenses*.[1] Here too was "a big case" that possessed considerable political salience at the time, bearing as it did so directly on
the East-West struggle over the role of the United Nations in
the period of the Cold War. The question put to the Court in
Certain Expenses by the General Assembly was answered in the
same year, 1962, as the judgment issued by the Court on
South Africa's preliminary objections to the initiation of contentious proceedings. Hence, the Court had essentially the
same composition in the two cases. Most intriguingly, the

---

[1] *See* Maechling, *supra* note 21 of chapter 2.

members of the Court most associated with strict construction-
ism in the South West Africa dispute were the principal tele-
ologists in *Certain Expenses*. Our discussion here will be limited,
then, to the relevance of the advisory opinion in *Certain Expenses* to my central argument that the Court needs a different
jurisprudential orientation if it is ever to play the important
role projected for it by the Charter of the United Nations.

Perhaps more than any other case to date, *Certain Expenses*
confronted the Court with a true opportunity to construe the
Charter in light of the kind of organization that the United
Nations had become by then.[2] Instead, the advisory opinion,
along with its one declaration, three separate opinions, and
five dissenting opinions, provides the industrious specialist
with a welter of arcane confusions.[3] The Court was asked to
respond to the following question: "Do the expenditures authorized by the General Assembly to cover the costs of the
United Nations operations in the Congo (ONUC) and in the
Middle East (UNEF) constitute 'expenses of the Organization'
within the meaning of Article 17(2) of the Charter?" The referral to the Court was made on the basis of a 52–11–32 vote,
indicating a substantial split within the United Nations at the
time as to whether a judicial determination would be helpful.[4]
Perhaps this split was too deep to enable, under any circumstances, the Court to play a useful independent judicial and
educative role. Not only was a substantial minority either opposed or lukewarm to the desirability of referring the question
to the Court, but also a significant number of states were in
fundamental disagreement about the underlying issues. In
such circumstances, the General Assembly's Resolution 1731
request for an advisory opinion, so it could receive "authoritative legal guidance as to obligations of Member States" with
respect to the financing of UNEF and ONUC, seemed to
dump a hopeless task into the lap of the World Court. What-

[2]*See, e.g.,* the comments to this effect by the distinguished Nigerian jurist, Elias, in
JUDICIAL SETTLEMENT OF INTERNATIONAL DISPUTES, *supra* note 8 of chapter 1, at 24,
26.

[3]This confusion is well-exposed by Stanley Hoffman in his essay *A World Divided
and a World Court Confused: The World Court's Advisory Opinion on U.N. Financing,* in
INTERNATIONAL LAW AND POLITICAL CRISIS 251 (L. Scheinman & D. Wilkinson eds.
1968).

[4]For exact text, *see* G.A. Res. 1731 (XVI), 16 U.N. GAOR Supp. (No. 17) at 54,
U.N. Doc. A/5100 (1962).

ever the judicial outcome, the losing side would almost assuredly treat it as nonauthoritative.[5]

The Court was placed in an even more awkward position by the defeat in the General Assembly of a French amendment to the resolution that would have asked the Court to determine whether the peacekeeping expenditures were "decided in conformity with the provisions of the Charter."[6] Given the position of France in the constitutional debates, the French amendment was likely designed to underscore doubts about the constitutionality of the entire peacekeeping role that had been adopted by the General Assembly as a matter of practice. The General Assembly majority did not want to validate such doubts by acting as if it were legally unsure of a general course of action it had followed since the so-called Uniting for Peace Resolution was passed in 1950, a resolution that enabled the United Nations to take action in the event the Security Council was paralyzed in a peacekeeping context by a veto by the Soviet Union or by any other permanent member.[7] At the same time, from a technical viewpoint, how could the Court assess whether the expenses incurred by the General Assembly fit within the purposes of article 17(2) if it did not consider whether they had been validly incurred? Disagreement also surrounded the question of how the Court should interpret the defeat of the French amendment in the General Assembly. Some of the judges felt that the Court should respect the Assembly formulation of the question, but decline, on such narrow terms, to answer the question.[8] Others felt that such a broader inquiry into the character of the Assembly's peacekeeping role was unnecessary because there could be no issue of impropriety so long as the Assembly was acting as it clearly was to uphold Charter purposes. The majority took the position that the defeat of the French amendment had no bearing on the proper scope of the

[5]See Gross, supra note 19 of chapter 2, for analysis of the relationship between the size of the majority making the request and the effectiveness of the resulting advisory opinion.

[6]For helpful comments on issues of authoritativeness relative to advisory opinions, see O. LISSITZYN, THE INTERNATIONAL COURT OF JUSTICE 84–90 (1951).

[7]See discussion of the French amendment in majority opinion, Certain Expenses, supra note 10 of chapter 2, at 156–57; but see Judge Spiropoulos's Declaration, at 180–81, and Judge Basdevant's dissent, at 235–38.

[8]G.A. Res. 377A (V), 5 U.N. GAOR Supp. (No. 20) at 10, U.N. Doc. A/1775 (1950); for text and some discussion see R. FALK & S. MENDLOVITZ, 3 THE STRATEGY OF WORLD ORDER: THE UNITED NATIONS 249–69 (1966).

Court's judicial inquiry and that the Court remained free to consider whether the underlying resolutions authorizing the two peacekeeping operations were in conformity with the Charter. In effect, the Court ended up treating the request *as if* the French amendment had succeeded in the Assembly. Yet obviously, such a course was awkward. Its propriety depended on the somewhat dubious argument that the majority in the General Assembly was concerned not to manifest doubts about its own course of action but did not intend thereby to foreclose judicial inquiry on the same issue.

It also would have been possible for the Court to refuse the request for advice, relying on the permissive language of article 65 of its Statute to the effect that the Court "*may* give an advisory opinion on any legal question" whenever an authorized body makes such a request.[9] However, as Guenther Weissberg observes, the Court as a matter of past practice:

> has acknowledged and accepted its status as a major participant in the activities of the Organization and has acted accordingly, notwithstanding the permissive language of Article 65(1) . . . . Only the most "compelling reason" could lead to a refusal to comply with a request and so far none has been found.[10]

Weissberg also states regarding the case involved in *Certain Expenses*, "[l]egally the endeavor to secure the opinion . . . was unquestionably sound; politically it showed little foresight."[11] Even as restrictively as it was framed, the question put to the Court raised an important issue regarding international treaty construction. However, because of the depth of the General Assembly's split on the merits of the case and on the relevance of seeking judicial advice for it, it was not very helpful for the Court to generate an advisory opinion that a significant portion of the United Nations, including such important states as France and the Soviet Union, both veto powers, were bound to regard as nonauthoritative. Further, given the positivist disposition of the Court, it might on balance have been more

---

[9]*E.g.*, Judge Quintana in his dissenting opinion interprets the defeat of the French Amendment as preventing ". . . the Court from bringing its judgment to bear on the legally decisive factor . . . ." *Certain Expenses, supra* note 10 of chapter 2, at 247; *see also* Judge Koretsky's comments in his dissenting opinion, at 253–54.

[10]Weissberg, *The Role of the International Court of Justice in the United Nations System: The First Quarter Century,* in THE FUTURE OF THE INTERNATIONAL COURT OF JUSTICE, *supra* note 10 of chapter 1, at 137.

[11]*Id.* at 138.

constructive to go the route allowed by article 65 and refuse to respond to the question in these circumstances in which the conditions of authoritativeness did not appear to exist. After all, even within the Court there existed an array of views on both substance and procedure in this dispute.

Judge Koretsky believed, in contrast to Weissberg, that a "compelling reason" did exist to refuse the Assembly request, namely, that "[p]olitical issues prevailed over juridical considerations." The problems involved in this question were not budgetary in character, but constituted "a basic constitutional problem," associated with "financial policy in peace-keeping matters, and, connected with it, a question of the powers and responsibilities of the principal organs of the United Nations, the political essence of which can hardly be denied." This understanding led the Soviet judge, with his conservative views of judicial function, to argue that since "the political aspect of the question posed to the Court is the prevailing one, the Court, to my mind, ought to avoid giving an answer to the question on the substance and ought not to find unwillingly that its opinion may be used as an instrument of political struggle."[12] But how else can the Court relate to controversies that have serious international implications except to function as "an instrument" of persuasion to one side or the other in a political struggle? The alternative logic, if consistently applied, would entail the Court's standing aside, at least in the discharge of its advisory functions, whenever a big case was presented. In all probability, this kind of passivity would further hasten the decline of the Court, especially in the setting of the United Nations, where its role as a constitutional court within the organization has been confirmed in an early and important series of advisory opinions.[13]

Judge Quintana in his dissenting opinion also seemed especially sensitive to the possible adverse political implications of the Majority Opinion: "To say that this new advisory opinion might decide the fate of the United Nations in the years to come would certainly be rash, but it may at least be affirmed

[12]All quotations from Judge Koretsky's Dissenting Opinion, *Certain Expenses, supra* note 10 of chapter 2, at 254.

[13]*E.g., Conditions of Admission of a State to the United Nations,* 1948 I.C.J. 57 (Advisory Opinion of May 28); *Reparations for Injuries Suffered in the Service of the United Nations,* 1949 I.C.J. 174 (Advisory Opinion of April 11).

that its effects would be far-reaching.[14] The anxious concern, however, seems to presuppose that the Court's decision would be taken as authoritative by the Member nations, or that the Court could function as a decisive instrument in the political struggle. As it turned out, the advisory opinion caused only a temporary ripple in the waters of the wider controversy over United Nations financing. It did not, perhaps unfortunately, exert much influence upon United Nations practice in this area.

There was another issue further complicating the alleged need of the General Assembly for "authoritative legal guidance" in this area. That was the San Francisco decision to withhold from the Court any power of judicial review in relation to controversial interpretations by other organs of the United Nations Charter. In effect, each principal organ of the United Nations makes its own determination of its legality in relation to the Charter and each Member State retains the discretion to ignore any nonbinding actions of the Organization that it regards as contradicting its own interpretation of the Charter. This structural constitutional decentralization played a crucial part in orienting the Majority in its reasoning in *Certain Expenses:*

> In the legal systems of States, there is often some procedure for determining the validity of even a legislative or governmental act, but no analogous procedure is to be found in the structure of the United Nations. Proposals made during the drafting of the Charter to place the ultimate authority to interpret the Charter in the International Court of Justice were not accepted; the opinion which the Court is in the course of rendering is an *advisory* opinion. As anticipated in 1945, therefore, each organ must, in the first place at least, determine its own jurisdiction.[15]

The role of the Court does include that of making constitutional appraisals, as the investigation carried out in *Certain Expenses* illustrates, but the weight of any such appraisal is "advisory," rather than "authoritative," even regarding the legal issue involved. There exists some confusion, however, as to the legal status of advisory opinions in the context of the Court.[16] Of course, the entire discourse of the discussion of

[14]*Certain Expenses, supra* note 10 of chapter 2, at 240.

[15]*Id.* at 168 (emphasis added).

[16]*See, e.g.,* Gross, *supra* note 19 of chapter 2, at 405–21, including especially quotation with approval of an excerpt from Judge Lauterpacht's Separate Opinion in the

the matter is itself positivist, and one therefore would not expect an advisory opinion to have had much greater political weight had the drafters of the Charter adopted the Australian proposal at San Francisco and given the Court full powers of judicial review. We see here the substantive incoherence of the Assembly's call for "authoritative legal guidance," considering the indeterminate and possibly marginal constitutional role given to judicial advice in situations of fundamental constitutional controversy.

As several judges have suggested, in consequence of the United Nations' constitutional decentralization, the contractual foundations of the United Nations system are very shaky, especially, as in this case, in confining the role of the General Assembly to the narrow limits agreed upon in San Francisco. The Dissenting Opinion of Judge Winiarski was most persuasive on this: "The intention of those who drafted [the Charter] was clearly to abandon the possibility of useful action rather than to sacrifice the balance of carefully established fields of competence, as can be seen, for example, in the case of the voting in the Security Council."[17] The majority in *Certain Expenses* carried the principle of institutional effectiveness to the *extreme* by imposing financial obligations on objecting members, even those who might have been expected to restrict their own obligations regardless of the size of the majority by exercising their veto power. It is the extremity of the claim, its "blank check" character, that needs to be apprehended. At issue here is not the shift of a residual peacekeeping competence to the General Assembly in light of the Security Council's inability to act in a variety of instances (an inability not generally appreciated as obstructive save in exceptional situations). The Charter, drafted historically in what was generally a pre–Cold War frame of reference, settled for institutional ineffectiveness for the United Nations in relation to the Great Powers, but it did not anticipate, it seems clear from the preparatory material, the extent to which one or more of the Great Powers would be integrally

1956 *South-West African Petitions,* in which it is said that "Whatever may be its binding force as a part of international law—a question upon which the Court need not express a view—it is the law recognized by the United Nations." *Supra* note 41 of chapter 3, at 46–47. To some extent Lauterpacht's view of authoritativeness is based on the Assembly's acceptance of the legal determination by the Court after the opinion has been issued.

[17]*Certain Expenses, supra* note 10 of chapter 2, at 230.

involved in virtually every important post-1945 threat to or breach of international peace, and involved in a way directly antagonistic to its geopolitical rivals. In the period up to 1962—that is, in the period of United Nations history and practice relevant for the Court in *Certain Expenses*—the problem of the United Nations' unanticipated institutional ineffectiveness had been handled, for better or worse, by means of United States leadership, a period that might more suitably be described as one of American "hegemony." The role of the United Nations in the Korean War (1950–52) was the high point of this unanticipated development. In this war, American foreign policy, in relation to a highly partisan and violent struggle between ideological adversaries in a divided country, was fully endorsed and ratified by the United Nations. The United Nations' formal participation in the Korean War consisted largely of blessing and legitimizing the American-led defense of South Korea, not directing or paying for it. This war also provided the context in which a de facto revision or adaptation of the Charter was achieved that enhanced the potential peacekeeping role of the General Assembly by means of the Uniting for Peace concept. UNEF and UNEC, although dealing with less blatantly Cold War issues than the Korean War, represented a new reliance on Assembly activism in the peacekeeping area, implemented (according to critics) by an allegedly Western-biased Secretary-General. It had become evident by the 1960s, however, that the General Assembly would never again be as easily dominated by the United States or by any other major Member as it had been in the first decade of its existence. Before long the United States had joined the Soviet Union in opposing General Assembly activism, although this opposition was exercised more in the realm of economic matters than was Soviet opposition to peace and security undertakings. The United States was no more inclined to regard General Assembly attempts to specify a new international economic order in the mid-1970s as authoritative than the Soviet Union was earlier prepared to submit to General Assembly claims in the peacekeeping area. From a Western viewpoint, the tame Assembly of the early 1950s had become very unruly by the late 1970s.

Judge Fitzmaurice in his thoughtful separate opinion in *Certain Expenses* draws attention to the problem:

[T]here is the fact that it would not be easy to draw a hard and fast line between necessary, essential and obligatory functions of the Organization, on the one hand, and merely optional, non-essential and permissive ones on the other. Changing concepts also are involved. Today, the humanitarian and aid-giving functions of the Organization are, if less imperative, hardly less important than its political functions, and may well contribute materially, or even be essential, to the success of the latter.[18]

Suppose the Assembly assesses opposing members for contributions to emergency development projects, and gives such undertakings its most urgent, insistent backing? One commentator, James Hogg, who views the majority in *Certain Expenses* as "sound" when "read in light of political realities," acknowledges that "[c]onceivably, adoption of the principles of this decision could operate to the disadvantage of the United States." He imagines, for instance, "vast programs for the economic development of underdeveloped countries" in which the United States is "invited to pay its allotted share whether it had voted for the programs in question or not." However, Hogg offers this line of reassurance: "Such an eventuality is not a practical possibility, however; the United States has sufficient political influence to foreclose such a vote. Were such a vote taken, this country could refuse to pay, and were voting rights suspended, the United States might feel forced to withdraw from the Organization." What Hogg considered "a purely theoretical" possibility for the United States, however, had already been realized as a practical reality for the Soviet Union.[19] Should a really "sound" decision by the Court have put one of the two superpowers in the position where its disagreement with the policy of the Assembly pushed it to the point that loss of voting rights or even withdrawal from the organization might well result?[20]

[18]*Id.* at 214–15.

[19]All quotations in this paragraph are from Hogg, *Peacekeeping Costs and Charter Obligations—Implications of the International Court of Justice Decision on Certain Expenses of the United Nations*, 62 COLUM. L. REV. 1263 (1962).

[20]In a central respect, the refusal of Soviet bloc states to feel "obligated" by an adverse advisory opinion had already been clearly exhibited in response to the East-West character of the controversy underlying *Interpretation of Peace Treaties, supra* note 10 of chapter 2, as was the willingness of "the victorious" side to drop the issue. Weissberg says of the Court's role here that "its contribution was in inverse proportion to its ability to affect the outcome." Weissberg, *supra* note 10, at 138.

Part of tendering a response to this question involves know-
ing whether it was really indispensable for the United Nations
to act in these two situations. Let us grant what is not altogether obvious in the Congo situation—that a convenient,
even though marginal, contribution was made to international
peace and security by letting the United Nations loose on
these two peacekeeping missions. But did that make such actions indispensable? Because of the increase in Third World
strength in the General Assembly, *it has become harder to discuss*
United Nations peacekeeping roles in the 1980s. Can we note
any real deterioration in the quality of international relations
as a consequence? In theory, the weakening of the United
Nations' capacity to intervene in strife-torn countries in order
to defend and uphold human rights constitutes a setback for
the forces of international peace and justice, even though the
earlier exercise of this capacity was not without its own costs
and ambiguities. Only exceptional circumstances and an overwhelming international consensus ever allowed the United
Nations to act justly, effectively, and in an atmosphere of generalized approval. This "reality" may disappoint United Nations enthusiasts, but it is a reflection of the world as it is.
Actions taken to make the United Nations stronger *prematurely*
only end up by making it weaker. The sequence of events that
followed the Court decision in *Certain Expenses,* including the
struggle over whether to invoke the article 19 suspension of
voting rights belonging to nonadherents in default, suggests to
me that the majority view was "unsound" because it pushed
through an unnecessary interpretation of the Charter that un-
realistically endowed the organization with the authority and
competence to insist that even permanent members of the
Security Council financially support General Assembly initiatives of which they disapprove in whole or in part. At its most
basic level, the policy trade-off is between the peacekeeping
effectiveness of the United Nations and universal participation
in its activities. What makes the United Nations valuable, perhaps indispensable, is that it represents a global forum that is
not a species of *alliance* of one part of the world's societies
against another. *The strongest Soviet policy case* in 1962 was the
contention that these Assembly-sponsored peacekeeping operations came dangerously close to converting the United
Nations Organization itself into a *Western-led alliance,* thereby

jeopardizing its paramount importance as global forum for communication and negotiation from all sides.

It also could be argued that the financing crisis showed that an indispensable part of the institution's effectiveness was its ability to assess members for their fair share of Assembly operations, however constitutionally dubious such a power was. One can make the argument that the level of United Nations indebtedness was so great at that time, especially that arising from the Congo operation, that some kind of firmer approach to the large number of countries in arrears was needed. The actual course of events belies this claim. An alternative financial strategy was devised later in the 1960s despite the continuing refusal of the delinquent states to contribute to the financing of the two peacekeeping operations of which they disapproved. Perhaps the majority judges on the Court *believed* that the future of the United Nations required an immediate financial rescue, or that their constitutional duty was primarily one of reinforcing the will of the Assembly majority on a matter clearly within its general sphere of competence. It is plausible to entertain these explanations because of the nature of the arguments that were advanced. Yet, this brings us back to the question of the Court's authoritativeness. How could a manifestly nonauthoritative advisory opinion make a practical contribution? Well, it could (and did, for a while) strengthen the resolve of the majority to push ahead with its position, deepening the crisis and producing the celebrated "do-nothing" seventeenth session of the Assembly. This new experience of institutional ineffectiveness led ultimately to an accommodation between the majority and members in arrears that was sought and found outside the framework of the 1962 majority opinion.

The crux of the majority's reasoning was most effectively, if too gently and obliquely, probed by Judge Bustamante of Peru. He described the central distinction relied upon by the majority between "enforcement" actions and "police or security" actions as "perhaps too subtle."[21] At least the distinction was too subtle to handle the problem of the distribution of functions between the Security Council and the General Assembly as contemplated by the Charter's exclusive assignment of all peacekeeping activities to the Security Council. To share the responsibility

---

[21]*Certain Expenses, supra* note 10 of chapter 2, at 296.

in the manner desired by the Assembly "would perhaps," according to Bustamante, require an amendment to the Charter.[22] There is in fact no way to give an *authoritative* endorsement to what the Assembly did on behalf of the United Nations without an amendment of the Charter as per the procedure set forth in article 108, namely, a two-thirds vote of the members including all permanent members of the Security Council.[23] Posing the issue in this way suggests the dependence of the organization upon the consent of all its principal members in order for the organization to adapt the Charter in fundamental ways to reflect changing circumstances. It confirms the validity of Judge Winiarski's conception of the Charter as sacrificing United Nations effectiveness for the sake of giving reassurance about sovereign rights to some members, allowing their opposition to proposed initiatives to prevent action by the United Nations.

As might be expected, the most indignant dissenting opinion was contributed by the Soviet member of the Court, Judge Koretsky. His argument, mired in an orthodox positivist (and utterly non-Marxist) comparison of Charter provisions and Assembly actions, was designed to make the principal points that the Assembly at best can do no more than recommend actions and procedures to the members, and that there was no legal way to overcome the initial departure from its competence in the authorizing resolutions for ONUC and UNEF. He argued that a later emphasis on the Assembly's authority to deal with budgetary matters cannot cure retroactively the invalidity of its peacekeeping role. With evident frustration Judge Koretsky gives his view, somewhat rhetorically, that "the Court must not shut its eyes to reality."[24] For Koretsky this reality involves adherence to "the strict observation of the Charter . . . the necessity of the strict observation and proper interpretation of the provisions of the Charter, its rules, without limiting itself by reference to the purposes of the Organization."[25] He adds, as if to clinch the argument, "otherwise one would have come to the long ago condemned formula:

[22]*Id.*

[23]Gross, *supra* note 19 of chapter 2, at 428, suggests a procedure somewhat easier to accomplish: "Short of a formal amendment one could envisage a procedure whereby the advisory opinion or its operative part would be accepted as authoritative for the future by a vote which corresponds to the requirement in Article 108 . . . ."

[24]*Certain Expenses, supra* note 10 of chapter 2, at 268.

[25]*Id.*

'The ends justify the means.' "[26] This is strange rhetoric coming from the only Leninist member of the Court. The strength of the positivist paradigm is so great at The Hague that even the Soviet judge seemed to be inhibited by it from talking directly about the issue of international public policy and the concrete social forces that were most influential in determining the course of Assembly action in this dispute.

In an important respect, Koretsky has the last word: "It has been said more than once that peace-keeping operations should be financed in another way" (than by way of article 17[2]).[27] And so they eventually came to be! The "political" strength of Koretsky's "legal" analysis was that it had the determined backing of the Soviet Union (as well as that of France and of a respectable number of lesser members). It was not "realistic" to cram a constitutional innovation of this magnitude down the throats of major objecting members. Interestingly, the sticking point was the obligation to pay. The Assembly minority apparently was prepared to live with the will of the majority in the Assembly so long as it was not compelled to contribute to the implementation of that will. There were alternative possibilities for solving the financial crisis, but each had its own formidable difficulties: relying on voluntary contributions, assessing only the supporters of the initiatives, or assessing the states whose activities required the expenditures in the first place. That these schemas, for various reasons, would not establish a principled basis for financing future peacekeeping operations merely underlines the current modesty of the limits upon institutional effectiveness. As secretaries-general are fond of stressing in their annual reports, the United Nations can rarely, if ever, do more than its members want it to do. The United Nations is mainly an arena (or a series of arenas) *of* the state system, not an alternative to it.

The Court's majority reiterated the attitude of the Assembly's majority as to the problems of institutional effectiveness. The international policy dimension was left largely unexplored in the majority opinion, in part because of the judicial method used, and thus the advisory opinion appeared to be both "a rubber stamp" for the Assembly and the champion of a politically nonsustainable position. The opinion lacked any

[26]*Id.*
[27]*Id.*

compelling sense of juridical necessity. Nor were its policy implications assessed in any instructive or useful way. Neither the issue of the decision's lack of authoritativeness nor the problems of the United Nations peacekeeping identity were creatively explicated.

A comparison along these lines with the South West Africa / Namibia line of litigation is suggested by the preceding analysis. Could it not be argued that the 1966 majority correctly deferred to the reality of sovereign rights in a system of nation states, imposing a more modest role upon the United Nations? And contrariwise, that the Court's advisory opinion in 1971 in that case was a ludicrous endeavor, trying to validate an overly sanguine conception of the United Nations institutional effectiveness by the forced insertion of a United Nations administration into the mandate territory over South Africa's objections? Wasn't the interpretative issue comparable, a matter of protecting the rights of the minority against the emergence of a hostile majority committed to redefining an original contractual relationship?

The differences between the two situations are significant. The contractual relationship embodied in the mandate was intertwined with a conception of sacred trust. The nature of the arrangement embodied an evolving morality as to the meaning of both "well-being" and self-determination for the territory's inhabitants. South Africa, as the main opponent of the United Nations' demands, did not represent either a politically or a morally significant challenge to the majority position. The pressures upon South Africa to relinquish the Mandate would persist no matter what the Court decided. The more teleological style of interpreting constitutional instruments was historically characteristic of the practice of the International Court of Justice (more so than it had been with the Permanent Court of International Justice), and therefore the 1966 majority *departed* from judicial expectations even in terms of the judicial method it used, presumably in order to accommodate pressing policy considerations.

In the case of *Certain Expenses,* a set of opposite considerations existed. The contractual relationship pertaining among principal members of the United Nations was the essence of the bargain struck in San Francisco. The ability to override the contract, the Charter, in order to enable the organization to promote its primary purposes was opposed by a substantial minority of the members, especially when it came to financing these purposes. The minority at the same time partially accommodated itself to *past* undertakings, despite the view that the authorization for such undertakings had been void. To push the financing issue, in this context, was to push the minority into a corner. Even the Assembly majority failed to sustain the kind of competence claimed in the ONUC and UNEF situations. The composition and the priorities of the United Nations organization have changed since 1962. Now even the United States, the original leader of the shift toward granting more power to the Assembly, has become wary of Assembly prerogatives and more favorably inclined in the interim toward a stricter construction of the Charter contract.

Furthermore, the technical grounds on which *Certain Expenses* was decided seem weak. In contrast to the case presented by the mandate, in which the directive to adjudicate seemed clear on its face, in the case of financing Assembly enterprises, it was necessary to rest a justification of the judicial opinion upon the dubious assumption of obligatory peacekeeping operations conducted by the General Assembly. Not only could the Assembly recommend, but also its recommendations, however grandiose, generated obligations even for those who were in the opposition.

Beyond these specific lines of criticism directed at the outcomes in relation to the circumstances of the two controversies, I want to contend more radically that *the entire* existent jurisprudential frame of reference for *all* viewpoints is generally unhelpful. It is unhelpful because it does not generally reveal and consider the underlying conflict that gives rise to the legal challenge. Judge Alvarez in his 1950 dissent and Judge Ammoun in his 1962 separate opinion do move beyond the positivist confines of the traditional law framework, acknowledging in clear language the larger issues at stake. Moving in this direction for making decisions and writing expositions would not eliminate controversy over the Court's proper role; in fact, it might heighten disagreements, but it would bring law and impartial adjudication into a clarifying relationship with the opposing tendencies at work in this historical era. The Court needs to reflect this opposition, being neither a relic of the past nor a handmaiden to those who seek a different future. "Law" cannot be "neutral" or "objective" with respect to contending interpretations of history and opposed positions of interest in the global system. Above all, the Court is uniquely qualified to offer, in its advisory capacity especially, an arena for discussing and perhaps even for resolving normative controversy. This opportunity exists particularly in big cases, where the legal form of the controversy sets the stage for an educative jurisprudence. But this kind of a reorientation of the Court's vision will not simply happen. It requires a deliberate effort to influence the consciousness and outlook of the Court's judges. Such a change cannot happen overnight. Appropriate legal education and theory are required, and the electoral process in the United Nations for World Court judges needs to emphasize the relevant criteria.

Of course, traditionalists of all kinds would resist such a proposed reorientation. They would attack it as an effort to politicize the Court, to make it into "a political football" "as bad as the General Assembly." They would claim that the current scorn for the activities of the Court would be increased and, what is worse, that the Court's potential for development would be destroyed. They would also argue that governments (and their legal advisors) would never submit legal disputes to the Court in an environment where the approach to and outcome of controversies were subject to such unpredictable arguments. Indeed, to the extent that positivist expectations about judicial style persist, there might well be a further deterioration of the Court's role, at least in the short run, in third-party adjudications.

My recommendations are shaped by the conviction that the Court's genuine mission should be advisory in the best sense of an educative or edifying jurisprudence capable of informing and enlightening the relevant community about the principles and policies at stake, as well as the relevance of pluralist jurisprudential perspectives. The Court is generally too cumbersome as it now functions to handle complex technical controversies among states that would be potentially susceptible to routine third-party procedures, although its adoption of streamlining rules has helped. Nevertheless, it remains generally true that innovative adjudicative and dispute-settlement techniques (*e.g.,* special courts, chambers, and the like) offer the best hope for the expansion of third-party procedures in international life within the overall framework created by the World Court apparatus.

CHAPTER VII

Can the World Court Succeed?

*More and more it seems to me that the philosopher, being of
necessity a man of tomorrow, has always found himself, and had to
find himself, in contradiction to his today: his enemy was ever the
ideal of today.*[1]

My central thesis is illuminated by Nietzsche's assertion: men
and women of today have dominated the discussion about the
future of the World Court. Their assessments and proposals
do not cut deeply enough into the jurisprudential fabric to
offer genuine hope or insight in the face of its current plight.
The current malaise surrounding the Court is a matter that
challenges us to find, in Nietzsche's sense, the perspective of
tomorrow and even of the day after tomorrow.

Provocatively, Nietzsche also asserts that "[m]an is finished
when he becomes altruistic."[2] The world political system is
structured by contending social forces organized into net-
works of interacting territorial states. These states have very
diverse histories, ethnic compositions, orientations, capabilities, endowments, and priorities. Governments, more precisely
government officials, act on behalf of these states both directly
in foreign policy and within the various arenas of statecraft,
including the United Nations. Their perspective, despite an
often misleadingly idealistic rhetoric, is shaped by considerations of perceived short-run self-interest. Neither altruism
(consideration for the well-being of humanity as a whole or
concern for those people and societies who are most materially
deprived) nor enlightened long-term self-interest (the importance for *each* state of a stable global system characterized by
intensifying interdependence) can be counted upon to exert
any sort of major influence on the shaping of international
institutional practices. The Court cannot be rescued, in other
words, either by good will or by ingenious tinkering.

[1]F. NIETZSCHE, BEYOND GOOD AND EVIL 137 (Vintage ed. 1966).
[2]F. NIETZSCHE, TWILIGHT OF THE IDOLS §35, at 87 (Penguin ed. 1968).

The evolution of international society in recent decades has created an ever more problematical context for the discharge of judicial functions as conventionally conceived by international law specialists in the Euro-American tradition.[3] Leo Gross concludes his report on behalf of a distinguished panel of the American Society of International Law by suggesting that the declining stature of the World Court "can only be explained by total opposition to the normative character of international law itself."[4]

It is true from *one* point of view that the Soviet bloc's and the Third World's criticisms of the makeup of the Court and of its inadequate conception of what constitutes applicable law are only part of the story, and a somewhat superficial and outdated part of it at that. The electoral procedures of the Court that are not subject to a veto have already produced a somewhat more representative membership since the rude awakening of 1966. At the same time, as Lyndell Prott has persuasively written, "all the evidence indicates that no real progress will be made until the Bench is *a better integrated group,* and that will not happen until its composition becomes more homogeneous, or a greatly increased workload builds up a group personality."[5] It may appear inconsistent to insist simultaneously on the need for a greater representativeness and a more integrated representation on the Court, and in a sense, it is. What is intended is a representative bench for the Court that can agree on a reorientation of judicial style appropriate for the current world system. This is perhaps an unrealistic objective. Yet if this kind of change is unrealistic, it is also unrealistic to believe that the Court somehow can be made more effective without such an underlying shift in values and perspective.

Additionally, the Court is necessarily part of the struggle

[3]*See, e.g.,* JUDICIAL SETTLEMENT OF INTERNATIONAL DISPUTES, *supra* note 8 of chapter 1; THE FUTURE OF THE INTERNATIONAL COURT OF JUSTICE, *supra* note 10 of chapter 1; for a critique along these lines see Prott, *The Future of the International Court of Justice,* 33 YEARBOOK OF WORLD AFFAIRS 284 (1979).

[4]THE FUTURE OF THE INTERNATIONAL COURT OF JUSTICE, *supra* note 10 of chapter 1, at 764.

[5]Prott, *supra* note 1 of chapter 3, at 286. She emphasizes the dissensus about the nature of judicial function as a main contributory factor to the "non-authoritativeness" of the World Court under current world conditions, and illustrates her point by reference to the *Nuclear Tests* cases, "where only six of the 15 judges supported the reasoning of the majority judgment."

concerning the normative character of international society. The alignments of states can be observed in such characteristic settings as the Law of the Seas Conference, the various sessions of the General Assembly calling for a new international economic order, and the movement to expand the conception of human rights to include the basic needs of a person. These settings reveal an intense Third World concern with certain directions of global reform, despite all the well-noted differences between African, Asian, and Latin American states about normative issues. This concern, however, manifests an overwhelmingly *legislative* emphasis, a series of demands that condition world stability on greater fairness in the division of the economic pie. The Euro-American defensiveness in these settings has to do with its own antilegislative stance arising from concerns *about protecting expectations created in the past*. This defensive posture involves sustaining as much of the legitimacy of the basic framework of rights and duties inherited from the past as possible. This defensive effort includes a positivist insistence that lawmaking is dependent for its validity on sovereign consent. This insistence helps us understand the reason why such a fierce debate rages around the question of whether to attribute, in many different circumstances, lawmaking effects to the formal acts of the General Assembly. This Western interest in its geopolitical and economic inheritance is masked by a kind of jurisprudential arrogance that claims for its contingent and self-interested views on law and judicial function the mantle of objective reality. It is contemptuous of all alternative images, dismissing them as "political." The essential drift of the argument is conveyed by Manley O. Hudson's comment that the Permanent Court of International Justice's exercise of advisory jurisdiction "has kept within the limits which characterize judicial action. It has acted not as an 'academy of jurists' but as a responsible 'magistrature.' "[6] Judge Fitzmaurice stresses this distinction drawn by Hudson and even adds italics to the quoted words for emphasis in his annex on judicial function, appended to his 1971 *Namibia* dissent.[7]

[6]M. HUDSON, THE PERMANENT COURT OF JUSTICE 1920–1942, at 511 (1943).

[7]*Legal Consequences for States of the Continued Presence of South Africa in Namibia,* *supra* note 75 of chapter 4, at 291–92. Edward McWhinney in his important book on the World Court calls attention to this distinction as illuminating the main line of jurisprudential conflict. E. McWHINNEY, THE WORLD COURT AND THE

What is missing in these explanations is both simple humility and its obverse understanding—the realization that views on "law" and "judicial function" are inevitably culture bound, geopolitically shaped, and historically conditioned.[8] There exists no single *prescriptive model* for what the World Court should be. Its own statute is vague and ambiguous. To rely on the Permanent Court of International Justice as a suitable model for the Court (a tendency reinforced by judicious references to its operations as the golden era of international adjudication) overlooks the International Court's drastically different context of operation. Perhaps much of the superficiality of assessments of why international adjudication is not working can be traced back to the original uncritical extension of the Permanent Court's framework to the altered world of 1945. In retrospect, the early Permanent Court years provide an image of a regional institution operating within a global framework. The role of the Permanent Court was facilitated by the character of the Versailles peace treaties and by its tendency to give rise to disputes, as well as by the homogeneous and moderate character of an international society that continued to be dominated by Europe. When conflicts among European countries emerged in the 1930s, the role of the Permanent Court of International Justice declined rapidly.

Immediately after World War II, because of the experience of the East-West anti-Axis Alliance, it was natural that continuities with the past would be stressed. But reference to the nature of judicial function in the period of the Permanent Court, as if it automatically pertained to the International Court of Justice period, has not encouraged rethinking basic

---

CONTEMPORARY INTERNATIONAL LAW-MAKING PROCESS 32–33 (1979). *See*, in this regard, Judge Fitzmaurice's Annex to his Dissenting Opinion in the *Namibia* proceeding, *Legal Consequences for States of the Continued Presence of South Africa in Namibia*, *supra* note 75 of chapter 4, at 229–317, esp. 302–04.

[8]Lyndell Prott aptly uses the phrase "legal ethnocentricism" to denote this attribute of the judicial process in the World Court. It encompasses the various elements of what she calls "judicial predisposition," including "preconceived possible solutions which are later justified by a choice among various acceptable methods of reasoning" as well as "all those habits of mind that influence the activity and jurisprudence of the judges of the International Court, whether these are possible methods, conceptual structures, judgment styles, legal remedies, or other factors which have been programmed by the judges' training." Her book is a pathbreaking study of international adjudication, especially in its detailed examination of such factors as "cultural patterning" of judicial behavior. L. PROTT, *supra* note 1 of chapter 3, at 192; wider discussion at 191–99.

issues of craft and orientation. For instance, it has been me-chanically argued that the present Court should necessarily discharge its advisory role in the spirit of a "responsible magis-trature," because this had been the approach adopted by the earlier Court. The Permanent Court *no longer* provides, if in-deed it ever did, a positive model for international adjudica-tion, in general, at the *global* level.[9]

Changes in the international political environment, specifi-cally changes in the patterns of conflict and the globalization of participation, have inevitably made the Court a very dif-ferent kind of institution in recent decades from the old court, no matter how similar the formal structure and proce-dures might appear. The essence of that difference is the collapse of the earlier consensus among the active partici-pants in international society about its normative character, as well as far greater diversification in the cast of characters. To act as if such crucial differences are irrelevant to the nature of judicial functioning is in fact to take sides in the controversy in a peculiarly overbearing and misleading fa-shion, even if this is done "innocently" or unconsciously (that is, in the spirit of upholding a so-called objective legal science).

The movements for national self-determination and decolo-nialization that occurred in the 1950s had a considerable im-pact on the tone and the content of United Nations operations, especially those centered in the General Assembly. Even so, and this point needs to be stressed, the Assembly even in its most militantly anti-Western moments remains *a pale reflection* of ac-tual political feelings and trends among the peoples of the world.[10] In actuality, the governments of the Third World gen-erally and often use anti-Western and antiimperialist rhetoric without meaning it, whereas many popular forces are sincerely committed to these postures. Numerous Third World govern-ments are linked by ties of dependence to Western economic and political power, and they maintain their domestic rule by

[9]Note remarks to this specific effect by Judge Alvarez in his individual opinion in the *Fisheries Case* (U.K. v. Nor.), 1951 I.C.J. 116, 146 (Judgment of December 18).

[10]This observation can be tested by comparing the intergovernmental focus of the call for a New International Economic Order (NIEO) with the insistence on internal, as well as international, justice in the documents of the Third World Forum and such representative statements of Third World intellectuals as the Cocoyac Declaration or the Poona Indictment. For these texts, see BASIC DOCUMENTS IN INTERNATIONAL LAW AND WORLD ORDER 415–24 (B. Weston, R. Falk & A. D'Amato eds. 1980).

repressive terror.[11] Such governments do not represent in any consensual respect the will of their people, nor do the members of the small elites ruling these countries, from whom World Court members are drawn, reflect the radical populism of their citizenries.[12] The public ideological displays put forth in the General Assembly are largely, although not exclusively, window dressing—concessions to pressures from below, pressures associated with world public opinion.[13] Such displays can be compared with the ritual endorsements by the United States and the Soviet leaders of disarmament goals.

As a consequence, it is not surprising that Third World and Soviet bloc presences in the Court, with a few exceptions to be noted, have been of such minimal consequence in reshaping the image of the Court, as well as in endowing the critical notions of law and judicial function with a new and more appropriate content. To be sure, by and large Third World judges have taken a somewhat more teleological approach to their judicial roles than have their Euro-American counterparts, but they have confined their deviation from Western legal culture to matters of interpretation and substance—in fact, to a technical option *within* the Euro-American paradigm.[14] As I have suggested earlier, the argumentation and even the citations relied upon have been orthodox, even if one emphasizes styles of legal reasoning as a yardstick. Marxism is now probably the most influential global political ideology in terms of intellectual adherence (even in the countries of the Third World governed by anti-Marxist leaders, and taking account of the anti-Soviet content of much contemporary Marxist analysis), yet it has had virtually no acknowledged impact upon the Court. Even Soviet-bloc judges, while taking positions in accord with Soviet foreign policy, have as yet made no attempt whatever to rethink judicial function in a global setting from a Marxist perspective. Soviet policy is intent on keeping the Court a feeble institution and, hence, does

[11]For example, by ties of indebtedness, aid and credit lines, military and paramilitary support, as well as personal allegiance.

[12]Admittedly there are considerable variations of political consciousness present in various countries; see for instance, Janice Perlman on the nonradical character of the Brazilian urban poor. J. PERLMAN, THE MYTH OF MARGINALITY (1976).

[13]Issues such as terms of trade, public indebtedness, and aid levels are genuine North-South controversies.

[14]*See* L. PROTT, *supra* note 1 of chapter 3, at 217–27, for dicussion of the variation of judicial styles of reasoning represented on the Court.

not favor modes of "strengthening" (from whatever perspective) the Court as an institution.[15]

At stake in this massive resistance to change by the Court are the issues of socialization, role-playing, and cultural hegemony. The members of the Court are socialized into accepting a certain conception of the range of permissible jurisprudence and of its appropriate derivation. They are also trained, by and large, to adopt a style of legal reasoning that falls within rather narrow logical confines. These features of legal education are "received" as if they were beyond questioning, whereas the apparent objectivity of their status is partly a matter of history, partly a question of geopolitics (or power). Some understanding of cultural hegemony as a mode of domination seems useful to explain the jurisprudential "consensus." There are certain factors that are so much a part of "the environment" that they are taken for granted even though they are actually a legacy of one form or another of domination. The educational patterns in the legal profession virtually the world over have been overwhelmingly based on Euro-American presuppositions and textual materials.[16] Very few independent reexaminations of these supposedly value-free presuppositions about the nature of the judicial function and whether they serve or disserve the needs of the excolonial peoples or various underclasses of the world have been made. Little social criticism exists along these lines of the Court as a judicial institution. As a consequence, legal thought-forms do not adequately take into account the changing global contexts, arenas of international law often seem sterile, and the great issues of the day are obscured rather than illuminated even when the World Court directly confronts them. Indeed, to the extent that there exists an alternative prescriptive model for the World Court, it is provided by the United States Supreme Court, a very special model of judicial function that *happened* to take its present shape at an early stage in American legal history.[17] This model

[15]Such Soviet negativism was recently evident in the 1970–74 General Assembly debates leading up to the do-nothing Resolution 3232, 29 U.N. GAOR Supp. (No. 31) at 141, U.N. Doc. A/9631 (1974). In the discussions, the Soviet Union opposed (successfully) even setting up a committee to study ways to improve the functioning of the Court.

[16]Of course, there are important variations within this framework.

[17]See the interesting discussion by E. McWhinney, *supra* note 7, at 65–68, where he writes of the United States Supreme Court as "a polar extreme" among judicial models that contrasts with the European civil law tribunal model that has consistently dominated the professional character of the Court's operations and outlook.

presupposes a far more integrated legal order with a much higher level of community respect for judicial determinations than exists globally. In fact, this more activist role for the Supreme Court (which has been best represented on the World Court by the evolutionary approach to judicial function of Philip Jessup) has been contested even within the United States. It has been especially challenged by a more passive view of judicial function (the so-called passive virtues) perhaps most trenchantly expressed in the writings and judicial opinions of Felix Frankfurter.[18]

In the economic sphere, it has been well understood by Third World leaders that formal political independence does not entail genuine economic independence for Third World countries. In cultural spheres, however, a similar understanding is much more rudimentary, especially because so many of the elites and often also the counterelites of these countries have been westernized by education and by social and intellectual conditioning. This masking of conditioning is particularly true in relation to international legal matters, where the claim of "science" is made to disguise the presence of arbitrary elements.[19] Western cultural hegemony in relation to the World Court has meant that this leading international judicial body operates overwhelmingly in relation to a set of symbols and procedures associated with legal positivism (blended by some judges and on some occasions with a dose of natural law).[20] This cultural hegemony is also evident in the general failure of Third World and non-Western members of the Court or other public officials to question the use of The Hague as the site for the World Court or to challenge, even symbolically, the retention of English and French as the Court's exclusive working languages.[21]

[18]On these issues, see A. BICKEL, THE LEAST DANGEROUS BRANCH: THE SUPREME COURT AT THE BAR OF POLITICS (1962).

[19]To this effect, see Johan Galtung's remarks about his own work: "Although written by a social scientist, the book is quite explicit in its critical attitude. This is not because I regard the book as some kind of extra-curricular activity, but because I regard social critique as an indispensable ingredient of social science analysis. So-called 'objective information' is usually conservatism in disguise. For the critique to be 'scientific,' a minimum requirement is that the value-pattern be made very explicit and the contrast with facts and trends reasonably thorough . . . ." J. GALTUNG, THE EUROPEAN COMMUNITY: A SUPERPOWER IN THE MAKING 6 (1973).

[20]E.g., Judge Tanaka's dissent in the 1966 South West Africa Cases, supra note 30 of chapter 1.

[21]These issues have gradually emerged on the international policy-making agenda in other settings. For instance, a Third World operating locus was made a sine qua

The Court will not be able to overcome its current difficulties, especially when and if it is confronted by a big, politically charged controversy, until its members come to embody a spirit of cultural *autonomy* and *pluralism* that reflects the principal attitudes in the world system on the leading normative issues of the day, including a range of views about the lawmaking processes at work in international life. The conservative idea of banishing the big case, of reserving the Court for technical, routine issues that stress adjectival, procedural matters, is not *politically* viable, given the composition of the United Nations and the electoral procedures set up by the Court's Statute (articles 2-15). If anything, pressure is likely to increase for judicial responses similar to those taken by the Court in its 1971 Namibia and its 1975 Western Sahara advisory opinions. New questions arise as to judicial style and jurisprudence suitable for a world system constituted by the diversity of states, cultures, and ideologies now active in the global arena. To what degree can Euro-American judges be induced to be responsive to the needs and aspirations of this new international setting?[22]

To achieve a spirit of autonomy involves both form and substance. It requires the Court to reconsider the audience for its proceedings and its overall role in the world system.[23] More concretely, such autonomy would naturally lead in the direction of a value-oriented and educative jurisprudence such as has already been prefigured to a degree in different ways in the contributions of Judges Alvarez and Ammoun. It is evident from the tone of the 1971 Namibia dissenting opinions by Judges Fitzmaurice and Gros, especially the former, that

---

non for a United Nations operating program in the environmental area. Arguments about convenience were rejected as the original recommendation of a Geneva location was replaced by Nairobi. From a functional perspective, there may be different costs borne by such reactions against cultural hegemony, including difficulty in recruiting prime talent, securing an adequate budget, being taken seriously as a problem-solving organ. Whether these costs are only short-term remains to be seen.

[22]Accordingly, such attention has been appropriately given to Judge Hardy Dillard's Separate Opinion in *Western Sahara*, especially that portion where he counsels against applying in a non-Western setting a concept of law "which now prevails in post-Reformation western-oriented societies." *Advisory Opinion on the Western Sahara*, *supra* note 74 of chapter 3, at 125; *see also* L. PROTT, *supra* note 1 of chapter 3, at 232; E. McWHINNEY, *supra* note 7, at 82–83.

[23]*See* Prott's very creative discussion of "audience" as an element of judicial style, *supra* note 1 of chapter 3, at 152–72; her study, in general, strikes a note compatible with my own, and has exerted a definite influence on the approach taken here.

the willingness of Euro-American policymakers to trust the Court in contentious disputes might be expected to decline even further if it moves toward a more representative and normatively responsive jurisprudence. As McWhinney notes, prospects for increases in contentious jurisdiction "are bleak," in any event.[24] McWhinney seems to propose, along the lines taken here, that the Court align itself with the dynamic political currents in the world, thereby encouraging a whole new direction of growth for the Court. He suggests that "[i]n presenting the names of candidates from countries other than their own, could not individual states contribute to an intellectual break-through [sic] by trying to offer judicial innovators who are not afraid of change in the World Community or in International Law itself?"[25] A willingness to encourage the Court to act as an academy of jurists, based on a shared view that the Court's primary mission is to contribute to the purposes of the United Nations, would reinvigorate the Court's judicial function by reference to the new political configurations and tendencies active in the world. This direction would entail a virtual reversal of Fitzmaurice's recipe for judicial reform, based on raising standards of professional competence.[26] There are dangers, even normative ones, associated with an excessive receptivity to political trends current in the world, but these dangers seem far less serious at present than do the dangers associated with the persistence of a posture of aloofness. Perhaps in the decades ahead, it might someday again be necessary to urge a greater aloofness on the Court. Such a rhythm of ebb and flow is healthy for the development of any governmental process, including the judicial process.

Nevertheless, it is fair to ask, judicial innovation *for what?* It is here that the strands of an educative jurisprudence appropriate to the Court's advisory jurisdiction in big cases becomes

[24]*See* E. McWhinney, *supra* note 7, at 166; *cf. also* L. Prott, *supra* note 1 of chapter 3.

[25]E. McWhinney, *supra* note 7, at 168.

[26]*E.g.*, Fitzmaurice, *Enlargement of the Contentious Jurisdiction of the Court*, in The Future Of the International Court of Justice, *supra* note 10 of chapter 1, at 461–98; *see also* Gross, *Conclusions, id.* at 727–86; or the anodyne General Assembly Resolution 3232, *supra* note 15; of especial relevance here is the consideration of judicial qualifications—do we give priority to professional criteria in relation to competence or should the search be for "judicial innovators"? The Court will positively evolve to the extent that the General Assembly and the Security Council face this question and resolve it in a generally consistent and progressive manner.

so central. I think that in very general terms the correct challenge was set forth by Judge Alvarez almost thirty years ago, a challenge clearly issued ahead of its time but one that now needs to be revived in a serious way. The essence of what Alvarez had to say was exceedingly simple: "[T]he Court has a free hand to allow scope to the new spirit which is evolving in contact with the new conditions of international life: there must be a renewal of international law corresponding to the renewal of this life."[27]

Judge Alvarez's view of the new challenge and the opportunity it presents was expressed in rather lofty and abstract language that was noncommittal in relation to the play of social forces. His main contention was that the old international law was overly "*juridical* and *individualistic*" (resting on the conjunction of sovereign wills) and was "more and more being superceded by what may be termed the *law of social interdependence*." He emphasized that:

> This *law of social interdependence* has certain characteristics of which the following are the most essential: (a) it is concerned not only with the delimitation of the rights of States, but also with harmonizing them; (b) in every question it takes into account all its various aspects; (c) it takes the general interest fully into account; (d) it emphasizes the notion of the *duties* of States, not only towards each other but also towards the international society; (e) it condemns the abuse of right; (f) it adjusts itself to the necessities of international life and evolves together with it; accordingly, it is in harmony with policy; (g) to the rights conferred by strictly juridical law it adds that which States possess to belong to the international organization which is being set up.[28]

Alvarez's tone and orientation is generally one of enlightened humanism, and it expresses the conviction that international interdependence had advanced in psychopolitical terms to the point where a universal global community perspective could be said to exist as an empirical matter. The prime task of the Court, accordingly should be to take account in its work of

[27]*Conditions of Admissions, supra* note 13 of chapter 6, at 67; Judge Alvarez in this Individual Opinion felt that General Assembly Resolution 171 (II), November 14, 1947, by its call for "progressive development" of international law by the Court had sanctioned his conception of judicial function.

[28]*Id.* at 69–70. To similar effect, Alvarez, Individual Opinion, *Fisheries Cases* (U.K. v. Nor.), 1951 I.C.J. 116, 145–53, esp. at 148–51; also Dissenting Opinion, *Admissions to the United Nations, supra* note 25 of chapter 2, at 12–21; Dissenting Opinion, *Status of South-West Africa, supra* note 25 of chapter 2, at 174–85.

what is happening. Judge Alvarez urged the Court to be empirical in the best sense of being *open* to new trends, rather than purporting to be *detached,* and hence an unwitting captive of past dogma.

The main limitation of the Alvarez approach lies in its idealism, in that special sense of exaggerating the extent and the quality of international harmony and of underestimating conflict, intense nationalistic tendencies, ideological antagonisms, and most of all, the importance of hierarchy and exploitation in international relations.[29] His outlook seems unaffected either by the East-West struggle or by the North-South schism. As a result, neither ideological nor cultural variables figure directly in Judge Alvarez's proposed reconstruction of international law. Judge Alvarez affirms that "one of the concerns of our time is the improvement of underdeveloped territories" from an economic point of view, but he regards this as justified "to obtain the best possible results for the benefit of the general community" and as attainable by the means of the voluntaristic dynamics of aid.[30] In this respect, Judge Alvarez appears well-intentioned but naive, out of touch with the harsher egocentric realities of the international political economy. His jurisprudence gets lost in a burst of altruistic enthusiasm; in other words, exactly what Nietzsche warns us against, as a guide to either understanding or action. The post-1945 history of international economic relations suggests the persistence of coercion as a shaping force and the corresponding marginality and ambiguity of voluntary aid programs.

On balance, the positive legacy of Judge Alvarez is more formal and stylistic than substantive. He emphasizes the crucial relevance of broad contextual changes at the global level to the proper discharge of judicial function by the Court. As an empirical matter, he stresses the discontinuity in historical context between the League period and the emergent United Nations period of international adjudication. He opens the way, then, for the Court to evolve its own new model of judi-

[29]My only significant differences with the excellent work of appraisal relating to the Court done by Prott and McWhinney arise from their failure to stress (or even articulate) the relevance of hierarchy in international relations to the perception and discharge of judicial function. To some extent this dimension of hierarchy is implicit in Prott's insistence that diverse cultural patterning underlies judicial behavior and cannot be "transcended" by a prescriptive or analytic account of *the* proper role of the World Court.

[30]*See Status of South-West Africa, supra* note 25 of chapter 2, at 174.

cial function and law.[31] His role as judge is as a conceptual liberator and precursor precisely because he starts from first principles and refuses to be confined by prevailing tradition of legal obscurantism. Judge Alvarez, without articulating a rationale, expressed his views in the spirit of an educative jurisprudence directly accessible to those without specialized legal training.[32] Since Judge Alvarez, no member of the Court has put the challenge of jurisprudential creativity so boldly or clearly.[33]

To some extent, the challenge offered by Judge Alvarez has been subsequently grounded in geopolitical social reality by several Third World members of the Court, particularly Judges Padilla Nervo and Ammoun. They have broken through the technicism of Euro-American judicial method to bring into "the field of awareness" issues of national self-determination, the anticolonial struggle, and the revolt against racism. Their views, however, have not been set forth in a systematic enough form to have had a sustained impact on either the judicial style of the Court or its substantive output.[34] Also, the extension of considerations of international hierarchy (nuclear versus non-nuclear states) to a novel area such as atmospheric nuclear testing led virtually the entire Court in the *Nuclear Tests Case* to evade substance and fall back on procedural technicism.[35]

The most important aspect of a new jurisprudence for the Court would entail a commitment to an educative mission in which the primary audience of the Court would, in addition to

[31] As such, he is a judicial antitype to the Lauterpacht-McNair-Fitzmaurice type of professionalized jurisprudence with an implicit conception of audience and style.

[32] There are a variety of educative jurisprudences, their impact and relevance a matter for analysis and appraisal. In this regard Roger Fisher's work on compliance, *supra* note 50 of chapter 1, is developed in the spirit of an educative jurisprudence. It differs in tone and spirit because its prescriptive focus is ahistorical and seems to presuppose a social, psychological, and cultural context unaffected by patterns and structures of hierarchy.

[33] A perceptive essay charts a similar course to that of Alvarez. Gordon, *Changing Attitudes Towards Courts and Their Possession of Social Decision Prerogatives*, in THE FUTURE OF THE INTERNATIONAL COURT OF JUSTICE, *supra* note 10 of chapter 1, at 336–64; McWhinney also moves in a similar direction when he affirms at the end of his book that "[t]he World Community is not, of course, bound to any static, Western constitutional law models of a Court and of the judicial function." E. McWhinney, *supra* note 7, at 168; *see also* discussion of Soviet models of law and lawmaking, at 130–41.

[34] *See, e.g., Western Sahara Opinion, supra* note 74 of chapter 3.

[35] Nuclear Tests Case (Austl. v. Fr.), 1974 I.C.J. 253 (Judgment of December 20); Prott, *Avoiding a Decision on the Merits*, 7 SYDNEY L. REV. 433 (1976); but consider also McWhinney's discussion of the Nuclear Tests Case, *supra* note 7, at 34–64, esp. at 61–64, where the rationale for procedural dismissal is defended.

the parties to a dispute, become a nonprofessional constituency of concerned *planetary* citizens. One crucial priority for this audience involves an awareness of the adverse normative effects of international hierarchy in its various political, economical, and cultural dimensions. The normative profile of such a jurisprudence would be generally "progressive" in the sense currently understood by the majority United Nations General Assembly, although contrary interpretations would also be represented. The World Court could become a much more genuine judicial arm of the United Nations, sensitive to the way the organization has evolved. In the process, the Court could well become, temporarily at least, an anathema to Euro-American or Western-oriented legal professionals who hitherto have generally given it their support.[36] Yet, to be "global" in its orientation, the new judicial culture would have to reach beyond a Third World agenda of global reform to embrace the interrelated agenda of concerns associated with a visionary world order perspective for all peoples and stages of development, including problems of avoiding nuclear war.[37]

Edward Gordon makes some imaginative comments about adapting the judicial culture of the Court to the broader tasks of social, economic, and legal reconstruction in the world. Gordon notes, for instance, that the same positive experience in adapting judicial operations to the requirement of socialist societies, such as Cuba, is useful as a guide for reforming the sense of judicial function at the global level. He is aware that anti-Communism has exacted a certain cultural price in terms of Western intellectual flexibility: "[W]e need merely observe that the disposition to reject the legitimacy of all Communist legal systems has the side effect of tainting even those features we might in more rational moments like to adopt for ourselves."[38] What attracts Gordon is the emphasis given in some Communist judicial arenas to the educative function of law in

[36]These groups might move even farther than they already have in the direction of favoring specialized courts for the settlement of particular kinds of disputes and of constituting regional courts for Trilateralist relationships.

[37]Such a perspective underlies the efforts of the World Order Models Project over the last decade; for summary images of its orientation(s), see ON THE CREATION OF A JUST WORLD ORDER, *supra* note 22 of chapter 1. In this transnational undertaking a central difficulty has been devising appropriate ways of reaching nonprofessional (in this context, non–social science) audiences.

[38]Gordon, *supra* note 33, at 340.

relation to society as a whole.[39] The role of these communist courts is above all else to embody the values of society in a vivid living form.[40] To be sure, these values are generally specified in these societies by the state (rather than by the people), but this does not necessarily detract from the example they provide of courts being used as arenas of *popular political education*.

Of course, some will attack the idea of such a popular jurisprudence as a debasement of *any* legal process, as especially corrupting of courts, as interfering with their stature as "impartial arbiters" of conflicting claims, and as tantamount to converting the judicial arena into a propaganda mill. As I have argued earlier, this position is itself *a* polemical stand about the way courts *ought* to behave. My outlook implies a different polemical stance, one that can be opposed as being self-defeating or futile given the world as it is, but *not* one that can be properly dismissed because it is "political" or "unscientific." All prescriptive models of judicial function are political and unscientific. The world system is *free* to construct the model of law and judicial function that best serves its needs and values as these are perceived by policymakers acting on behalf of the range of participants in international life.

My argument is directed particularly toward the policy-making constituency of the world political system, especially in the Third World, where I expect a more receptive audience among leaders and their advisors than I do in the West. The essence of the appeal is to reevaluate the role and character of the World Court from a visionary perspective. It is necessary to promote the self-interest of the non-Western countries in a global system in which the structures of power and authority

[39]The educative orientation of courts seems more a function of a revolutionary mood than a reflection of socialism, especially of bureaucratic socialism. The revolutionary jurisprudence of the anti-Marxist Iranian Revolution is also predominantly concerned with popular education, in this instance with inculcating the values of an Islamic Republic. At the same time, Soviet variants of legal "Byzantinism" certainly demonstrate that being "socialist" does not necessarily produce an educative jurisprudence. That is, law with a revolutionary orientation tends to be expressive about its motives and goals, whereas law with a counterrevolutionary orientation tends to evolve some kind of protective mystique. Issues of "audience," "authority," and "knowledge" are all present here.

[40]Gordon refers to the experience of Cuban popular tribunals as illustrative, especially their tendency "to encourage popular acceptance of the norms of a new social order. . . ." Gordon *supra* note 33, at 355.

continue to be weighted against change. I want to argue that the potentials for a reorientation of consciousness within the United Nations have been barely explored, and that one structure where such a creative possibility exists is the World Court. It is an intriguing possibility partly because virtually everyone agrees that the Court is not working well. The standard diagnosis of international lawyers has been to account for the disappointment by blaming it on a regressive refusal by sovereign governments to entrust their disputes to third-party procedures. My diagnosis suggests that national governments have indeed been regressive, but in a different sense, in their failure to reconstitute the Court in light of their values and goals *freely* considered.

In a formal sense I am proposing that normative life be breathed into article 9 of the Court's Statute:

> At every election, the electors shall bear in mind not only that the persons elected should individually possess the qualification required, but also that in the body as a whole the representation of the main forms of civilization and of the principal legal systems of the world should be assured.

And as for qualifications, article 2 says:

> The Court shall be composed of a body of independent judges, elected regardless of their nationality from among persons of high moral character, who possess the qualifications required in their respective countries for appointment to the highest judicial offices, or are jurisconsults of recognized competence in international law.

If these provisions are themselves construed in a teleological spirit, then the whole notion of a "qualified" nominee can be detached from Euro-American legal ideology.

Detached for what purpose? What is the content and the drift of an educative jurisprudence? Is there any point in extending and reproducing the ferment and partisanship of the General Assembly in the calmer confines of the World Court? I believe that the search for "judicial innovators" who would be generally acceptable to the General Assembly through the nominating and electoral process will result in three kinds of change:

—an upsurge in reliance upon the Court's advisory functions by coordinated organs of the United Nations;

—a greater willingness by the Court to engage in judicial activism to deal with the inequities of the past and present, especially as these are evident in North-South relations;

—a concern about longer term issues of world order, including questions touching on war and peace, mass poverty, oppression of various types, and ecological decay, as well as the interrelationships between these elements.

Yet why should citizens of the United States (or any other OECD country) make or support such a proposal? Is this not an example of a disguised form of altruism that assumes the shape of "third worldism" and is attractive mainly to intellectuals in the richer countries of the North who feel alienated from the governing processes and value patterns of their own society? My conviction is that this proposed reorientation of the World Court could become part of a broader strategy of international adjustment to the changing realities of international life in the present transition period that is generally beneficial to most of the peoples (although certainly not to all of the special interests) in the richer and more technologically oriented countries.

The United States' political consciousness, for example, is dangerously opposing the flow of history, especially by its continuing efforts to oppose foreign national revolutions. These efforts produce an unacceptable image of the "reasonableness" of the status quo that can only be sustained, if at all, by militarist means—given the self-destructive character of contemporary war, it is a dangerous form of disorientation.[41] In contrast, accommodating the flow of history, above all letting revolutionary nationalism run its course, supposes that the stability of the state system in the nuclear age will finally depend upon combining equity and ecological planning to a sufficient degree to discourage large-scale recourse to warfare.

Even if we grant that this kind of analysis may hold true, the short-term reaction of elites and their citizens in the North is likely to be highly antagonistic to any effort to confer a potential for legislative action upon the World Court. After all, the history of the South West Africa/ Namibia dispute suggests that even in such a one-sided situation, the Court lacks the leverage to overcome or even to erode South Africa's recalci-

[41]For an analysis of this American distance from historical circumstances in a different context, see Falk, *The Panama Treaty Trap*, 30 FOREIGN POL. 68 (1978).

trance, or to cause the material interests of morally outraged states to be set aside. The French refusal to participate in the *Nuclear Tests Case* after its Preliminary Objection (and its withdrawal from the Optional Clause after the Court agreed to enjoin French atmospheric testing as a Preliminary Measure) suggests that even law-oriented states cannot be pushed very hard by judicial pressures and that the Court is likely to relent quite rapidly if the defendant state rejects its authority.[42] Certainly one would expect an immediate reaction of hostility to this proposed reorientation in professional and official circles dominated by the Euro-American ethos. This reaction may produce a wave of withdrawals by these states from even the present degree of acceptance of compulsory jurisdiction. It is probable that the reliance on the Court for contentious proceedings, at least by Western governments and those closely aligned with them, would diminish to the vanishing point. Yet, given the current marginality of the Court, any further decline along this dimension would be slight and should not be feared.

Recalling Nietzsche's admonition at the beginning of this chapter, our reorientation is aimed, not at today, but at tomorrow and the day after tomorrow. It is a call to those with authority or influence at the primary level of the sovereign state to reinterpret the potential relevance of the Court to the fulfillment of an enlightened conception of national goals, one that suggests the importance of global reform. As a first step, it calls for greater normative self-awareness by the weaker members of international society and an increased understanding that international law and its institutions provide a framework of opportunity, if only they could be reconceptualized in a world-interested way. The non-Western participants in the world's political processes have a stake in the Court's adapting its received tradition of jurisprudence to their special goals; they have a stake in using their political influence within the United Nations in the election of judges and in the framing of questions for advisory responses by the Court. Such a strategy cannot succeed if it is followed opportunistically in a shallow way—there must be a serious commitment to reconstituting the World Court as a serious global institution. The

---

[42]*See Nuclear Tests Case, supra* note 35, at 276; on the French role, see E. McWHINNEY, *supra* note 7, at 36–43.

appropriate nominees to the Court must be judicial innovators in the profound sense, not functionaries whose judicial behavior is predicated on statist affiliations that could be charted in advance or prescribed.

This reorientation does not entail a capricious style of judicial response. It does not rest upon idealism or altruism, or on any false illusions about the withering away of the state system.[43] It does assume that a large number of governments representing disadvantaged states have a deep and self-interested commitment to global reform of a specific type (redistributive *within* the confines of a state system) and that virtually all governments acknowledge the need for predictable minimum standards and procedures for managing international relations in a growing number of technical domains. To vindicate their proclaimed identity, judicial innovators, World Court judges, would have to operate successfully to realize both of these decision-making functions.

In effect, what the World Court should become is an academy of jurists, responsive primarily to the prevailing normative sensitivities of the General Assembly, although maintaining as well a more principled and long-range point of view on the overall global agenda. It should be an academy of jurists that seeks to persuade a nonprofessional audience of individuals concerned about global policy that in the Court's view deserves respect. It should test and reflect the diverse ideologies of law and justice active in political life at all levels of social organization in relation to specific controversies and legal disputes. The educative worth of the Court's work will depend on the emergence over time of a panhuman values framework that allows diverse cultural and ideological orientations to communicate their points of agreement and disagreement. As a practical matter, the Court's advisory role would, at first, be likely to expand and its role in legal disputes among states to decline.

In its essence, the new jurisprudence proposed for the Court would consist of two elements now generally absent or downplayed:

[43]A possible qualification relates to our endorsement of Judge Tanaka's natural-law response to the protection of basic human-rights, see chapter 4. This separation of the human-rights subject matter from the individualist and voluntarist behavior of governments moves the new international law in the direction advocated in more sweeping terms by Judge Alvarez. To the extent that it endows General Assembly law-declaring resolutions with authoritative weight concerning human rights standards, it combines sociological with naturalistic criteria of legal content.

—first, a panhumanistic framework of global commitments, mainly derived from the Principles and Purposes of the United Nations as set forth in its Charter;

—second, a series of explorations from diverse cultural, ideological, and national perspectives of the proper resolution of a particular legal dispute, thereby exposing the plural character of the present world system and providing the foundations for the future development of a new world law responsive to the altered character of the world.

Index

Index